Trade Diversification in the Least Developed Countries

About UNCTAD

The United Nations Conference on Trade and Development (UNCTAD) is the principal organ of the General Assembly in the field of trade and development. It was established as a permanent intergovernmental body in 1964 in Geneva as a result of the first session of the Conference, with a view to accelerating economic growth and development, particularly that of the developing countries. UNCTAD discharges its mandate through: policy analysis; intergovernmental deliberations, consensus-building and negotiations; monitoring, implementation and follow-up; and technical cooperation. These functions are interrelated and call for constant cross-fertilization between the relevant activities. UNCTAD members aim to achieve steady sustained growth in all countries and to accelerate the development of developing countries, so that all people can enjoy economic and social well-being.

UNCTAD is composed of 188 member States. Many intergovernmental and non-governmental organizations participate in its work as observers. The UNCTAD secretariat forms part of the United Nations Secretariat. With a staff of about 480 and located at Geneva, the Secretariat is headed by a Secretary-General, currently Rubens Ricupero (Brazil). UNCTAD's annual operational budget is approximately $55 million drawn from the United Nations regular budget. Technical cooperation activities, which have developed as a result of UNCTAD's sectoral expertise financed from extrabudgetary resources, amounted to approximately $22 million in 1995.

The most recent Conference, UNCTAD IX, was held in Midrand (Johannesburg), South Africa from 27 April to 11 May 1996. The theme of the Conference was 'Promoting growth and development in a liberalizing and globalizing world economy'.

The Conference, which brought together over 2000 senior officials from 134 countries (including five Heads of State and Government and sixty-two Ministers, and Heads of the main international institutions), adopted the Midrand Declaration, submitted by the President, Alec Erwin, Minister of Trade and Industry of South Africa.

UNCTAD IX agreed on a major reform of the organization in order to focus its work 'on a new priority trade and development issues of central importance on which it can make a substantial impact' on people's lives in developing countries, in particular the least developed among them (LDCs).

The Declaration gives a strong political boost to international cooperation for development and to UNCTAD as the focal point within the United Nations for the integrated treatment of development and inter-related issues in the areas of trade, finance, technology, investment and sustainable development. The Declaration calls for greater partnership between developed countries, developing countries and the least developed countries. It also emphasizes the benefit of involving the civil society in the partnership for development.

Trade Diversification in the Least Developed Countries

Edited by

Chandra Kant Patel and Samuel Gayi

United Nations Conference on Trade and Development, Switzerland

Edward Elgar Publishing

Cheltenham, UK • Lyme, US

Published by
Edward Elgar Publishing Limited
8 Lansdown Place
Cheltenham
Glos GL50 2HU
UK

Edward Elgar Publishing, Inc.
1 Pinnacle Hill Road
Lyme
NH 03768
US

A catalogue record for this book
is available from the British Library

Library of Congress Cataloguing in Publication Data
Patel, Chandra, 1941–
    Trade diversification in the least developed countries / edited by Chandra
Patel and Samuel Gayi.
    Includes bibliographical references and index.
    1. Developing countries—Commercial policy.   2. Exports–
–Developing countries.   3. Foreign trade promotion—Developing
countries.   4. Trade regulation—Developing countries.   I. Patel,
Chandra, 1941–   .   II. Gayi, Samuel.
    HF1413.P375   1997
    382'.3'091724—dc20   96–35157
                                                                              CIP

ISBN 1 85898 514 5

Printed and bound in Great Britain by
Hartnolls Limited, Bodmin, Cornwall

Contents

Tables

EXPLANATORY NOTES TO THE TABLES

Two dots (..) indicate that the data are not available, or are not separately reported.
One dot (.) indicates that the data are not applicable.
A dash (–) indicates that the amount is nil or negligible.
Details and percentages do not necessarily add up to totals, because of rounding.

Contributors

Lena Chia, United Nations Conference on Trade and Development,
Switzerland

Gérard Fischer, United Nations Conference on Trade and Development,
Switzerland

Samuel Gayi, Faculty of Social Sciences, University of Science and
Technology, Kumasi, Ghana

Willem van der Geest, Queen Elizabeth House, Oxford University, UK

Colin Kirkpatrick, Development and Project Planning Centre, University of
Bradford, UK

Gabriele Köhler, United Nations Conference on Trade and Development,
Switzerland

Lev Komlev, United Nations Conference on Trade and Development,
Switzerland

Chandra Kant Patel, United Nations Conference on Trade and Development,
Switzerland

Khalil Rahman, United Nations Conference on Trade and Development,
Switzerland

John Weiss, Development and Project Planning Centre, University of
Bradford, UK

Abbreviations

ACP	African, Caribbean and Pacific (group of states)
AIDS	acquired immune deficiency syndrome
ASEAN	Association of South-east Asian Nations
BOT	build-operate and transfer
CFA	Communauté financière africaine
c.i.f.	cost, insurance and freight
CMEA	Council for Mutual Economic Assistance
DCs	developing countries
DMECs	developed market-economy countries
ECA	Economic Commission for Africa
ECOWAS	Economic Community of West African States
EEC	European Economic Community
EC	European Community (or Communities)
EIB	European Investment Bank
EIU	Economist Intelligence Unit
EPZ	export-processing zone
ESAF	Enhanced Structural Adjustment Facility
ESCAP	Economic and Social Commission for Asia and the Pacific (formerly ECAFE)
ETS	economic time series (UNCTAD database)
EU	European Union
FAO	Food and Agriculture Organization of the United Nations
FDI	foreign direct investment
FY	fiscal year
GATS	General Agreement on Trade in Services
GATT	General Agreement on Tariffs and Trade
GDP	gross domestic product
GNP	gross national product
GSP	generalized system of preferences
IDA	International Development Association
IFPRI	International Food Policy Research Institute
IMF	International Monetary Fund
ITC	International Trade Centre
LDCs	least developed countries

MFA	Multi-fibre Arrangement
MFN	most-favoured nation
NGO	non-governmental organization
NIEs	newly industrializing economies
ODA	official development assistance
OECD	Organization for Economic Cooperation and Development
PTA	Preferential Trade Area
QRs	quantitative restrictions
R&D	research and development
REER	real effective exchange rate
RTAs	Regional Trade Areas
RMG	ready-made garment
SAF	Structural Adjustment Facility
SAP	structural adjustment programme
SDR	special drawing right
SITC	Standard International Trade Classification
SME	small and medium enterprise
SOEs	state-owned enterprises
SSA	Sub-Saharan Africa
TNC	transnational corporation
UNCTAD	United Nations Conference on Trade and Development
UNDP	United Nations Development Programme
UNICEF	United Nations Children's Fund
UNIDO	United Nations Industrial Development Organization
UR	Uruguay Round
WTO	World Trade Organization

Preface

The experience of a number of countries in rapidly altering the composition of their exports towards higher value-added products, has renewed interest in issues such as the essential requirements of a successful diversification programme, and how diversification is influenced in turn by growth in the aggregate volume of output. The process of trade liberalization under way in many LDCs also raises the question of whether the overall objective of market opening itself will set in motion processes that could lead to greater diversification of trade.

The generally poor performance of LDCs in recent years in respect of both output and trade throws into sharp focus the reasons why the long-stated policy objectives regarding trade diversification have not led to sustained export growth characterized by horizontal and vertical diversification of exportables. This failure is all the more worrisome, given the undoubted potential that exists in many LDCs to secure much faster rates of export expansion. It is also a matter of concern that the preferences accorded to LDCs under arrangements such as the Lomé Convention and the generalized system of preferences (GSP), not to mention direct external financial support for trade expansion, have so far not influenced, to any significant extent, their export performance.

Against this background, the Paris Conference reviewed the causes of poor export performance in LDCs and outlined policies – both domestic and international – likely to play a role in strengthening the diversification process.

In response to the recommendations in the Paris Programme, the UNCTAD Secretariat undertook a number of studies on trade-diversification policies and experiences in a number of LDCs with a view to understanding better the issues involved in formulating a practical and viable programme of trade diversification and to share the results of these experiences with a wider group of countries.

Country studies were undertaken for eight LDCs: Bangladesh, Benin, Cape Verde, Haiti, Lao People's Democratic Republic (PDR), Mozambique, Niger and Uganda. The publication separately reviews the overall experience with trade-policy reforms and performance in a number of African LDCs. An overview chapter brings together the country and regional experiences, draws attention to a number of common policy issues and provides general policy guidance on the scope and content of successful diversification policies. The final chapter reviews the implications of the Uruguay Round, which was concluded after the country studies had been completed, for the trade-diversification potential of LDCs.

A number of consultants together with staff of the Least Developed Countries Division were involved in preparing the studies. This research was made possible by generous support from the government of Italy which provided financial assistance through a comprehensive project on trade diversification. A large number of government officials and private-sector institutions shared information, extended research support and provided valuable comments on drafts. The UNCTAD Secretariat wishes to express sincere appreciation to them and to UNDP officials in the countries covered for their cooperation and support.

The views expressed are those of the authors and do not necessarily reflect those of the officials interviewed, of the governments concerned, or of the United Nations.

Chandra Kant Patel
Coordinator
UNCTAD/Italy Trust Fund Project
on Trade Diversification

1. Trade diversification in the LDCs: an overview[1]

Chandra Kant Patel, Samuel Gayi and Willem van der Geest

1 OBJECTIVES AND SCOPE OF DIVERSIFICATION

A major objective of trade-diversification policies has been to reduce dependence on a limited number of commodities that are subject to major price and
volume fluctuations or even secular declines and to enhance earnings from
trade. A related objective is to reduce dependence upon one or a limited number
of geographical destinations. The diversification objective is also linked to the
expansion of opportunities for exports and improvement of backward and
forward linkages to domestic inputs and services.

This overview presents some of the salient findings of the discussion on trade
diversification emerging from a set of country studies prepared by the
UNCTAD Secretariat and the outcome of a meeting organized by UNCTAD on
this subject.[2] It highlights the main issues and draws some policy conclusions.

Trade diversification is generally premised on three interrelated objectives:
stabilizing earnings, expanding export revenues, and upgrading value added.
Most analyses distinguish 'horizontal diversification' into new products within
the same sector, from 'vertical or diagonal diversification' into processing of
domestic or imported inputs which entails a shift from the primary to the
secondary and tertiary sectors.

Via *horizontal diversification*, LDCs can reduce the variability of their
export earnings by exploiting the booms of some commodity markets when
others are experiencing slumps (see Johnson 1991:22). Modifying the commodity composition would help smooth export revenues because the instability
index for a particular group of commodities tends to be systematically lower
than that for any of its constituents, indicating that price stability gains from
diversification are obtainable.[3] While this is only a partial solution, since export
earnings are also determined by the variation of supply volumes and the costs of
inputs, the risk-reducing case for diversification, nevertheless, remains strong.[4]

Trade expansion through diversification also contributes to an acceleration of the growth process. Knowledge and experience gained from one economic activity tend to benefit others in an economy:

1. broad scientific and technical training (as well as learning by doing) enhances technological capability;
2. forward and backward linkages are facilitated as the output of one activity becomes the input of another; and
3. some advantages, associated with economies of scale and increased sophistication of markets, accrue to certain services and institutions like banking, financial instruments and markets, telecommunications, maintenance and repair facilities (Johnson 1991:23).

These 'dynamic effects' or 'secondary' advantages may well enhance the attainment of the value-added objective of diversification which is addressed primarily by *vertical* or *diagonal* diversification into manufactures or services.

Before discussing the experience and performance of the LDCs in trade diversification, some issues which require careful analysis in the design and harmonization of trade-diversification strategies, need to be signalled. The first relates to the potential consequences of simultaneous horizontal diversification by many LDCs into 'new' primary products for world market prices of these products if diversification leads to *significant* shifts in supply. Individual countries will, no doubt, be price takers, but there is the possibility of:

1. oversupply which may lead to falling prices (because of low income elasticity of demand); and/or
2. increased competition through which larger and well-established producers may drive out new producers, for example, forcing down prices through economies of scale and/or improving efficiency.

Are LDCs as a group likely to suffer reduced export earnings along the lines of the 'fallacy of composition' argument? Would this apply only to 'stagnating' product markets, and not to 'expanding' product markets?[5] These questions raise issues that are crucial to diversification policies and indicate the need for policy coordination among LDCs.

The second concern relates to the scope of domestic policies introduced to achieve (trade) diversification, the most common of which, in recent years, has been a policy of trade liberalization which aims at moving the domestic prices of traded goods towards international price levels. Conventional trade-liberalization policies adopted in recent years include: reducing controls on trade (direct and indirect, including tariffs); replacing direct interventions by price mechanisms; and, introducing a more neutral framework of incentives for trade, for example, by exchange-rate adjustment. Trade liberalization is expected to contribute to trade diversification by promoting the growth of internationally-traded output, and by aligning the composition of existing production with the respective country's comparative advantage.

As a consequence of shifts in thinking on trade policy, the context in which trade-diversification programmes are being designed and implemented has undergone important changes. In the first place, LDCs, are increasingly undertaking trade-policy reforms of which market liberalization is often an important component. Diversification objectives and goals (as defined above) therefore need to be placed in the wider context of macroeconomic reforms, the aggregate objective of which is to place significantly greater reliance on markets and the development of market-friendly policy regimes and private-sector incentives. This process has been given a significant momentum as a result of the Uruguay Round, the implications of which for LDCs are analysed in Chapter 11. Equally important is the process of economic globalization, resulting in the need for policy makers to take into account the cross-border enlargement of economic spaces. The policy challenges to LDCs as a consequence of this and of efforts to secure higher levels of foreign investment and trade with neighbours (and Regional Trade Areas (RTAs)) have resulted in a set of trade-diversification objectives significantly wider than addressed heretofore. They are wider in the sense that they necessarily involve economic policy reforms, embracing exchange rate, fiscal policy reforms and reorientation of pricing policies, as they influence tradables in particular. On the other hand, the role of the governments is now circumscribed to a greater degree than before. It is no longer taken for granted that the public sector itself needs to directly invest in productive activities for export promotion or directly or indirectly support import-substituting investment.

This changed perception about the role of the public sector has put greater premium on the design and implementation of trade-diversification policies in which governments assume an important, albeit qualitatively different role.

2 RECENT TRENDS IN DIVERSIFICATION PERFORMANCE

The assessment of the diversification performance of LDCs requires three caveats. First, the trade data of many LDCs, which underpin the discussions and analyses, suffer from gaps in coverage. For example, although informal-sector trade is significant in many LDCs, informal cross-border trade flows[6] are often excluded from the trade statistics. Consequently, trade statistics tend to be somewhat biased in favour of the large-scale and modern sector. Informal cross-border trade, if documented, would modify the export profile of many LDCs, and diversification may actually be slightly broader than portrayed by the official trade statistics.

Second, trade diversification in LDCs has to be analysed within the context of the extraordinarily low levels of (recorded) export revenue they obtain.[7] In 1991, the total value of merchandise exports of LDCs as a whole stood at $12.1 billion, corresponding to about 6.6 per cent of their combined GDP and accounting for 1.6 per cent of the total merchandise export earnings of all developing countries, and less than 0.4 per cent of world merchandise exports.[8] The small base of total trade flows in each of the LDCs magnifies the degree of dependence, and makes it difficult to appreciate actual improvements in the degree of diversification achieved, since shares in world markets remain negligible.

Third, a comprehensive indicator of trade diversification, measuring differences among countries, is difficult to define, because diversification is a multi-faceted process and individual LDCs emphasize different aspects of it to take account of differences in the size of their economies and populations, their geographical situation and, perhaps most importantly, historical legacies.

Nevertheless, there are some measures which are useful and indicative of the level of diversification of a country: product concentration, defined as the share of the three main export products in total export earnings, which illustrates the extent of export diversification; and geographical concentration, defined as the share of the three main trading partners in total exports which indicates the degree of exposure to demand variations in particular markets which may arise from economic fluctuations, shifting tastes and preferences and, last but not least, protection and trade barriers.

Based on these diversification measures, the performance of LDCs, as a group, leaves much to be desired. Throughout the past decade, concentration of exports on two or three products remained pervasive and, with few exceptions, these export products were in the commodity, or un- and semi-processed goods category: only five of the 28 LDCs, for which there are comparable export data, reduced their commodity dependency; and 26 of these continue to derive more than 70 per cent of their earnings from commodity exports (see Tables 1.1 and 1.2).

Commodity concentration is extremely high in 13 LDCs, of which nine are in Africa. Throughout the 1980s, these LDCs depended on coffee, cocoa or cotton as their main export product with major consequences for their export earnings because of the downward trend, and wide annual fluctuations in the prices of cocoa and coffee.[9] Product concentration, where one, two or three products constitute more than half of total export receipts, remains a profound problem for most LDCs, especially in the case of commodities characterized by low-income elasticities of demand.

However, a scrutiny of the export configuration making up the remaining half of export turnover shows a more differentiated picture. The number of products exported by LDCs to the world market is in fact increasing, albeit slowly, indicating some embryonic diversification. For example, a disaggrega-

Table 1.1 Dependence of LDCs on commodities for export earnings (number of countries)

Region	Percentage of commodities* in total exports earnings					
	Average 1979–81 (%)			Average 1991–93 (%)		
	>70	70–50	<50	>70	70–50	<50
Africa	23	5	2	21	5	4
Developing Asia and Pacific Oceania	3	–	–	3	–	–
South and South-east Asia	2	2	1	2	2	1
Developing America	–	–	–	–	–	–

Note: * Commodities include total primary commodities as defined in the UNCTAD *Commodity Yearbook* (SITC Section 0–2 (less groups 233, 244, 266, 267), Section 4, division 68 and item 522.56), plus SITC Section 3 (mineral fuels and related materials), diamonds. (SITC group 667), and non-monetary gold (SITC group 971).

Source: UNCTAD Secretariat data. Includes all least developed countries for which consistent data are available.

tion to the three-digit level of the SITC classification, measured by the total number of products LDCs are exporting, indicates that a number of them have succeeded in diversifying their export base and hence are beginning to 'surface' in selected product markets, including manufactures (Table 1.2).

Three worrying features of this nascent diversification must be noted. First, with the exception of textile fabrics, some of the product groups emerging are at the lower end of the scale in terms of unit values and degree of processing and value added, so linkages and vertical or diagonal diversification are minimal. Second, increasing LDC market shares may merely be indicative of the progress achieved in other developing countries which are vacating this market and moving into higher value-added product groups, leaving the economically less attractive ones to the LDC economies. Third, changes in the relative weight of commodities versus manufactures in the export composition of a given LDC over time may also reflect a case of 'false diversification': the price decline of commodities may be the sole cause of the apparent increase in diversification (see UNCTAD 1994a:57ff).

Nevertheless, diversification is feasible, and the modest shift observed in the export patterns of LDCs flags the need for supportive measures.

Geographical diversification has been advocated for a variety of reasons, but mainly to reduce the vulnerability of LDCs to:

Table 1.2 Share of main commodities in LDCs' total merchandise exports (percentage)

Country/territory	1979–1981 (average)	Share*	1991–1993 (average)	Share*
Afghanistan	fruits 29%, gas 29%, carpets 10%, hides 7%, cotton 6%, nuts 2%, crude materials 2%	68	fruits 21%, hides 8%, nuts 8%, cotton 6%, crude materials 4%	37
Angola	petroleum 76%, precious stones 11%, coffee 9%	96	petroleum 88%, precious stones 5%, gas 1%	94
Bangladesh	jute/jute products 69%, leather 10%, tea 6%, fisheries 5%	85	textiles 50%, jute/jute products 18%, fisheries 8%, leather 6%, tea 2%	76
Benin	palm kernels/oil 26%, cocoa 25%, cotton/textiles 18%, cement 5%, groundnuts 3%, cotton seed 1%	69	cotton 66%, petroleum 16%, cotton seed 6%, wheat flour 2%, palm kernels/oil 1%	88
Burkina Faso	cotton 40%, live animals 22%, hides 4%, rubber tyres 4%, sesame seeds 3%	66	cotton 46%, gold 14%, live animals 10%, hides 4%, vegetables 1%	70
Burundi	coffee 77%, precious stones 8%, gold 7%, tea 2%, crude materials 2%, cotton lint 2%	92	coffee 71%, tea 12%, tobacco 4%, crude materials 3%, hides 2%, refined sugar 2%, cotton lint 2%	87
Cape Verde	fisheries 38%, crude minerals 19%, fruits 16%, vegetables 9%	73	fisheries 49%, fruits 25%, hides 2%	76
Central Af. Republic	precious stones 29%, wood 27%, coffee 18%, cotton 12%, crude materials 4%, tobacco 2%	74	precious stones 56%, live animals 14%, cotton 10%, wood 9%, coffee 4%, crude materials 1%	80
Chad	cotton/textiles 63%, live animals 30%, hides 2%	95	cotton 43%, live animals 30%, crude materials 2%	75
Comoros	spices 66%, copra 4%	70	spices 78%	78
Equatorial Guinea	cocoa 78%, wood 15%, coffee 3%	96	wood 45%, cocoa 14%	59
Ethiopia	coffee 64%, hides 14%, petroleum 7%, vegetables 3%, crude materials 2%, sesame seeds 2%	85	coffee 56%, hides 15%, gold 11%, crude materials 5%, vegetables 2%	82
Gambia	groundnuts/cake/oil 65%, fisheries 9%, palm kernels 1%, gold 1%	75	groundnuts/cake/oil 13%, fisheries 5%, vegetables 3%, cotton 3%	21
Guinea	bauxite/alumina 91%, live animals 2%, coffee 2%, cocoa 1%	95	bauxite/alumina 74%, precious stones 14%, live animals 3%, cotton 2%, rice milled 2%, coffee 1%	91
Guinea Bissau	fisheries 31%, groundnuts 29%, palm kernels/oil 19%, cotton 11%, cashew nuts 5%	79	cashew nuts 63%, fisheries 10%, cotton 6%, palm kernels/oil 3%, groundnuts 2%, wood 2%	79
Kiribati	copra 59%, fertilizers 23%, fisheries 10%	92	copra 59%, fisheries 12%, crude materials 2%	73
Liberia	iron ore 55%, rubber 16%, wood 13%, natural abrasives 6%, coffee 5%	84	iron ore 8%, rubber 6%, wood 7%	21
Madagascar	coffee 44%, spices 22%, refined petroleum 6%, fisheries 5%, meat 3%, sugar 2%, cotton fabrics 3%, crude minerals 2%	72	spices 22%, fisheries 16%, coffee 12%, sugar 3%, cotton fabrics 5%, fruits 4%, sugar 3%, crude minerals 3%	50
Malawi	tobacco 47%, sugar 17%, tea 14%, groundnuts 5%, cotton 3%	78	tobacco 72%, sugar 6%, tea 9%, cotton 2%, coffee 2%	87
Maldives	fisheries 73%, textiles 11%	84	fisheries 77%	77
Mali	live animals 50%, cotton 34%, gold 8%, groundnut oil 3%	92	cotton 45%, live animals 23%, gold 3%, groundnut oil 1%	71

Table 1.2 (contd.)

Country/territory	1979–1981 (average)	Share*	1991–1993 (average)	Share*
Mauritania	iron ore 70%, live animals 18%, fisheries 7%	95	iron ore 45%, fisheries 28%, live animals 9%, petroleum 2%	82
Mozambique	nuts 20%, sugar 11%, fisheries 10%, tea 8%, cotton lint 7%, wood 5%, copra 4%	41	fisheries 47%, nuts 10%, cotton lint 9%, sugar 4%, copra 3%, fruits 2%, wood 1%	66
Myanmar	rice milled 40%, wood 24%, vegetables 5%, tin 4%, precious stones 4%, fisheries 3%, rubber 3%, jute 2%, tungsten 2%	69	wood 29%, vegetables 18%, rice milled 8%, fisheries 7%, sesame seeds 6%, spices 2%, precious stones 2%, copper 1%, rubber 1%	55
Nepal	jute/jute products 18%, hides 17%, cereals 13%, wood 11%, carpets 6%, live animals 4%, vegetables 4%, spices 2%	48	carpets 44%, textiles 14%, vegetables 4%, live animals 2%, spices 2%, jute/jute products 2%, hides 1%	62
Niger	uranium 82%, live animals 9%, vegetables 2%, cereals 2%, tobacco 1%, skins 1%	93	uranium 71%, live animals 14%, vegetables 4%, tobacco 1%	89
Rwanda	coffee 66%, tea 10%, tungsten 5%, tin 5%, crude materials 3%, hides 2%	81	coffee 55%, tea 25%, tin 3%, crude materials 3%, hides 3%, tungsten 1%	83
Samoa	copra 50%, cocoa 21%, taro 11%, fruits 6%	82	vegetables 40%, fruits 30%, copra 14%, beer 8%	84
Sao Tome and Principe	cocoa 87%, copra 6%	93	cocoa 70%, copra 1%	71
Sierra Leone	precious stones 42%, coffee 14%, cocoa 11%, rutile 10%, bauxite 6%, palm kernels/oil 3%, fish 2%	67	rutile 45%, bauxite 20%, precious stones 10%, fisheries 5%, cocoa 5%, rutile 5%, coffee 3%	75
Solomon Islands	fisheries 35%, wood 24%, copra 20%, palm oil 12%, cocoa 1%	79	fisheries 37%, wood 36%, copra 7%, palm oil 9%, cocoa 4%	80
Somalia	live animals 80%, fruits 9%, hides 5%, crude materials 2%	94	live animals 65%, fisheries 11%, fruits 3%, hides 2%, crude materials 1%	79
Sudan	cotton 40%, groundnuts 13%, cereals 11%, gum arabic 7%, live animals 6%, sesame seeds 6%	64	cotton 26%, live animals 13%, gum arabic 10%, sesame seeds 8%, sugar 8%, cereals 6%, groundnuts 3%	49
Togo	fertilizers 46%, cocoa 14%, petroleum 13%, coffee 10%, cement 6%, cotton 5%	73	fertilizers 31%, cotton 20%, coffee 4%, cocoa 3%, wheat flour 3%	55
Uganda	coffee 97%, cotton 1%	98	coffee 62%, cereals 5%, tea 5%, fisheries 5%, cotton 4%, sesame seeds 4%, vegetables 4%, tobacco 3%	72
United Republic of Tanzania	coffee 28%, cotton 11%, spices 10%, cashew nuts 6%, sisal 6%, natural abrasives 3%, tea 4%, tobacco 3%, vegetables 3%	49	cotton 21%, coffee 20%, tea 6%, tobacco 6%, gold 12%, cashew nuts 3%, spices 2%, vegetables 2%, sisal 1%	47
Zaire	copper 50%, petroleum 13%, coffee 13%, cobalt 9%, cobalt 6%, zinc 2%	72	copper 30%, petroleum 23%, cobalt 20%, precious stones 11%, coffee 5%, gold 2%	73
Zambia	copper 84%, cobalt 2%, precious stones 2%	88	copper 80%, cobalt 9%, precious stones 2%	91

Note: * Share of first three main commodities of exports in per cent.

Source: UNCTAD Secretariat calculations.

1. fluctuations arising from changes in the level of demand for imports, currency fluctuations, or other developments in their principal export markets;
2. tariff and trade disputes; and
3. 'linkage' pressures (that is, attempts by their powerful trading partners to utilize economic leverage to force concessions on non-trade issues) (Moss and Ravenhill 1989:521).

There has been little change in the geographical concentration of LDC exports,[10] as the developed market economies remain the major markets for LDCs, and accounted for more than 70 per cent of their total exports in 1990, about half of which went to the EC.

Long-term changes in this geographical pattern have occurred in only a few LDCs, probably because geographical and product diversification are closely linked: markets for manufactured exports tend to be more diversified than those for commodities. Among the LDCs, only Bangladesh substantially increased its share of exports going to developed-country markets, in particular to the United States, from 43 per cent in 1975 to 71 per cent in 1990. Overall, the share of developed countries as destinations for LDCs' exports has diminished from about three-quarters in 1980 to about two-thirds in 1990.[11] This limited geographical diversification may also be indicative of a shift towards south–south trade which may be advantageous to LDCs if intraregional trade flows can generate economies of scale and economies in transport costs.

Another, often neglected, facet of diversification is the restructuring of imports. Trade and current-account deficits are high in most LDCs given the very low level of export earnings, although some have succeeded in cushioning these imbalances by attracting concessional aid and remittances from emigrant workers. The deficits reflect, among other things, the lack of diversification of these economies, and the associated high dependence on imports, not only of capital goods but also of low- and medium-income consumer goods, and primary goods such as cereals, edible oil and other low-income consumables. The import of primary commodities (*excluding fuel*) as a percentage of total imports of all LDCs has not changed over the last 25 years, remaining at about 25 per cent between 1966 and 1991.[12]

Accordingly, export orientation needs to be coupled with a certain degree of import substitution. Trade, and related microeconomic policies, must develop a judicious mix of export-oriented production and sustainable import substitution within an overall macroeconomic policy framework that does not condone inefficient import substitution industries. Indeed, too much reliance on export promotion to the neglect of domestic production may actually fail its objective of diversifying the domestic production structure. As the experience of the East Asian countries suggests, export diversification and import substitution are complementary, since the pursuance of one to the neglect of the other may create structures detrimental to long-term economic development (Amsden 1993; Bhuyan 1986:210).

3 CASE STUDIES: MAIN ISSUES ARISING

This section summarizes some of the main issues revealed by the case studies, highlights the constraints on trade diversification, and examines the national and international policy issues involved in promoting trade diversification. The first part presents the major characteristics of the macroeconomic reforms initiated by the case study LDCs during the 1980s and identifies three categories of constraints to trade diversification exposed by the reforms. The second part discusses the national policies which could ease the constraints, identified in part one, and enhance the diversification efforts of LDCs. The focus of part three is complementary donor or international support measures to improve the efficacy of national diversification policies.

3.1 Economic Reforms and Constraints to Diversification

Like many other developing countries, the LDCs studied have, during the 1980s, initiated a process of macroeconomic and administrative reforms aimed at:

1. reducing macroeconomic disequilibria by reducing fiscal and balance-of-payments deficits (or maintaining them at sustainable levels); and
2. attaining greater outward orientation in order to improve the efficiency of resource allocation.

The policy measures adopted to achieve these have included liberalization of domestic, import and export trade, exchange-rate adjustments (devaluation), privatization of public enterprises and deregulation of the economic environment under the banner of structural adjustment.[13]

In some of the case studies, macroeconomic policy changes and opportunities for trade diversification have to be analysed within the context of a post-war economic and political rehabilitation process (Uganda and Mozambique). For these LDCs which suffered economic stagnation or internal conflicts, the initial strategy is not one of diversifying exports *per se*, but rehabilitating production to regain market shares in their traditional export products or sectors where basic domestic know-how can readily be tapped and trade channels more easily reopened. These traditional sources of foreign-exchange earnings can contribute to reestablishing a viable balance-of-payments position during the process of diversification. Moreover, extensive infrastructural and institutional development will have to materialize before these countries can fully realize their potential for export expansion and opportunities for export diversification and efficient import substitution.

In a second group of countries studied (Benin, the Lao PDR and Mozambique), reforms are being superimposed on economies previously biased against outward orientation or the market mechanism: that is, economies previously modelled on 'socialist' policies.

The island economies (Cape Verde and Haiti) face a different set of constraints to diversification compared to the other LDCs studied, given their geographically-limited resource base and inherent limitations to achieving economies of scale, both of which make it difficult for them to attract sustainable financial inflows.

Alongside the above, all the country case studies reveal two significant issues. First, they demonstrate some potential for trade diversification: both recorded trade and estimates of informal-sector trade flows indicate that there is an emerging trend towards diversification. Second, almost all of them exhibit a 'dual' economic structure: a small urban or formal economy coexists with a large, and often vibrant, informal sector in which trade activities are reportedly very large.

The overwhelming size and significance of the informal sector in the overall economy of these LDCs may modify their economies' response to macroeconomic policy reforms which, by their design, are geared to impact on the formal sector. Trade-diversification policies may therefore have to take into consideration the 'porousness' of national frontiers which facilitate informal cross-border trade.[14]

The LDCs studied suffer from almost similar trade-diversification constraints which are due to the limitations on their economic development, given their high levels of poverty and records of economic stagnation (and social disintegration attributable to civil wars and/or political instability). The constraints on the trade-diversification potential in these LDCs can be loosely grouped into three categories:

1. *political and economic policy constraints* which may be relieved by reforms and/ or international cooperation;
2. *endowment-related and structural constraints* which may be difficult to overcome in the short term, or even in the long term; and
3. *country- or location-specific constraints*.

Policy constraints relate to the following:

- political difficulties (resulting from political instability in most cases) and lack of government commitment;
- administrative (civil/public sector) inefficiency, including corruption and rent-seeking behaviour;
- inadequate land management and tenure institutions;
- a non-transparent macroeconomic framework;
- restricted access to international markets.

Endowment-related and structural constraints include:

- inability to reap economies of scale in production and distribution of goods and services because of a country's small population and low per-capita income levels or the production of similar goods by other countries in the region;
- long distances to import and export markets;
- threat of environmental degradation, given the pivotal role of natural resources in expanding trade or exports;
- ineffective financial intermediation;
- an underdeveloped private sector;
- weak technological capability and its concomitant low levels of human capital in engineering, entrepreneurial and managerial skills;
- inadequate infrastructure.

The above general restrictions to trade diversification are exacerbated by some *country- or situation-specific constraints* which deserve to be emphasized:

- transit and/or transportation costs (land-locked and island countries);
- demographic and labour constraints (for example, the Lao PDR); most recently, the AIDS pandemic is creating a new dimension to this constraint (for example, Uganda);
- political stalemate (for example, Haiti), and the need to establish security of property rights and political stability (for example, Haiti, Mozambique and Uganda);
- limited availability of natural-resource inputs, for example, water for industrial use (for example, Haiti), and proneness to natural disasters and a fragile natural ecology (for example, Bangladesh, Cape Verde, the Lao PDR and Niger);
- exchange-rate rigidity – CFA-zone countries (for example, Benin and Niger).

Conversely, some advantages may be conferred by the regional location of specific countries. For example, LDCs in the Asian region are in a position to benefit from the economic dynamism of the region either specifically through increasing intra-Asian trade, or generally from spillover effects of economic growth particularly in the 'second-tier NIEs' (newly industrializing economies).[15]

The main conclusion from the case studies conducted, as well as from other broader-based investigations into the trade performance of LDCs, is that the choice of policy instruments, and the sequencing of reforms, need to meet the

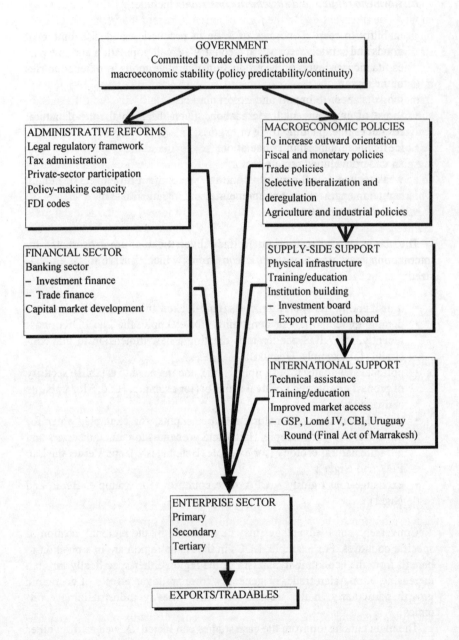

Figure 1.1 Policy and institutional framework for trade diversification

specific institutional and structural characteristics of each LDC. In addition, supply-side interventions in the form of agriculture and industrial policies and physical infrastructure provision are a prerequisite to overcoming the constraints to successful diversification (see UNCTAD 1994a).

Thus, economic and administrative reforms have to be concluded and/or initiated to provide the necessary macroeconomic, administrative and political framework.[16] These reforms at the national level would, no doubt, have to be complemented by policies at the international level for their full efficacy to be realized (see Figure 1.1).

Some tentative suggestions have been made, in the studies presented, regarding possible products or sectors into which the individual countries might be able to diversify. While this is a useful exercise, it should be emphasized that it would be important to carry out the necessary reforms and to create the conditions for competitive production in order to identify with more certainty the items that can be efficiently produced. In-depth feasibility studies would need to be made on the competitive production of specific products for the international market in order to be able to identify policy priorities and sectoral strategies for each country.[17]

3.2 National Policies for Trade Diversification

Trade diversification calls for a sophisticated array of macro-, sectoral- and micro-policy initiatives and instruments which take into account resource endowments, formal- and informal-sector production and trade patterns, and institutional capacities of each LDC. The selection and implementation of policy options to change the economic environment require a political leadership committed, in particular, to diversification, and to development generally. Specifically, the role of government is crucial for four separate, but related, reasons.

First, the government needs to be committed to implementing vital fiscal and monetary policies to create an overall framework which generates macroeconomic stability and policy predictability or continuity. The Haiti case study draws attention to how macroeconomic instability (precipitated by political crisis) can instigate the cancellation or withdrawal of new investments and wreck a burgeoning trade-diversification process.

Second, the administrative system needs to be reviewed, as discussed below, in order to facilitate export and import trade. Discretionary measures that may be required to attain the value-added objective of trade diversification (for example, targeting of incentives) should be based on administrative transparency and accountability.

Third, governments need to pursue agricultural and industrial development policies conducive to broadening and upgrading the productive base.

Fourth, the government has to improve the quality of physical infrastructure, and to launch or strengthen various institutions to promote investment, and to facilitate the acquisition and adaptation of technological innovations. There is a role for a governmental body (for example, an Export Promotion Council) responsible for the search for and identification of new markets and for disseminating market information to entrepreneurs and traders on a systematic basis.

In summary, governments should provide public goods, including economic and physical infrastructure, education and training facilities, and the legal, regulatory and promotional framework conducive to the conduct of private business. The policy framework, in particular trade and exchange-rate policies, should not discriminate against production for export. An added dimension in the fine-tuning of trade policy, especially in LDCs, is the role of the informal sector both in production and trade. Given the importance and predominance of the informal sector as a source of employment and livelihood for large segments of the population, policy recommendations have to be sensitive to and supportive of this sector. It is essential that informal establishments capable of sustainable growth are not asphyxiated by new trade regimes, but rather enabled to continue contributing to the diversification of production and trade.

Overall, the case for a 'refined' or 'selective' role of government in the trade-diversification strategies of the LDCs studied, and more generally in economic-policy formulation and implementation of LDCs, is evident.

The rest of this section discusses salient policy reforms that have to be intensified or initiated at the national level to resolve the *policy and endowment-related and structural constraints*.

Removing policy constraints
A key policy recommendation in the structural adjustment programmes of the 1980s, was to improve competitiveness via exchange-rate adjustment, which in practice generally implied devaluation. The exchange rate influences the relative prices at which traded and non-traded goods are produced and sold. Specifically, a devaluation is expected to enhance the competitiveness of a country's traded-goods sector through:

1. increasing profitability of export production via an increase in the domestic currency unit of the value of exports;
2. increasing demand in foreign markets for a country's exports by reducing the foreign price of these exports; and
3. switching domestic expenditure away from imports to import substitutes via an increase in the domestic currency price of imports.

The extent of nominal devaluation which has taken place in LDCs is well documented (see UNCTAD 1992a:PartI). A nominal devaluation does not, however, automatically imply that exportable goods are sold more cheaply in international markets. The price of export goods is also determined by the impact of domestic inflation on the export sector.[18]

The regional case study on Africa, presented in this book, analyses the impact of recent trade-related reforms (that is, exchange-rate liberalization) undertaken in the 1980s, on the growth and composition of output and exports in African developing countries. It concluded that exchange-rate policy has not been an effective means of stimulating the export sector; that reductions in foreign-exchange availability due to deteriorating income terms of trade causes import compression and retards economic growth; and finally, that the aid inflows play an important complementary role in the liberalization process by maintaining investment levels, and therefore strengthening the supply response to price changes (Kirkpatrick and Weiss, Chapter 2 in this book).[19]

These results call into question the nature of recent adjustment programmes in LDCs, and perhaps, cast doubt on the desirability of a large devaluation as a first stage of the process. Certainly, they underscore the fact that while exchange-rate depreciation may be necessary, it may not be a sufficient condition for improving export performance in LDCs. Supply-side or structural constraints have to be eased to improve the efficacy of exchange-rate adjustments, specifically, and adjustment programmes generally (see UNCTAD 1994a:57–67). Indeed, as discussed below, the success of trade-policy reforms to attain trade diversification also requires international support, finance, technical assistance and improved market access.

The success or failure of export-diversification policies and strategies will depend considerably on administrative efficiency, transparency and account-ability which can be enhanced by:

1. simplifying and streamlining tariff structures and customs procedures and reducing quantitative restrictions; and
2. limiting government intervention to those activities for which it has the financial and managerial capabilities.

Any intervention by government has to be transparent, disciplined and based on rigorously-defined performance criteria for specific sectors or industries. The aim of such interventions should be to complement, and not substitute for, the working of markets, bearing in mind that, in the LDCs' context, markets are frequently weak or dysfunctional (see UNCTAD 1994a:43ff).

The following is an illustrative list of measures towards liberalized trade and export promotion which could be tailored to meet specific institutional weaknesses of LDCs:

- removal or reduction of quantitative restrictions (QRs);
- tariff adjustment to levels reflecting economic objectives. Selective tariff structuring has been used in some developed countries successfully (see UNCTAD 1994c:viii, 49–76);

- export promotion and improved trade-facilitation programmes;
- quality control, especially of exports, to ensure that all exporters adhere to international standards so as not to jeopardize export opportunities; and
- development of a legal and regulatory framework favourable to private investment, domestic as well as foreign.

Specific export incentive schemes to promote non-traditional exports may take the form of:

- export performance benefit scheme, for example, tax benefits;
- duty drawbacks whereby an exporter is entitled to a refund of customs duties or sales taxes on imports of raw materials for the manufacture of its export products;
- duty rebates on the import of capital equipment and spare parts; and
- bonded warehouse facilities against back-to-back letters of credit.

Resolving endowment-related and structural constraints

Retraining and on-the-job-training schemes may have to be instituted with both the public and private sector acting in concert to meet the requirements of new technology necessary for diversification. Given financial constraints, educational expenditure may have to be focused on providing basic – primary and secondary – education. Vocational training, post-secondary education and continued education programmes have a significant role to play and need to tap innovative sources of expertise and of finance (see UNCTAD 1994a:159). Technical and managerial skills' training may be of higher priority in the short run, but institutions capable of undertaking basic, R&D-type research will be required in the longer-term perspective to support and generate innovations that facilitate diversification.

In an attempt to improve financial intermediation, some LDCs are undertaking financial-sector reforms with modest results, but banking services in most LDCs are inefficient and domestic capital markets are non-existent or thin. Ongoing reforms have to be concluded and new ones must be initiated in the LDCs with a view to improving competition in the provision of banking services premised on market-determined interest rates, easing barriers to entry and exit of financial and non-bank financial institutions, stimulating domestic savings, improving the efficiency of resource allocation, and providing services crucial to diversification, in particular trade and investment finance,[20] and export insurance. Policies should also aim at the development of domestic capital markets, and the liberalization of foreign-exchange markets.[21]

Regarding the role of informal finance, measures are required to create a nexus between formal and informal finance (see Ghate 1992).

Given a sound government investment policy, foreign direct investment (FDI) can be an important source of finance and assistance in diversifying export trade into manufacturing. Furthermore, FDI can accelerate access to technology, disseminate new products and processes, upgrade managerial skills and develop export markets, sometimes by diverting trade (that is, taking advantage of unfilled quotas or of preferential tariff treatment for LDCs). Their improved policy stance on investments notwithstanding, many LDCs have received very little of the increased FDI flows to developing countries since the mid-1980s: for example, LDC share of FDI inflows to developing countries declined from an annual average of 2.2 per cent in 1991 to 0.6 per cent in 1992.[22]

Within this overall picture, FDI has been playing a growing role in certain LDCs, mainly because of the emergence of Japan and the NIEs as sources of FDI. For example in Bangladesh, nearly one-third of the foreign investment projects approved by its Board of Investment from 1977 up to July 1991 (excluding those relating to the Chittagong export-processing zone) originated from East and South-east Asia. Entrepreneurs from these countries have also been present in some African LDCs (Lesotho, Mozambique, Malawi and Madagascar), participating in export-oriented ventures, although Japan's FDI stock in African LDCs has been dominated by investment in flags of convenience in Liberia.

Foreign investors and expatriate know-how, sometimes even without any actual direct greenfield investment, have been playing a growing catalytic role in launching new export sectors in some LDCs. Examples include the promotion of garments exports from Bangladesh and horticultural products from Africa (Rhee and Belot 1989).

From the experience of developing countries that have successfully attracted sizeable FDI inflows, LDCs can attract increased levels of FDI if policy and structural constraints are alleviated as discussed above (see also, UNCTAD 1994b). In addition, foreign investors should be eligible to borrow working capital from domestic banks under terms similar to those for domestic investors.

Other conventional measures employed to attract FDI, however, need careful consideration in the LDC context. These include forms of tax abatement and arrangements for salary and profit repatriation, and abolition of double taxation. A major component of LDC policy on FDI should be a careful *targeting* of sectors and sources of FDI. This requires a national investment board, a code on FDI, and subsequently a strict adherence to the policy adopted. Efficiency and transparency in the investment board's decisions is a core condition for ensuring that inflows of FDI are mutually beneficial to the investor and the host country.

'Export platforms', the best known of which are export-processing zones (EPZs), are one means of improving the performance of non-traditional exports (see Kirkpatrick and Weiss, Chapter 2 in this book, for the preconditions for this form of export promotion). EPZs are, however, not essential if access to imported inputs at world prices can be guaranteed by some of the measures already discussed, for example, effective duty-drawback schemes or removal of tariffs on intermediaries.

Finally, with reference to property laws, a system of recording ownership of land and other assets, streamlining tenurial arrangements and giving them legal backing are crucial elements of diversification as they improve predictability and reliability of the overall economic framework.

3.3 International Policies Towards Trade Diversification

The capacity of LDCs to achieve a significant degree of trade diversification is partly determined by external factors which can reinforce or counteract the results of domestic-policy initiatives. Supportive international policies could help address two interrelated objectives: access to international markets, and the ability to reap economies of scale in the production and distribution of goods and services.

The question of improved access to international markets for LDC exports is crucial in the light of recent developments in the global trade-policy environment. Market access for items of export interest to LDCs would be affected by the Final Act of the Uruguay Round, and as discussed later (see Chapter 11 on the Uruguay Round in this book) there is a compelling case for external support measures to mitigate possible adverse consequences on LDCs arising from the Uruguay Round agreement.

In consonance with the significant positive changes in the policy environment for FDI in LDCs in recent years, the governments of FDI home countries could facilitate the flow of foreign investment to LDCs by initiating and improving investment guarantee schemes, so as to underwrite some of the financial risks entailed in investing and engendering new technology in LDCs, and by designing fiscal and other incentives for investment in LDCs. By reducing the risk to individual enterprises these measures would enhance the flow of risk-bearing capital.

On the broader question of international development cooperation, two main issues need to be addressed. First, the sequencing of structural adjustment programmes (SAPs) and trade-reform policies (and associated conditionalities) must be reviewed taking into account the special characteristics of LDC economies. Second, there is the need for an increase in the volume of balance-of-payments support, and, more generally, donor assistance to enhance trade expansion and diversification in LDC economies (see UNCTAD 1994a:Chapter III), in order to contain the short-term stabilization problems.

In the longer term, international support measures must be geared towards improving the competitiveness of LDCs in the multilateral trade environment engendered by the Uruguay Round. This would involve increased financial and technical assistance to the LDCs to help them assuage their structural constraints and enhance supply capacity through major investments in physical infrastructure and human-capacity development. Given the low levels of income and savings in most of these LDCs, the resources needed for these investments exceed those that their domestic economies can generate in the short to medium term, hence the need for generous donor support.

NOTES

1. An earlier version of this chapter was published in UNCTAD (1992b).
2. Report of the Expert Group Meeting on Trade Diversification in the Least Developed Countries (TD/B/LDC/GR/3), Geneva, May 1995.
3. For example, the price variability of all tropical beverages taken together (14 per cent in 1982–90) was less than that of coffee (16.8 per cent), cocoa (15.1 per cent) or tea (19.1 per cent) alone. The instability index is defined as the percentage deviation from the time trend of prices.
4. At a different level, the risk-reducing argument for diversification has forcefully been made for economies which are primarily agricultural, and have a large share of population dependent on the agricultural sector. Fluctuations in agricultural output are often severe for reasons which are beyond human control, such as weather or natural disasters. But whatever their causes their impact is likely to fall on particular segments of the sector, perhaps specific localities or particular farm groups. In many African LDCs, the primary objective of diversification would thus be to reduce the food insecurity of vulnerable households (see Report of the Secretary-General of the United Nations 1991 and ECA 1990).
5. 'Expanding' product markets are those that are large (in terms of global export value), dynamic (in terms of export value growth rates), and reliable (displaying stable, or even increasing unit prices). For the fallacy of composition argument as it applies to LDCs, particularly Sub-Saharan Africa (SSA), and for a discussion of commodity markets, see UNCTAD (1993b:25–35, 101) and UNCTAD (1994a:39ff).
6. Throughout this chapter, the term 'informal cross-border trade' is used to refer to a broad gamut of activities ranging from traditional informal cross-border trade to smuggling and contraband trade.
7. The data for this section, unless otherwise stated, are UNCTAD Secretariat estimates based on various publications.
8. LDCs' total primary commodity exports (excluding fuels) as a share of the world total fell by more than half, from 3.3 per cent in 1966 to 1.4 per cent in 1991, indicating that world trade expansion over this period (from $65.2 billion to $3,424.7 billion) had not been matched by a proportionate expansion of LDC trade (UNCTAD Secretariat estimates).
9. For example, the average annual composite indicator prices of cocoa and coffee (New York/London) have fluctuated, but generally declined since 1980 reaching their lowest points in 1992, although they have both slightly recovered since then (UNCTAD 1994e, various issues). The variability in commodity prices for coffee, cocoa and most food crops during 1982–90 was less than that for the preceding period 1970–82 (UNCTAD 1991a:396), but this reduced variability should be seen in the context of secularly declining prices for tropical beverages, cotton, tobacco and vegetable oilseeds.
10. A study on Sub-Saharan Africa covering the period, 1958–86, however, concluded that African countries enjoyed some measure of success in geographically diversifying their trade. Most notable is the decline in the relative importance of former colonial powers in both exports and imports of the three-country grouping adopted. However, while these developments have reduced the vulnerability of African countries to external pressure from one major trading partner, it was observed that this has been offset by the increasing propensity of the EC to behave as a single entity in international economic relations (see Moss and Ravenhill 1989:521).

11. Both Comtrade and Department of Trade data render the same picture (ETS database).
12. Indeed, even for mainly primary commodity-exporting LDCs, primary products make up about one-fifth of all their total imports in 1966-80, falling marginally to about 18 per cent in 1989 and 1991 (see UNCTAD 1991a:81 and UNCTAD 1993a:85).
13. The adjustment programmes of most of these countries are supported by IMF/World Bank conditional funding through structural adjustment facilities, but Cape Verde did not make use of these facilities (see country case study).
14. It may be observed *ex ante* that the effects of individual policy measures on informal-sector trade flows may differ depending on whether products involved are 'reexports' from, or main exports of, the country from which the trade originates; or indeed, products for which the potential exists for the country to diversify into 'officially'.
15. See Madhur 1994.
16. Macroeconomic policies for diversification in LDCs will need to be supported by a wide range of incentives for micro-enterprises (see UNCTAD 1992a:Part I).
17. As cautioned by Johnson, although it is sometimes possible and easy to give concrete examples of what to diversify into, it is not necessary to do so, as 'one does not know *ex ante*' (Johnson 1991:24ff.).
18. Such relative price movements are captured by the concept of 'real' or 'real effective' exchange rate (REER): the nominal effective exchange rate (a weighted average of the nominal value of a country's currency in terms of the currencies of its trading partners) corrected for relative inflation rates between the country and its trading partners. It is normally expressed as an index. For a discussion of the statistical relationship between movements of REER and real export earnings as well as export volumes, see UNCTAD (1992a:Part I) and Kirkpatrick and Weiss (Chapter 2 in this book).
19. Also, UNCTAD studies on a sample of LDCs and other countries, based on data for REER and export earnings, revealed no significant association between devaluation and export growth (UNCTAD 1992a:22–9).
20. For an in-depth assessment and evaluation of trade financing in developing countries, see UNCTAD (1991c).
21. See UNCTAD (1992a, 1992b) and ESCAP (1992) for a discussion of interest rates, pricing and marketing arrangements in LDCs and reforms being undertaken. Research on selected LDCs has revealed that some LDCs have a problem of excess liquidity, indicating the paucity of bankable projects and hence investment activities, rather than savings and capital, constitute their bottleneck.
22. In absolute terms, FDI inflows to all LDCs in 1992 (roughly US$0.3 billion) was about equivalent to the inflows to Pakistan during that year. For a more detailed account of FDI trends in LDCs, see UNCTAD (1994b and 1994d:60–65).

REFERENCES

Agosin, M. and D. Tussie (1993), *Trade and Growth: New Dilemmas in Trade Policy*, New York: St Martin's Press.

Amsden, A.H. (1993), *Structural Macroeconomic Underpinnings of Effective Industrial Policy: Fast Growth in Five Asian Countries*, UNCTAD Discussion Paper no. 57.

Baban, R. and I. Greene (1992), *The Export Performance of Sub-Saharan Africa, 1970–1990: A Survey*, IMF Working Paper 92/55, Washington.

Bevan, D., A. Bigsten, P. Collier and J.W. Gunning (1987), *East African Lessons on Economic Liberalization*, Aldershot: Trade Policy Research Centre.

Bhuyan, A.R. (1986), 'Trade Policy for Development', *Journal of Management Business and Economics*, vol. 12, no. 2 (Apr.) pp. 194–214.

Davenport, M. (1994), *Possible Improvements to the Generalized System of Preferences*, UNCTAD/ITD/8, Geneva: United Nations.

Deanne, J. (1991), *Foreign Direct Investment, The Neglected Twin of Trade*, The Group of Thirty, Paper 33, Washington.

Economic Commission for Africa (ECA) (1990), *Survey of Economic and Social Conditions in African LDCs, 1989–1990*, April, Addis Ababa: United Nations.

Economic and Social Commission for Asia and the Pacific (ESCAP) (1992), *Mobilization of Financial Resources in ESCAP Least Developed Countries*, Bangkok: ESCAP.

GATT (1994), 'Increases in market access resulting from the Uruguay Round', *News of the Uruguay Round of Multilateral Trade Negotiations*, Geneva: GATT.

Ghate, P.B. (1992), *Informal Finance: Some Findings from Asia*, Manila/Oxford: Oxford University Press.

Jaffee, S. (1992), 'Enhancing agricultural growth through diversification in Sub-Saharan Africa', in S. Barghouti, L. Garbus and D. Umali (eds), *Trends in Agricultural Diversification, Regional Perspectives*, World Bank Technical Paper no. 180, pp. 61–92, Washington: World Bank.

Johnson, O. (1991), 'Economic Integration in Africa: Enhancing Prospects for Success', *Journal of Modern African Studies*, vol. 29, no. 1, pp. 1–26.

Kirchbach, F. von (1990), *Competitiveness of Exports from the Preferential Trade Area in International Markets 1984 to 1988*, ITC/DTC/90/1302, Geneva: United Nations.

Lall, S. (1993), 'Trade Policies for Development: A Policy Prescription for Africa', *Development Policy Review*, vol. 11, pp. 47–66.

Madhur, S. (1994), 'Trade Reform and Performance in Selected Least Developed Countries in Asia', Background Paper submitted to UNCTAD Trade Diversification Project (unpublished).

Mayer, J. (1993), 'Diversification experience in least developed countries', mimeo, Geneva.

Mayer, J. (1994), 'Analysis of the Evolution of Commodity Dependence, Diversification and Interrelationship with Economic Characteristics of Developing Countries', mimeo, Geneva.

Moss, J. and J. Ravenhill (1989), 'Trade Diversification in Black Africa', *Journal of Modern and African Studies*, vol. 27, no. 3, pp. 521–545.

Report of the Secretary-General of the United Nations (1991), 'Implementation of diversification in the commodity sector in Africa at the national, subregional and regional levels with the support of the international community', A/46/324/add.1, New York.

Rhee, Y.W. and T. Belot (1989), *The Role of Catalytic Agents in Entering International Markets*, World Bank Industry and Energy Working Paper no. 5, Washington.

Shafaeddin, M. (1994), *The Impact of Trade Liberalization on Export and GDP Growth in Least Developed Countries*, UNCTAD Discussion Paper no. 85, Geneva.

Streeten, P. (1993), 'The Special Problems of Small Countries', *World Development*, vol. 21, no. 2, pp. 197–202.

Taylor, L. (1993), 'The Rocky Road to Reform: Trade, Industrial, Financial, and Agricultural Strategies', *World Development*, vol. 2, no. 4, pp. 577–590.

UNCTAD (1990), *Diversification, Processing Marketing and Distribution, Including Transportation, with a View to Identification of Special Needs and Problems of the Least Developed Countries*, TD/B/C.1/312, Geneva: United Nations.

UNCTAD (1991a), *Commodity Yearbook*, New York: United Nations.

UNCTAD (1991b), *Handbook of International Trade and Development Statistics, 1990*, New York: United Nations.

UNCTAD (1991c), *Trade Financing in Developing Countries: An Evaluation of Existing Schemes and Future Requirements*, Geneva: United Nations.

UNCTAD (1992a), *Trade and Development Report 1991*, New York: United Nations.

UNCTAD (1992b), *The Least Developed Countries 1992 Report*, New York: United Nations.

UNCTAD (1992c), *Analysis of National Experiences in Horizontal and Vertical Diversification, Including the Possibilities for Crop Substitution*, TD/B/CN.1/14, Geneva: United Nations.

UNCTAD (1993a), *Commodity Yearbook*, New York: United Nations.

UNCTAD (1993b), *Trade and Development Report 1993*, New York: United Nations.

UNCTAD (1993c), *The Role of GSP in Improving LDCs' Access to Markets: Some Recent Developments*, TD/B/39(2)/CRP.7, Geneva: United Nations.

UNCTAD (1993d), 'Evaluation of the Draft Final Results of the Uruguay Round by African Countries', African MTN Project, mimeo, Geneva.

UNCTAD (1993e), *Situation and Prospects for Commodities. Identification and analysis of factors affecting commodity markets with a view, inter alia, to reducing distortions*, TD/B/CN.1/13, Geneva: United Nations.

UNCTAD (1994a), *The Least Developed Countries 1993–1994 Report*, New York: United Nations.

UNCTAD (1994b), *Foreign Direct Investment to the Least Developed Countries and Other Developing Countries Outside Africa*, E/C.10/1994/6.11, Geneva: United Nations.

UNCTAD (1994c), *Trade and Development Report*, New York and Geneva: United Nations.

UNCTAD (1994d), *World Investment Report, 1994*, 'Transnational Corporations, Employment and the Work Place', New York and Geneva: United Nations.

UNCTAD (1994e), *Monthly Commodity Price Bulletin*, various issues, Geneva.

2. Trade diversification in Sub-Saharan Africa and in the African LDCs: efforts, constraints and results

Colin Kirkpatrick and John Weiss

1 TRADE DIVERSIFICATION: CORE ISSUES

The main objective of trade-diversification programmes and measures is to boost earnings from trade and reduce dependence on commodities that are vulnerable to major price and volume fluctuations or declining price trends (UNCTAD 1992:77). The concept of diversification is therefore multidimensional, and incorporates the separate, though related, objectives of trade expansion, earnings stability and increased value-added content. These three facets of trade diversification need not always be mutually consistent, and an assessment of the net impact of various policy initiatives may involve weighing, in terms of relative importance, the separate indicators of trade-diversification performance.

At the national level, trade-diversification programmes will involve an array of macro-, sectoral- and micro-policy initiatives and instruments. These measures must in turn take account of differences between countries in terms of the size, resource endowments, trading and production patterns, and institutional capacities.

The focus of this chapter is on trade diversification in African least developed countries.[1] Trade diversification is considered in terms of its trade expansion dimension, particularly the production of non-traditional, manufactured exports which, historically, have been characterized by superior terms of trade and growth performance. It is reasonable to assume that progress in trade expansion will also contribute to improved earnings stability and increased value-added content.

The chapter also concentrates on one component of trade-diversification policy, namely trade liberalization, which is understood to mean a movement in the relative domestic prices of traded goods towards international price levels. In practice, a policy of trade liberalization will involve the reduction of controls on trade, including tariffs, the replacement of direct interventions by price mechanisms, and the introduction of a more neutral framework of incentives for exportable production and imports. Trade liberalization is expected to contribute to trade diversification primarily by promoting the growth of internationally-traded output, but also by altering the product composition of existing production towards higher value-added products and by increasing the share in total exports of products characterized by lower price and earnings volatility. Many African least developed countries undertook trade liberalization measures during the 1980s.

2   TRADE LIBERALIZATION IN AFRICAN LDCs IN THE 1980s

The past decade was characterized by an increasing concern with the reform of domestic economic policy in many African least developed countries, given the need to tackle deep-rooted structural imbalances and to counter the adverse effects of an increasingly hostile external environment. It was widely acknowledged that Africa's structure of product and export trade had failed to respond to the fundamental shifts in the pattern of world trade and production that occurred during the 1970s, and that a reorientation of policy was needed to shift the structure of production towards products with greater growth potential. As a result, many African countries embarked on major programmes of economic-policy reform and trade liberalization, with the aim of inducing significant structural change and diversification in domestic production and external trade, by altering the pattern of incentives and raising the profitability of the tradables sector.

Much of this adjustment effort was undertaken in response to the structural adjustment conditionality attached to World Bank and IMF lending although in some instances, policy reform and trade-liberalization programmes were undertaken autonomously.

During the 1980–88 period, some 34 Sub-Saharan Africa (SSA) countries had adjustment loans with the World Bank and attracted 25 per cent of all World Bank adjustment lending commitments. On a regional basis, they accounted for almost half of all loan agreements (World Bank 1989). Similarly, since the introduction in 1986 of the IMF's Structural Adjustment Facility (SAF) – augmented in 1987 by the Enhanced SAF (ESAF) – some 30 SSA countries have adopted adjustment programmes under these arrangements (Nsouli 1993).

Trade-policy reform has been a prominent element within these adjustment efforts, featuring in almost 60 per cent of World Bank structural adjustment loans (SALs) to SSA (Table 2.1), while exchange-rate conditionality resulted from IMF conditionality.

Table 2.1 Content of World Bank lending operations: 1980–1988

Type of policies	Share of loans with loan-agreement conditions in various policy areas (%)*	
	All countries (183)	SSA (84)
1. Supply-side, growth-oriented policies		
Trade policies	58	58
Sectoral policies		
Industry	22	30
Energy	15	12
Agricultural	45	62
Financial sector	31	26
Rationalization of government finance and administration	51	57
Public enterprise reforms	44	58
Social policy reforms	11	13
Other	28	42
2. Absorption reduction policies		
Fiscal policy	51	69
Monetary policy (Money supply targets)	16	14
3. Switching policies		
Exchange rate	16	18
Wage policy	13	23

Note: * Based on an analysis of 180 SALs and SECALs to 61 developing countries. Numbers in brackets are total number of loans.

Source: World Bank (1989).

3 TRADE LIBERALIZATION AND DIVERSIFICATION PERFORMANCE

3.1 Estimation of a Trade-liberalization Index

Since the extent to which trade reforms have been implemented in LDCs has varied considerably during the 1980s, we construct a simple index of liberalization to allow a quantitative comparison and ranking of African LDCs by the extent to which they introduced liberalization measures in the 1980s.[2]

Of necessity the approach must be approximate since detailed data on the extent of liberalization are available for few economies. Here we apply three proxy measures of trade liberalization: changes in the share of imports in GDP; changes in the share of import tariffs in total government revenue; and the average foreign-exchange premium in the parallel market. The assumption is that economies undergoing trade liberalization will have an increasing share of imports in GDP, will rely less heavily on import tariffs and will experience a declining parallel market premium for foreign exchange (World Bank 1992a).[3] Countries are classified into 'high', 'medium' and 'low' liberalization categories by each of the three measures. Each category is given a numerical score and the overall index for a country is derived by averaging the total scores for the three criteria. Thus each criterion – import share in GDP, import tariffs in total revenue and the parallel market premium – has equal weight.[4] Further details of the procedures followed and the ranking of countries is given in the appendix, and the country coverage is listed in Appendix Table 2A.1.

Once countries are ranked by their score on the liberalization index, it is possible to compare average performance for groups of countries defined in terms of the orientation of their respective trade policies.

Table 2.2 compares several indicators for the 1980s for the country groupings of high, medium and low liberalizers. The performance indicators are

Table 2.2 Average performance in 1980s by country groups

Group[a]	Growth of exports[b]	Growth of manufacturing[c]	Indicator: export diversification[d]	Growth of GDP[f]
High liberalizer (6)	2.88	1.53	−1.96	4.60
Medium liberalizer (4)	3.98	7.05	−3.40	3.70
Low liberalizer (15)	−0.52[e]	1.41[e]	0.03[e]	2.27[g]
Average: high–medium (10)	3.31	4.29	−2.60	4.20
Average: very low (5)	0.70	1.30	8.70	4.95

Notes:
a.   Number of countries in brackets.
b.   Average annual growth in per cent, 1980–91.
c.   Average annual growth in per cent, 1980–90. Data are available for less countries than for exports.
d.   Change in percentage points share of the three major exports in total exports; a negative sign indicates diversification.
e.   Significantly different from average for high–medium group at 1 per cent level.
f.   Average annual growth 1986–90 in per cent with GDP valued at current price $.
g.   Significantly different from average for high–medium group at 10 per cent level.
The countries covered are the 25 African LDCs listed in Appendix Table 2A.1.

Source: Calculated from data in UNCTAD (1993a).

average annual growth of total exports (1980–91), average annual growth of manufacturing (1980–90), a measure of export diversification over the 1980s, and GDP growth. The diversification indicator is the share of the three main exports of a country in total export value; changes in this ratio are calculated for the 1980s. Data come from UNCTAD sources, principally UNCTAD (1993a) and from the World Bank (1992a).

The results show a consistent tendency for countries with low scores on the liberalization index to perform poorly during the 1980s in terms of all three criteria. For the low-liberalization grouping, average export growth was negative, manufacturing growth was low and no export diversification took place. Average GDP growth was also lower than for the other groups, although by this criterion there is less divergence in performance. For the five countries at the very bottom of the index scale (the very low liberalizers) performance was worse than the group average for the low liberalizers by two of the four criteria.

On the other hand, in general, the countries with a high value of the index tended to perform better than average for African LDCs as a whole. The high and medium liberalizers displayed both positive export and manufacturing growth and higher export diversification during the 1980s. Their GDP growth was also higher than for other countries. However, the link between higher values of the index and performance is not consistent, since the medium-liberalizer group shows a superior performance to the high group by all three

Table 2.3   Average performance in selected indicators by country groups: 1986-1990

Group[a]	Growth of exports[b]	Indicator growth of manufacturing[c]	Growth of GDP[e]
High liberalizer (6)	4.26	3.76	10.90
Medium liberalizer (4)	15.69	8.99	8.00
Low liberalizer (15)	1.94[d]	2.55[d]	5.00[f]
Average: high–medium (10)	8.83	6.37	9.74
Average: very low (5)	3.40	1.25	9.26

Notes:
a.   Number of countries in brackets.
b.   Average annual growth, 1986–91.
c.   Average annual growth, 1986–90. Less countries are covered than for exports.
d.   Significantly different from average for high–medium group at 1 per cent level.
e.   Average annual growth 1986–90 with GDP valued at current price $.
f.   Significantly different from average for high–medium group at 5 per cent level.
The countries covered are those of Appendix Table 2A.1.

Sources: Calculated from data in UNCTAD (1993a) and World Bank (1992a).

indicators, and surprisingly, the very low-liberalization group has a relatively good GDP performance. Simple linear regression tests correlating country values of the index with export growth over the 1980s reveal a positive, but statistically weak relationship; higher values of the index do appear to be related to better export performance.[5] Regression tests for the other performance indicators, manufacturing growth and export diversification, reveal no significant relationship with the index.

A similar pattern is revealed if we consider only the second half of the 1980s. In general, performance in most LDCs improved in the later period compared with the decade as a whole. Again when countries are grouped by values of the index, there is a clear tendency for the low-liberalizer group to perform poorly and for the medium group to outperform the high liberalizers, except in terms of GDP growth (see Table 2.3).

3.2 Structural Change During the 1980s

A useful indicator of structural change during the 1980s is the share of the manufacturing sector in GDP. For most African LDCs, manufacturing is a small part of national economic activity. Only in 9 countries did it exceed 10 per cent of GDP in 1990 (see UNCTAD 1993a). Over the 1980s, the manufacturing sector had increased its share in GDP in 15 countries, but remained constant or decreased in 16 countries (see Table 2.4).

Table 2.4   Change in share of manufacturing in GDP in 1980s: selected LDCs

Change[a] (%)	Number of countries
above 10%	1
>5 to 10%	1
1 to 5%	13
zero	8
−1 to −5%	7
below −5%	1

Notes:
a.   Change in share of manufacturing in GDP between 1980 and 1990.
b.   The extreme value of 25 per cent recorded for Zambia is likely to be due to misclassification of manufacturing and other activities. This shows the performance registered.
The 31 countries covered are: Benin, Botswana, Burkina Faso, Burundi, Cape Verde, Central African Republic, Chad, Comoros, Djibouti, Equatorial Guinea, Ethiopia, Gambia, Guinea, Guinea Bissau, Lesotho, Liberia, Madagascar, Malawi, Maldives (normally regarded as an Asian LDC), Mali, Mozambique, Niger, Rwanda, Sierra Leone, Somalia, Sudan, Tanzania, Togo, Uganda, Zaire and Zambia.

Source: Calculated from data in UNCTAD (1993a).

Table 2.5   Change in share of manufacturing in GDP in 1980s: African LDCs classified by values of the liberalization index

Group[a]	Change[b] (%)
High liberalizer (6)	1.50
Medium liberalizer (4)	4.30
Low liberalizer (14)	−0.23[c]
Average: High–medium liberalizer (10)	2.20

Notes:
a.   Number of countries in brackets.
b.   Change in share of manufacturing in GDP between 1980 and 1990; average for groups of countries.
c.   Extreme value for Zambia is omitted. Average is significantly different at 5 per cent level from the average for the high–medium group.
The country coverage is that of Appendix Table 2A.1, with the omission of Mauritania.

Source: Calculated from data in UNCTAD (1993a).

This indicator of structural change can be linked with our liberalization index. Table 2.5 groups countries by their score on the liberalization index and gives the average change in manufacturing as a proportion of GDP for these groups. As with the performance indicators used earlier (export growth, manufacturing growth and export diversification) there is a clear tendency for the high- and medium-liberalizer groups to perform differently from the low liberalizers. On average the share of manufacturing declined in the latter group, and rose in high and medium liberalizers. Again the medium group showed greater structural change than the high liberalizers. Regression tests on cross-country data give a positive, but insignificant relation between the value of the liberalization index and the degree of structural change.

3.3   Interpretation of Analysis with Liberalization Index

What we find in Tables 2.2 to 2.5 is that, in general, countries in SSA, and among them the LDCs, can be placed in two broad groupings. The majority, with low values on the liberalization index, show a very weak performance during the 1980s, while a smaller number, in the medium- and high-liberalizer groups, have a stronger but none the less far from satisfactory performance. This result appears to support the conventional view that economic policy reform, particularly in terms of trade liberalization, contributes to the restoration of growth. None the less, these results are far from conclusive: two major caveats need to be noted. First, the use of group averages disguises significant cross-country variations in performance. For example, the growth rate of total exports among the high- and medium-liberalizer group ranged from −1.1 per cent in Lesotho to 12.7 per cent in Botswana. A similar variation is evident in the degree of export diversification, with the share of three major exports increasing in Botswana from 88 to 91 per cent, and falling in Lesotho from 71 to 56 per cent.

Second, the value of the index reflects a combination of policy changes (for example, exchange-rate management and tariff reforms) and changes in an economy's external position. A relatively favourable shift in the terms of trade, for example, will increase export receipts, which in turn allows higher imports and reduces the premium on foreign exchange. Both of these latter effects will show up as a rise in our index.[6] The index itself is too crude to isolate the influence of different policy shifts, or to distinguish these policy shifts from other external factors which affect performance. Thus, while there may be little doubt that stronger economies tend to have higher values for the liberalization index, to assess how much of this strength is derived from policy reform *per se* ideally requires a focus on the circumstances of particular economies. Equally, the composite nature of the index means that it is not possible to identify the impact of particular policy instruments applied in the liberalization process. To address this second criticism, an attempt is made in the next section to disaggregate the analysis by examining the impact of exchange-rate changes on the performance outcome.

4   EXCHANGE RATES AND DIVERSIFICATION PERFORMANCE

An alternative composite measure of the effects of policy change is the real exchange rate. Perhaps the clearest indication that conventional liberalization measures have had only a weak impact in African LDCs comes from the lack of linkages between export growth and diversification on the one hand and real exchange-rate adjustments on the other. In African LDCs, a range of exchange-rate policies were pursued during the 1980s. The majority of countries pursued a pegged exchange-rate policy at the start of the 1980s, but there was subsequently a move to greater flexibility in exchange-rate management. By 1992, five countries had adopted a relatively free-floating system (Gambia, Sierra Leone, Sudan, Uganda and Zaire), while nine others had moved to a form of managed, adjustable-rate system (Madagascar, Mozambique, Zambia, Guinea, Guinea Bissau, Maldives, Mauritania, Sao Tome and Principe, and Somalia). Even where fixed or pegged exchange rates continued, step-wise adjustments were used in a number of cases. Countries in the franc zone also experienced changes in their exchange rates in response to movements of the franc in relation to these currencies (see IMF Annual Report, various issues).

This increased flexibility saw major shifts in real exchange rates in a number of African LDCs, with real depreciation in the majority of cases.[7] Table 2.6 summarizes the position for 20 African LDCs. Real exchange-rate changes are shown for two reference periods: period 1 compares the annual average real effective exchange-rate index for 1980–85 and 1986–90 and period 2 gives the change in the index between 1985 and 1990.[8] In both cases, a broadly similar picture emerges; for period 1, only 4 out of 20 countries experienced an exchange-rate appreciation (Sudan, Rwanda, Cape Verde and the Central African Republic (CAR)) and in period 2, only three countries had a real exchange-rate appreciation (Sudan, CAR and Botswana). The majority of countries had real depreciations of more than 10 percentage points in both periods, with a number of countries experiencing major real depreciations of more than 50 percentage points (Madagascar, Zambia, Uganda, Tanzania and Zaire in period 1 and Tanzania, Burundi, Ethiopia, Madagascar and Sierra Leone in period 2).

Of the countries covered by the liberalization index, those in the high–medium-liberalizer group pursued a variety of exchange-rate policies during the 1980s. Four were in the franc zone (Benin, Burkina Faso, Chad and CAR) and experienced a nominal appreciation against the US dollar. Six others (Gambia, Guinea, Malawi, Botswana, Lesotho and Burundi) adjusted their exchange rates over the decade and experienced nominal devaluations of varying magnitudes. However, the liberalizing economies did not experience larger than average real exchange-rate depreciations: the low-liberalizer group on average showed the largest real exchange-rate depreciation (see Table 2.6).

Table 2.6 Average real exchange-rate change by liberalizing groups

Group	Period 1[a]	Period 2[b]
High liberalizer (3)	–17.40	–17.70
Medium liberalizer (4)	–13.03	–15.50
Low liberalizer (13)	–46.07	–40.26

Notes:
a.   1986–90:1980–85.
b.   1990:1985.
Change refers to percentage point change in real exchange-rate index. See note 8. The country coverage is the same as in Appendix Table 2A.1, but omits Benin, Guinea and Chad from the high-liberalizer group and Djibouti and Somalia from the low-liberalizer group.

Source: Calculated from data in World Bank (1992a).

Table 2.7 Changes in the real exchange-rate

	Period 1[a]		Period 2[b]	
Real exchange rate	Number of countries	Average export growth[c]	Number of countries	Average export growth[c]
Appreciation	4	1.13	3	6.93
Depreciation				
0–10%	1	–1.10	5	9.84
10–30%	9	4.44	6	2.97
30–50%	3	–1.50	3	5.40
above 50%	5	–1.80	5	–1.98
Average for low-depreciation group[d]	14	3.10[c]	14	6.27[e]

Notes:
a. 1986–90:1980–85.
b. 1990:1985. See note 8.
c. Simple average export growth for country groups.
d. Countries with appreciation or depreciation below 30 per cent.
e. Significantly different at 1 per cent level from average for economies with depreciation above 30 per cent.
The country coverage is Botswana, Burkina Faso, Burundi, Cape Verde, Central African Republic, Gambia, Ethiopia, Guinea, Lesotho, Liberia, Madagascar, Mali, Mauritania, Niger, Rwanda, Sierra Leone, Sudan, Togo, Uganda, United Republic of Tanzania, Zaire and Zambia.

Sources: Calculated from data in World Bank (1992a) and UNCTAD (1993a).

Table 2.7 groups countries by the degree of real exchange-rate change in both periods and also shows average annual export growth for the country groups (classified by the real exchange-rate change). It is clear that there is no simple relationship between greater real exchange-rate depreciation and higher export growth. Generally, countries with the greatest real depreciation (more than 50 per cent) tended to have the lowest export growth, and particularly in reference period 2, countries with appreciations or low depreciations tended to show higher export growth.

Statistical tests for a correlation between real exchange-rate changes and export growth reveal a statistically very weak and unexpectedly positive relationship in period 1 and no relationship in period 2 which implies real depreciations have not been associated with export growth.[9] Further regressions testing for a correlation between real exchange-rate change and change in export diversification (defined by change in the share of the three major exports in total exports) and manufacturing growth reveal no significant relationship.

It is also possible to examine the relation between real exchange rates and structural change, as measured by the change in the share of manufacturing in GDP. Grouping countries by the extent of real exchange-rate change in Table 2.8, it appears that those with appreciating rates or lower depreciation on average have experienced a greater structural shift towards manufacturing as there is a decline in the share of manufacturing in economies with the largest real exchange-rate depreciations. This unexpected relationship is further supported by cross-country regression tests which show a statistically significant positive correlation between changes in the real exchange rate and the change in the share of manufacturing in GDP over the 1980s; namely a depreciation of the real exchange rate is associated with a fall in the share of manufacturing.[10]

Table 2.8   Change in the share of manufacturing in GDP in 1980s: African LDCs classified by real exchange movements

Real exchange rate[a]		Change in manufacturing share in GDP[b]
Appreciation	(4)	2.25
Depreciation		7.00
0–10%	(1)	–
10–30%	(8)	–
30–50%	(3)	1.67
above 50%	(4)	–2.50
Low depreciation[c]	(13)	1.23[d]

Notes:
a.   Number of countries in brackets.
b.   Change between 1980 and 1990: average for country group.
c.   Countries with an appreciation or depreciation below 30 per cent.
d.   Significantly different at the 1 per cent level from the average for countries with a depreciation above 30 per cent.

Source: Calculated from data in UNCTAD (1993a).

4.1   Interpretation of the Analysis with the Real Exchange Rate

The result that countries with appreciations or modest depreciations in their real exchange rates have had greater structural change and the absence of a strong negative relation between change in the real exchange rate and exports appears contrary to expectations. Adjustment of the real exchange rate is a central feature of conventional policy-reform packages, and the expectation is that, for economies in internal and external imbalance, a real depreciation, combined with cuts in domestic expenditure, will be required to restore equilibrium.[11]

Recent studies come to divergent views on the importance of the real exchange rate for export growth in Africa. Diakosavvas and Kirkpatrick (1990) find real exchange-rate changes to be a necessary but not sufficient condition for export growth, while Balassa (1990) and Gylfason and Radetzki (1992) stress the importance of nominal and real devaluations. Mosley and Weeks (1993:1591) report that 'liberalization unaccompanied by a real exchange rate depreciation appeared to be worse than useless, in that it lead to results inferior to the sample average. The explanation for this is clear: liberalization unaccompanied by real devaluation will immediately increase imports without necessarily assisting export performance'. UNCTAD (1992), however, reports no significant relationship between changes in the real exchange rate and export growth.

The solution to the apparent paradox between 'conventional wisdom' and the African LDC experience may be that the real exchange rate is a complex indicator that reflects both underlying conditions facing an economy, the 'fundamentals' as well as short-term policy changes, such as in exchange-rate or fiscal policy. Thus, for example, favourable external shocks like terms-of-trade improvements or higher aid flows will appreciate the real rate, while unfavourable shocks will cause it to depreciate. An appreciation may thus reflect favourable circumstances rather than, for example, inappropriate domestic policies. Similarly, a real depreciation may indicate weakening external circumstances or adverse internal shocks such as droughts or natural disaster. In summary: higher export growth may create an appreciation of the real rate, and lower export growth a depreciation, rather than causation running the other way.

Some support for this interpretation is provided by considering average terms-of-trade movements for countries classified by their degree of real exchange-rate change. For our second period, 1985–90, there is a clear tendency for countries with appreciations or modest depreciations (less than 30 per cent) to have a lower rate of terms-of-trade decline than countries with larger depreciations. For the first group, the average annual decline is 0.65 per cent, while for countries with depreciations of more than 30 per cent it is 6.71 per cent.[12]

The ineffectiveness of exchange-rate devaluation in stimulating manufacturing growth and diversification may also reflect the import-intensive nature of manufacturing activities in many African economies. The higher cost of imported inputs, combined with low substitution elasticities, can lead to a contractionary supply-side impact on the manufacturing sector. The likelihood of a weak supply response to exchange-rate changes is increased in primary and natural-resource-export-dependent economies like many in SSA, where there is limited opportunity for switching production in response to price signals.[13]

Additional supply-side constraints may have contributed to the limited responsiveness of the export sector to exchange-rate changes. In the LDCs, with inadequate infrastructure, imperfect markets and lack of capital, non-price

Table 2.9 Export growth and real exchange-rate misalignment

Parallel market premium[a]	Period 1[b]		Period 2[b]	
	Number of countries	Average export growth[c]	Number of countries	Average export growth[c]
Zero	8	1.92	7	6.23
5 to 30%	6	3.73	10	5.66
30 to 100%	3	2.30	..	..
Over 100%	8	−0.30	8	2.40

Notes
a. Average of nominal parallel to official rate.
b. As for Tables 2.6 and 2.7.
c. Simple average export growth for country groups.
Country coverage as per Appendix Table 2A.1.

Sources: Calculated from data in World Bank (1992a) and UNCTAD (1993a).

factors can prevail over price factors in influencing the output response (Mosley and Smith 1989). In a number of African LDCs, the abolition of export-marketing boards in the context of structural adjustment and market-liberaliza-tion programmes, has led to a fragmentation of the marketing system to inexper-ienced small traders at a time when requirements on world commodity markets in terms of quality and timely delivery have become more stringent (UNCTAD 1993b). A combination of these factors could, in part, explain why countries with a high liberalization index have not been the most successful in terms of export diversification, and why those with large exchange-rate depreciations experienced low export growth.

Another related explanation is that the economies that experienced larger real exchange-rate depreciations none the less failed to align the actual real rate with the sustainable long-run equilibrium rate. In other words, the problem may be the level of the real rate rather than its rate of change, so that even with rapid depreciations such economies failed to reduce the gap between the actual and the equilibrium rate. Some support for this possibility is provided in Table 2.9 which uses, as an approximate indicator of real exchange-rate overvaluation, the ratio of the parallel to the official nominal rate. Countries are grouped by the size of the parallel market premium. In both reference periods there is a tendency for those with the highest degree of overvaluation to have the weakest export performance. This result cannot be conclusive, however, since because of data limitations the country coverage in Table 2.9 differs from that in Tables 2.6, 2.7 and 2.8. Nevertheless, it would allow a rehabilitation of conventional policy reasoning since it implies that the complementary expenditure reduction measures necessary to generate an appropriate real exchange-rate adjustment were not pursued and thus, despite nominal devaluations, the real target was not hit.

5 EXTERNAL FACTORS AND DIVERSIFICATION PERFORMANCE

The capacity of African LDCs to achieve a significant degree of trade diversification is determined partly by external factors, which can act to reinforce or undermine the result of domestic-policy initiatives. Export performance will be the result of a complex interplay between the process of trade liberalization and exchange-rate policy, and fluctuations in the external economic environment. Two external factors which will loom large in influencing trade performance in African LDCs are movements in the terms of trade, and external resource inflows. We consider each in turn.

5.1 Terms of Trade

African LDCs are vulnerable to the highly volatile movements in the world prices of their major export commodities. The instability in prices is superimposed on the longer-run downward trend in the real purchasing power of their exports.[14] The supply constraints that are characteristic of much of Africa's export sector limit the capacity for generating a compensating expansion in export volume. The impact of the terms of trade on income growth can be indirectly tracked by considering the movement in the purchasing power of exports (income terms of trade). There is substantial empirical evidence that demonstrates the binding nature of the foreign-exchange constraint on growth in low-income economies.[15] The tightening of external financing compresses imports, which contributes to a decline in growth rates of gross domestic product.

The behaviour of the purchasing power of exports index over the 1980s displays variation across countries, reflecting differences in the composition of exports and in export supply elasticities. In African LDCs, the growth of GDP and the income terms of trade shows a positive relationship for a fair share of countries and for sets of countries grouped by GDP growth rates (see Table 2.2). This result confirms the import-constrained growth argument.

5.2 Aid Inflows

The African LDCs are heavily dependent on official development assistance for their external financing. The impact of aid inflows on economic performance, and in particular on trade diversification, is complex and difficult to quantify with precision. An economy's capacity to make a sustained improvement in performance in response to trade liberalization will be determined by the supply elasticities of the traded-goods sector. The medium- and long-run sustainability of a supply response will in turn depend upon the investment which is made in expanding the productive capacity of the export sector. There are convincing reasons, and supporting empirical evidence, for arguing that in African LDCs, public investment is complementary to private investment. Moreover, publicly-provided infrastructure and other inputs are a necessary catalyst in '*crowding in*' private-sector investment (White 1992; Mosley et al. 1992). Aid inflows may therefore have a role to play in the liberalization process, by maintaining investment and hence facilitating the supply response to demand and price shifts. For example, aid may offset the deleterious effects, on investment, of devaluation decisions following the reduction in the implicit subsidy on imported capital goods.[16]

The stimulus to export supply capacity can be offset, however, by the impact on the real exchange rate, if aid inflows subsequently induce an appreciation of the real exchange rate. This mechanism has now been established on theoretical grounds, and observed empirically.[17] The increase in domestic demand associated with inflows increases the demand for importables and non-tradables, and causes the relative price of non-tradables to export tradables to appreciate, thereby weakening the export response to the liberalization programme. This real exchange-rate effect is not a problem as long as aid continues to flow in, if it compensates for any reduction in foreign exchange earned by domestic output. However, the economy remains vulnerable to a decline in inflows, which would damage the recovery process.

There is a positive relationship when average growth performance and the ODA–GDP ratio are juxtaposed: higher average growth performance is associated with higher inflows (see Table 2.10). This would corroborate the argument that the net impact of inflows on economic growth during a period of structural adjustment and trade liberalization is positive.

5.3 Private Inflows

The late 1980s saw a significant shift in the pattern of external financial flows to developing countries, with commercial bank loans being replaced by bond and equity portfolio flows and greater foreign direct investment (FDI). For the African LDCs, with large official debt burdens and limited financial market development, access to international financial markets is likely to remain limited. FDI offers greater potential for the LDCs, and can be a source not only of finance, but can also assist LDCs in diversifying their export trade into manufacturing, by providing access to technology, upgrading managerial skills and

*Table 2.10 GDP growth and purchasing power of exports, and aid inflows**

	Average annual GDP growth rate, 1985–90	Average growth rate of purchasing power of exports	ODA/GDP ratio (per cent)
Countries with GDP growth rate < 2 per cent			
Sudan	1.9	−2.2	6.7
Niger	1.2	−6.8	16.7
Comoros	1.2	−1.3	25.9
Somalia	1.1	−8.0	29.6
Sao Tomé and Principe	1.0	−10.3	48.6
Benin	0.8	−0.5	12.3
Central African Republic	0.8	0.0	17.0
Zaire	0.7	−0.9	7.0
Rwanda	−1.0	−2.2	11.6
Liberia	−1.3	−5.0	7.4
Average for < 2 per cent	0.6	−3.7	18.3
Countries with GDP growth rate between 2–5 per cent			
Uganda	4.9	−7.8	8.0
Cape Verde	4.7	2.9	35.8
Guinea-Bissau	4.5	−0.4	53.1
Mozambique	4.4	−10.5	34.2
United Republic of Tanzania	4.2	−7.3	21.3
Ethiopia	4.1	−3.0	16.4
Burundi	3.8	−0.5	17.7
Guinea	3.4	−1.6	12.2
Burkina Faso	3.2	0.3	11.6
Mauritania	3.0	3.2	24.3
Madagascar	2.9	−1.2	11.7
Malawi	2.9	2.2	22.3
Togo	2.9	−1.6	14.0
Chad	2.6	4.5	24.8
Sierra Leone	2.6	−2.0	8.2
Equatorial Guinea	2.5	10.3	31.9
Zambia	2.3	−2.0	14.0
Djibouti	2.0	5.2	29.2
Average for between 2–5 per cent	3.4	−0.5	21.7
Countries with GDP growth rate > 5 per cent			
Botswana	9.9	10.6	6.8
Lesotho	7.5	−3.0	29.3
Gambia	5.6	0.0	38.9
Mali	5.4	3.7	23.1
Average for > 5 per cent	7.1	2.8	24.5

Note: * GDP growth rates refer to average annual growth 1980–1990, purchasing power of exports refers to average growth rate 1985–1991, ODA/GDP ratio refers to 1985–1990.

Source: UNCTAD (1993a: Annex table 7 and 25).

developing export markets. As recent research has illustrated, favourable cost structures and the quality of infrastructure are determining factors in FDI (Pfefferman and Madarassy 1993 and UN 1992).

Given their weak position in these areas, FDI inflows to non-oil-exporting African countries account for less than 3 per cent of all FDI inward flows to developing countries. For most SSA countries FDI contributes an insignificant proportion of gross capital formation (UN 1992).

Only for a small number of African economies have FDI inflows increased significantly in recent years, with investors from the East Asian newly industrializing economies establishing export-oriented manufacturing ventures in, for example, Lesotho, Mozambique, Malawi and Madagascar. But for the majority of African LDCs, the prospects of attracting major foreign investment inflows are likely to remain limited, until supply bottlenecks can be addressed and the trade-liberalization reforms adopted are seen to represent a permanent shift in policy orientation.

5.4 Intraregional Trade Development

The development of intraregional trade within SSA has frequently been proposed as a means to increase trade diversification. Generally, there has been a growing trend towards regionalism in international trade.[18] In Africa, however, the experience has been very different, despite the significant number of regional agreements adopted during the past three decades (see Table 2.3).[19]

Economic theory provides no presumptions as to the economic gains or losses from regional integration schemes. The formation of a regional trading agreement gives rise to both trade-creation and trade-diversion effects, and whether the net effect is positive or negative depends on the size of the two effects. In general, trade creation is expected to be significant where members differ with respect to resource endowment, have low transport costs and already have a significant share of intraregional trade and low common external protection (IMF 1993). In addition to these static effects, regional arrangements can have significant dynamic effects on the growth of output, arising from the expansion of investment and technological gains.

In Africa, the impact of the various regional arrangements on trade integration has been negligible, and the share of intragroup trade in most of the groups has remained small. Official trade statistics indicate that trade among SSA countries that belong to the various regional groupings as well as among SSA countries as a whole, is a fraction of each country's total trade and has remained roughly constant over the years (Table 2.3). High regional transportation costs have increased potential trade-diversion effects, while the creation of inefficient manufacturing activities behind protective barriers has limited potential trade creation effects. Finally, exchange-rate controls and balance-of-payments problems have created serious practical difficulties.

Liberalization of trade and reform of exchange-rate policy in African LDCs has contributed to creating the conditions for realizing increased benefits from trade expansion among neighbouring countries. The measures adopted need to be flanked by active regional cooperation in reducing non-tariff impediments by harmonizing customs and trans-shipment procedures, enhancing communications and transport links, or defining common technical standards of product specification and quality assessment.[20] As a broader policy approach, 'Open' regionalism, which aims at a common external tariff set at the level of the least protective member, which does not attempt to control unilateral trade-liberalization measures, and which cooperates on the reduction of artificial non-tariff barriers to neighbouring markets, would be crucial in expanding intraregional trade among the African LDCs.

6 CONCLUSIONS

The 1980s were difficult years for the least developed countries of Africa. Average real income levels declined, export growth was limited, and the pattern of export trade remained concentrated on a limited range of primary products. The 1980s also saw many African LDCs engaging in trade-liberalization programmes, aimed at generating economic recovery and trade diversification through a process of structural adjustment.

This chapter has sought to analyse the impact of trade liberalization, including exchange-rate policy in African least developed countries, on growth and composition of output and exports. In particular, it has examined the degree to which trade liberalization has contributed to achieving greater trade diversification in the African LDCs.

The results of the empirical analysis indicate that our index of trade liberalization has been positively correlated with an improvement in economic performance at the aggregate level. But an assessment of the causal nature of the cross-country correlation between the trade-liberalization index and performance presents a number of methodological difficulties. The performance outcome in individual countries is likely to have been affected by policy changes that are not 'captured' in our trade-liberalization measure, and by changes in the external policy environment over which the policy maker has little or no control. The influence of the additional factors is assessed by examining the influence on performance of changes in the exchange rate, the terms of trade and foreign-resource inflows.

The analysis of real exchange-rate changes for African LDCs does not confirm the conventional expectation that exchange-rate depreciation will contribute to export growth and greater structural change. This suggests that exchange-rate policy will be a relatively ineffective means of stimulating the export sector and that in some countries at least, real exchange-rate movements tend to follow, rather than cause, shifts in key parameters.

Consideration of the empirical evidence for the 1980s between economic performance and terms-of-trade movements is consistent with the view that African LDCs' growth is constrained by foreign-exchange availability. A tightening of the foreign-exchange constraint resulting from deteriorating income terms of trade compresses import availability and retards economic growth. The inflow of foreign aid appears to have the opposite effect on performance. The supply of aid can play an important role in the liberalization process, by maintaining investment levels, hence strengthening the supply response to price changes. Thus aid can offset the deleterious effect on investment which follows the reduction of the protection-related implicit subsidy on imported capital goods.

The experience of those developing countries that have successfully diversified their exports offers some guidance on the appropriate strategies for trade diversification in the African LDCs. But the choice of policy instruments, and the sequencing of the reform measures, need to address the specific institutional and structural characteristics of the African LDCs. For a low-income economy, with limited experience in non-traditional export markets and with serious internal supply bottlenecks and constraints, a wholesale, across-the-board programme of trade liberalization is likely to lead to unanticipated and even perverse performance outcomes.

In considering the means of improving non-traditional export performance in African LDCs it may be helpful to distinguish between different types of export-promotion strategies. At present the most widely publicized involves 'export platforms'. Here foreign investors are induced, *inter alia*, by a combination of fiscal incentives, low labour costs, and access to imported inputs at world market prices, to set up production specifically for the export market. Export-processing zones (EPZs) have been a popular institutional form for this type of export-oriented production but they are not essential, since access to imported inputs at world prices, a critical condition for the success of export platforms, can also be assured by either an effective duty-drawback scheme or by removal of tariffs on intermediates.

In Africa, Mauritius is a well-known example of a successful EPZ. Among African LDCs, Chad and Lesotho, in particular, have had some success with 'export platforms', achieving annual rates of export growth of about 20 per cent in the late 1980s.[21] However, the extent to which this experience can be replicated on a large scale elsewhere in the region is open to doubt. It is not obvious that there is a sufficiently large pool of foreign investors interested in establishing export platforms in the relatively high-risk environment of Africa to allow many countries to pursue this route. Furthermore there are well-known limitations to this strategy relating to the highly 'footloose' nature of production and the difficulty in establishing efficient linkages with the local economy. Thus, while for a few countries there may be scope for this form of export promotion, one must be sceptical as to whether it would stimulate major diversification.

A second type of export-promotion strategy involves the balancing of incentives for sale in domestic and export markets (so-called neutrality of incentives) to ensure that an increasing proportion of additional output is sold externally. Macroeconomic stability and economic recovery, removal of the major bias against exports created by high protection for import substitutes and duty-free access to imported inputs are prerequisites. Provided major real exchange-rate misalignments are avoided, the actual level of the real rate may be less important than the achievement of relative exchange-rate stability. Export growth in this case is 'organic', in that it emerges as part of a general programme of economic rehabilitation rather than being the driving force for recovery.

In Africa, success with this strategy will depend on the ability to overcome critical supply-side constraints. The limitations of existing infrastructure are well known, but recent work on African industries has focused on its extremely weak technological capability in the sense of the ability to apply, adapt and modify new technology in the process of industrial production (Lall 1993 and Pack 1993). In many industries, lack of technological capability, which is linked with low levels of human capital development, particularly in engineering and managerial skills, is seen as the key explanation for weak supply response to liberalization. The policy requirement is therefore to both expand education and training and to provide incentives to firms to employ these skills.

This interpretation of the supply-side problem can be linked with the role of further import substitution in Africa. Unless technological capability is brought in wholly from outside, by foreign investors, it must be developed locally. Elsewhere, for example in parts of South-east Asia and Latin America, there is evidence that experience gained from local production for the domestic market has been essential in allowing producers to learn to adapt and modify technology successfully.[22] Higher technological capability has allowed subsequent export growth in these economies. This argument suggests that there may be a stronger case than is allowed in current policy discussions for maintaining positive, but modest, tariff protection for local industry, with some selectivity in favour of those with greater technological dynamism. However the errors of past policies must not be repeated. Average tariff levels must not be excessive, and there must be a timetable for phased tariff reductions.[23] Further to avoid serious anti-export bias, additional incentives, such as tax measures or credit provision, must be offered to exporters to maintain broad neutrality of incentives. As technological capabilities grow, this set of tariff and subsidy measures will become less significant.

Although an export-promotion strategy may hold some attraction for African LDCs, it remains none the less a long-term programme. If more diversified exports are to emerge it is likely to be as a consequence, rather than as a direct cause of recovery. As yet, as we have seen, what recovery there has been in Africa is fragile and tentative. Relatively little structural change in African exports can be expected before supply-side obstacles are overcome.

NOTES

1. Not all LDCs are in the Sub-Saharan African grouping which is a geographical classification. In this text, Sub-Saharan Africa (SSA) refers to all countries south of the Sahara, including those not classified as LDCs, while African LDCs refers to the following 33 countries: Benin, Botswana, Burkina Faso, Burundi, Cape Verde, Central African Republic, Chad, Comoros, Djibouti, Equatorial Guinea, Ethiopia, Gambia, Guinea, Guinea-Bissau, Lesotho, Liberia, Madagascar, Malawi, Mali, Mauritania, Mozambique, Niger, Rwanda, Sao Tome and Principe, Sierra Leone, Somalia, Sudan, Togo, Uganda, United Republic of Tanzania, Yemen, Zaire and Zambia.
2. The approach adopted is broadly similar to that used in World Bank (1983) for an index of price distortions.
3. Comparative data are not available for the entire set of countries for each of the variables chosen in the analysis that follows. Therefore, the country average displays slight variations. The similarity in policies as well as constraints appears, nevertheless, to render the results representative.
4. The question of which weighting to apply to various criteria is a fundamental problem in this type of analytical work. The expedient of using equal weights, while approximate, is common: for example, see World Bank (1983) and Agarwala (1983).
5. The relation tested across countries is $EX = a + b\ INDEX$ where EX is export growth and $INDEX$ is the index. Using average export growth for the 1980s the result found is

$$EX = -2.86 + 0.15\ INDEX$$
$$(1.47)$$

   $\bar{R}^2 = 0.09$; $n = 25$; t ratio in brackets.
   The $\bar{R}^2$ is very low and the b coefficient is significant only at the 19 per cent level.
6. However, in this case terms-of-trade movements do not appear to be a significant influence on country scores on the index. The high- and medium-liberalizer groups on average experienced a decline in their terms of trade in both periods, while in the first half of the 1980s, low liberalizers on average experienced a terms-of-trade improvement.
7. Exchange-rate data come from World Bank (1992a). The real exchange rates given are real effective rates where nominal exchange-rate movements are adjusted for relative price changes in a country and its trading partners. Real indices are defined so that a decline gives a depreciation; see World Bank (1992a, Table 3.9).
8. Percentage changes refer to changes in the index between the average annual figure for 1980–85 and that for 1986–90 in period 1 and changes between the index value for 1985 and 1990 in period 2.
9. For period 1 simple linear regression of the relation $EX = a + b\ RER$ where EX is export growth and RER is change in the real exchange rate gives a very low $\bar{R}^2$ and a positive coefficient b which is significant at the 10 per cent level. The results are for period 1

$$EX = 2.65 + 0.04 \; RER$$
$$(1.61)$$

$\bar{R}^2 = 0.11; \; n = 22.$

For period 2, however, using World Bank instead of UNCTAD export data, there is no significant relationship.

10. The relation is $MAN = a + b \; RER$ where MAN is change in the share of manufacturing in GDP and RER is change in the real exchange rate. The result for the 1980s is

$$MAN = 1.88 + 0.04 \; RER$$
$$(3.51)$$

$\bar{R}^2 = 0.40; \; n = 18; \; t$ ratio is in brackets.
The coefficient b is significant at the 1 per cent level.

11. For a seminal statement of the 'dependent economy' two-sector model that lies behind this reasoning, see Dornbusch (1980).

12. The difference between the average for the two groups is significant at the 1 per cent level. Data on terms-of-trade movements refer to the barter terms of trade and come from World Bank (1992a, Table 5.15).

13. For a recent empirical confirmation of this argument, see, for example, Faini and de Melo (1990).

14. It should be recognized, however, that part of the decline in the terms of trade may be due to trade liberalization. If trade liberalization causes a significant shift in supply, the world price may be lowered. The adverse terms-of-trade effect of trade liberalization is likely to be concentrated on the agricultural exports of LDCs. See Bleaney (1992) for elaboration of this argument.

15. See, for example, Hemphill (1974). For an empirical application to Sub-Saharan African countries, see Lopéz and Thomas (1990).

16. This argument is developed in Collier and Gunning (1992).

17. For an application of the argument to a sample of Sub-Saharan African economies, see van Wijnbergen (1985). The argument is applied to Uganda by Lawrence et al. (1993) and to Ghana by Younger (1992).

18. See Kirkpatrick (1994), and de Melo and Panageriya (1993) for details on the recent growth in intraregional trade.

19. For details on the history of African regional trading arrangements see IMF (1993: annex III) and de la Torre and Kelly (1992).

20. For a discussion of the importance of regional cooperation in non-tariff areas, in the context of Asian regional cooperation, see Elek (1992).

21. World Bank data imply considerably higher growth rates than those reported in UNCTAD (1992 and 1993a) for the decade as a whole. World Bank (1992a, Table 6.1).

22. For a survey of the evidence, see Weiss (1990; Chapter 6).

23. What is an appropriate average level of nominal protection for a low-income economy is open to different interpretations: Rodrick (1992) suggests that it might be as high as 50 per cent. For a discussion of the type of protection strategy noted here, see Cody et al. (1990).

REFERENCES

Agarwala, R. (1983), *Price Distortions and Growth in Developing Countries*, World Bank Staff Working Paper no. 575, Washington, DC: World Bank.

Balassa, B. (1990), 'Incentive policies and export performance in Sub-Saharan Africa', *World Development*, vol. 18, no. 3, pp. 383–92.

Bleaney, M. (1992), *Liberalization and the Terms of Trade of Developing Countries: A cause for concern?*, CREDIT Research Paper no. 92/13, University of Nottingham.

Cody, J., R. Kitchen and J. Weiss (1990), *Policy Design and Price Reform in Developing Countries*, New York: St. Martin's Press.

Collier, P. and J. Gunning (1992), 'Aid and exchange rate adjustment in African trade liberalizations', *Economic Journal*, vol. 162, no. 413, pp. 925–39.

de la Torre, A. and M.R. Kelly (1992), *Regional Trade Arrangements*, IMF Occasional Paper 93, Washington, DC: IMF.

de Melo J. and A. Panageriya (eds) (1993), *New Dimensions in Regional Integration*, Cambridge University Press: Cambridge and New York.

Diakosavvas, D. and C. Kirkpatrick (1990), 'Exchange rate policy and agricultural exports in sub-Saharan Africa', *Development Policy Review*, vol. 8, no. 1, pp. 29–42.

Dornbusch, R. (1980), *Open Economy Macroeconomics*, New York: Basic Books.

Elek, A. (1992), 'Trade policy options for the Asia–Pacific region in the 1990s: the potential of open regionalism', *American Economic Review, Papers and Proceedings*, pp. 74–8.

Faini, R., F. Clavijo and Senhadji-Semhali (1992), 'The fallacy of composition argument, its relevance to LDCs manufacturers exports', *European Economic Review*, vol. 36, pp. 865–74.

Faini, R. and J. de Melo (1990), 'Adjustment, investment and the real exchange rate in developing countries', *Economic Policy*, October, pp. 492–519.

Foroutan, F. and L. Pritchett (1993), 'Intra-Sub-Saharan Africa trade: is it too little?', *Journal of African Economies*, vol. 2, no. 1, pp. 75–105..

Greenaway, D. and O. Morrissey (1993), 'Sequencing lessons from adjustment lending programmes', *Kyklos*, vol. 46, pp. 120–36.

Gylfason, T. and M. Radetzki (1992), 'Does devaluation make sense in the least developed countries?', *Economic Development and Cultural Change*, vol. 40, no. 1, pp. 1–25.

Hemphill, W. (1974), 'The effects of foreign exchange receipts on imports of less developed countries', *IMF Staff Papers*, vol. 21, pp. 637–77.

International Monetary Fund (IMF) (1993), *World Economic Outlook 1993*, Washington, DC: IMF.

Kirkpatrick, C. (1994), 'Regionalization, regionalism and East Asian economic cooperation', *The World Economy*, vol. 17, no. 2, pp. 191–202.

Lall, S. (1993), 'Trade policies for development: A policy prescription for Africa', *Development Policy Review*, vol. 11, no. 1, pp. 47–65.

Lawrence, P., D. Belshaw and M. Hubbard (1993), 'Aid, exchange rates and incentives for tradeables in Uganda: the contradictions of structural adjustment', paper presented to Development Studies Association Annual Conference, University of Sussex, September.

Lopéz, R. and V. Thomas (1990), 'Import dependency and structural adjustment in sub-Saharan Africa', *World Bank Economic Review*, vol. 4, no. 2, pp. 195–207.

Mosley, P., J. Hudson and S. Horrell (1992), 'Aid, the public sector and the market in less developed countries: a return to the scene of the crime', *Journal of International Development*, vol. 4, no. 2, pp. 139–150.

Mosley, P. and L. Smith (1989), 'Structural adjustment and agricultural performance in sub-Saharan Africa 1980-87', *Journal of International Development*, vol. 1, no. 3, pp. 321–355.

Mosley, P. and J. Weeks (1993), 'Has recovery begun? Africa's Adjustment in the 1980s revised', *World Development*, vol. 21, no. 10, pp. 1583–606.

Nsouli, S. (1993), 'Structural adjustment in Sub-Saharan Africa', *Finance and Development*, vol. 30, no. 3, pp. 20–23.

Pack, H. (1993), 'Productivity and industrial development in sub-Saharan Africa', *World Development*, vol. 21, no. 1, pp. 1–16.

Pfefferman, G.P. and A. Madarassy (1993), *Trends in Private Investment in Developing Countries*, International Finance Corporation Discussion Paper no. 14, Washington.

Rodrik, D. (1992), 'Conceptual issues in the design of trade reform for industrialization', *World Development*, vol. 20, no. 3, pp. 309–20.

Shafaeddin, S.M. (1993), 'Risks of marginalism of Africa in international trade', paper presented to the Development Studies Association Conference, University of Sussex, September.

UNCTAD (1992), *The Least Developed Countries 1991 Report*, New York: United Nations.

UNCTAD (1993a), *The Least Developed Countries 1992 Report*, New York: United Nations.

UNCTAD (1993b), 'Government policies affecting coffee export marketing', Workshop for Senior Policy Makers, Nairobi, mimeo, 29 November–3 December.

United Nations (UN) (1992), *World Investment Report*, Transnational Corporations as Engines for Growth, New York: United Nations.

van Wijnbergen, S. (1985), *Aid, Export Promotion and the Real Exchange Rate: An African Dilemma?*, World Bank Country Policy Department Discussion Paper no. 54.

Weiss, J. (1990), *Industry in Developing Countries*, London: Routledge.

White, H. (1992), 'The macroeconomic impact of development aid: A critical survey', *Journal of Development Studies*, vol. 28, no. 2, pp. 163–240.

World Bank (1983), *World Development Report*, Washington, DC: World Bank.

World Bank (1989), *Review of Adjustment Lending II: Adjustment Lending Policies for Sustainable Growth*, Washington, DC: World Bank Country Economics Department.

World Bank (1992a), *Africa: Development Indicators*, Washington, DC: World Bank.

World Bank (1992b), *Adjustment Lending and Mobilization of Public and Private Resources for Growth*, Washington, DC: World Bank Country Economics Department.

Younger, S. (1992), 'Aid and the Dutch disease: Macroeconomic management when everyone loves you', *World Development*, vol. 20, no. 11, pp. 1587–97.

APPENDIX

Trade-Liberalization Index

The three measures of liberalization are changes in imports in GDP, change in import tariffs in government revenue, and the average foreign-exchange premium in the black market. Data for the 1980s only are used. Using the first criterion, import to GDP ratios are averaged for the two periods: 1980–85 and 1986–90. If there is a rise of more than 5 percentage points of GDP between the two periods the country is placed in the 'high' liberalization category. If there is a rise of zero to 5 percentage points it is placed in the 'medium' category and if there is a fall in the ratio, the country is placed in the 'low' liberalization category.

Similarly, by the second criterion, the share of import tariffs in government revenue is averaged for the two periods 1980–85 and 1986–90. If the share of import tariffs falls by more than 5 percentage points the country is placed in the high category; if it falls by zero to 5 percentage points it is placed in the medium category and if it rises it is placed in the low category.

For the third criterion, the ratio of the parallel market to the official exchange rate is averaged for the period 1986–90. If the premium is zero to 5 per cent, the country is placed in the high-liberalization category; if it is 5 to 30 per cent, it is placed in the medium category and if it is more than 30 per cent it is placed in the low category.

A high category is given a score of 5, a medium category a score of 3 and a low category a score of 1. The totals for each country are added and then averaged and the final result is shown as a percentage. Only countries for which data on all three measures are available are included in the analysis. The resulting indices for 25 African LDCs are given in Appendix Table 2A.1. The higher the value of the index, the more liberalized the economy was during the 1980s.

For the purposes of comparison between groups of countries, the individual-country indices in the table are also placed in high, medium and low groupings. Since it is not possible to divide the countries into three groups of equal size there is a skewed distribution with roughly half of the countries in the high and medium groups and the remainder in the low category.

Table 2A.1 African LDCs – liberalization index

Country	Index
High	
Benin	36.7
Burkina Faso	36.7
Chad	36.7
Gambia	36.7
Guinea	36.7
Malawi	36.7
Medium	
Botswana	30.0
Burundi	30.0
Central African Republic	30.0
Lesotho	30.0
Low	
Ethiopia	23.3
Madagascar	23.3
Mali	23.3
Mauritania	23.3
Niger	23.3
Somalia	23.3
Togo	23.3
Uganda	23.3
United Republic of Tanzania	23.3
Zaire	23.3
Djibouti	16.7
Rwanda	16.7
Sierra Leone	10.0
Sudan	10.0
Zambia	10.0

Source: Calculation based on UNCTAD database.

3. Trade diversification in Bangladesh: prospects and constraints

Willem van der Geest and Khalil Rahman

1 ECONOMIC STRUCTURE AND POLICY CONTEXT

1.1 Overview of Diversification Performance

During its brief history, Bangladesh has achieved a remarkable degree of diversification. The dominance of the agricultural sector remains, but its contribution to GDP declined from 58 per cent at the time of independence to approximately 36 per cent by the early 1990s (see Table 3.1). Real GDP grew at an average of 4.2 per cent per annum between 1980 and 1993, but much of this growth was in public administration (including defence), trade and professional services, and the transport, storage and communication sectors. The industrial sector had been relatively stagnant throughout the 1980s: by 1992–93 the share

Table 3.1 Share of GDP by sector of origin

	1990–91	1991–92	1992–93	1993–94*
Agriculture	37.6	36.8	35.9	35.0
Manufacturing	9.8	10.1	10.6	11.0
Power, gas, water and sanitation	1.3	1.5	1.6	1.7
Construction	6.1	6.1	6.1	6.2
Transport and communication	11.8	11.8	11.8	11.8
Trade services	9.1	9.1	9.1	9.0
Housing services	7.5	7.5	7.5	7.4
Public administration and miscellaneous	16.7	17.1	17.5	18.0

Note: * Projection.

Source: Government of Bangladesh, Planning Commission (1994).

of manufacturing in GDP was 10.4 per cent. However, behind this picture of stagnation, some structural changes were taking place: the decline of the jute industry was balanced out by an increase in the textiles sector.

The trade performance of Bangladesh during the 1980s reveals a profound influence of this economic diversification process which resulted in a dramatic change in the pattern of merchandise (see Table 3.2). At the beginning of the decade raw jute and jute products accounted for approximately two-thirds of total export earnings, but their value and share in export earnings (in US dollars) have declined sharply since then. The ready-made garment (RMG) industry has become the country's main export-earning industry, and accounted for about one-third and 43 per cent of total export proceeds in fiscal year (FY) 1988–89 and 1990–91, respectively.

Explanations for the relative 'success' of trade-diversification efforts focused initially on the positive impact of the textile quota. For Bangladesh, this ensured market access while limiting the opportunities of competitors, and attracted international traders and subsequently investors (in the first instance from the Republic of Korea and India). However, at the present stage of development of the garment industry, the quota is no longer a major impetus to further expansion of the industry. Nevertheless, the gradual elimination of the Multi-Fibre Arrangement (MFA) under the Uruguay Round will intensify the competition for market outlets for the RMG sector.

The World Bank's structural adjustment programme (SAP) in Bangladesh focuses on industrialization as a precondition for reducing un- and underemployment. In this context, trade diversification becomes an important issue. Trade reforms, carried out under the first and second Industrial Sector Credit (ISC I and II), included comprehensive import-liberalization measures which increased competition in the domestic markets and led to limited growth of domestic industry.[1]

1.2 Structural Constraints to Industrialization

Bangladesh's industrial base is narrow and contributes less than 15 per cent to GDP, of which manufacturing, with a high import content, comprises about half.

The manufacturing sector is beset with numerous problems including: low labour productivity (see below), the restrictive size of the domestic market, inefficiency and sustained losses in large public-sector enterprises, underutilization of productive capacities owing particularly to lack of forward and backward linkages, and lack of physical and institutional infrastructure. These are exacerbated by the lack of accountability, and the prevalence of a large number of 'sick' units, reflecting inefficient choices by the nationalized industrial finance institutions. As of December 1992, 1,555 'sick' industrial units had been identified (World Bank 1993).

The country's industrialization prospects are also restricted by its vulnerability to frequent natural disasters. For example, the direct adverse impact of the 1991 cyclones on the country's balance of payments was estimated to be US$600 million (United Nations 1991).[2]

1.3 Natural and Human Endowments

The natural-resource endowments of Bangladesh are very limited. In comparison with African LDCs, for example, low per-capita land base provides a serious constraint on production. Similarly, fuelwood ratio per capita is low.

Budgetary allocations for human-resources development, in particular for education and health, in per-capita terms, have remained among the lowest in the world. The traditional indicator for the status of human-resource development, literacy rate, indicates that Bangladesh is *below* the average for the LDCs. Un- and under-employment of labour is widespread, but the bulk of the labour force will need skill-enhancing training as labour productivity is low. However, the Human Development Index (HDI)[3] stands at 0.186, slightly above that of other LDCs.

With respect to water resources, an area where Bangladesh differs markedly from other LDCs, the central concern is how to manage the extremes of drought and floods.

2   EXTERNAL-SECTOR PERFORMANCE

2.1   The Trade Sector

The performance of the external sector during the early 1990s showed marked improvement over preceding years. The annual trade deficit averaged $1.9 billion during 1990–93, down from $2.2 billion during 1988–90, due to an increase in the export growth rate and reductions in the level of imports.

The budget deficit remained well above its target of 7 per cent, except in FY 1991–92; but the current-account deficit has been less than 7 per cent of GDP since 1985–86, due, in part, to the slow implementation of aid programmes and projects caused by the limited availability of domestic public resources to execute projects, which compressed imports.

Export performance
The locus of dynamism in export performance lay in the continued expansion of non-traditional items, in particular, RMG, most recently, silk textiles. Earnings from RMG alone stood at $1,240 million in 1992–93, double the level of 1989–90, constituting more than 50 per cent of total exports revenues. Other non-traditional items included frozen shrimp, fish, frog legs and leather, with the composition of leather goods graduating towards a larger share of finished

products (see Table 3.2). Thus, the structure of exports has changed rapidly since 1985–86, when raw and processed jute and jute goods constituted 50 per cent of export earnings.

A closer look at the 'new' export products reveals the high degree of product specialization in the garment industry. Using disaggregated 4-digit trade statis-

Table 3.2 Value of total exports by commodity ($ millions)

	1985–86	1989–90	1990–91	1991–92	1992–93
Primary commodities					
Raw jute	124	125	104	85	74
Frozen shrimps, fish and frog legs	115	138	142	131	165
Other fish products	5	8	6	4	9
Tea	33	39	43	32	41
Fruits and vegetables	15	9	6	6	9
Tobacco	1	1	2	2	2
Betel leaves	4	0	1	1	2
Crude fertilizers	0	1	0	1	2
Lizard skins	1	–	–	–	–
Tortoise and turtle meat and shells	1	0	0	2	2
Manufactured goods					
Jute manufactures	294	331	285	179	195
Jute speciality products	1	–	73	123	97
Textiles, including silk and silk waste	0	–	0	0	29
Ready-made garments	131	609	736	1,064	1,240
Handicrafts	2	5	5	9	5
Bamboo and bamboo products	0	0	0	1	0
Leather and leather products	61	179	137	149	151
Newsprint	7	3	4	1	1
Paper	0	1	–	5	2
Cellophane	0	–	1	–	–
Pharmaceuticals and crude drugs	0	0	1	1	2
Glycerine	1	1	0	0	0
Urea	3	17	36	21	51
Naphtha	14	8	14	3	15
Furnace oil	0	9	19	5	21
Wire and cables	0	8	2	0	0
*All others**	5	31	100	169	263
Total	819	1,524	1,718	1,993	2,378

Note: * Includes items for which details are not shown or available separately.

Source: Government of Bangladesh, Planning Commission (1994).

tics, there are seven garment products for which the export earnings in 1988 exceeded tk 500 million (Government of Bangladesh, BBS 1994b:137).

The rapid growth of merchandise exports from $819 million at the start of the Third Five Year plan in 1986 to $2.4 billion in 1992–93 has also reshaped the direction of trade (Table 3.2). In 1985–86 the largest markets for Bangladeshi products were the United States and Canada. However, by the end of the decade the EC markets had surpassed the North American market although the US remained the largest single destination for merchandise exports from Bangladesh. Exports to the Far East also increased, in particular, to Japan (fish and prawns) and China (Government of Bangladesh, BBS 1994b:125–8).

Considering the changes in the geographical pattern of imports, Bangladesh's geographical trade diversification and product trade diversification, to some extent, seem to have complemented each other (see Table 3.3).

Instruments to promote non-traditional exports

The improved performance of non-traditional items needs to be seen in the context of supportive government policies and measures. These include a flexible exchange-rate system involving a series of mini-devaluations of the taka from 1990 onwards, as well as specific incentive schemes spelled out in the Board of Investment's policy statement (Government of Bangladesh, BOI 1994). The major incentives included:

1. liberalization of the holding of foreign-exchange accounts;
2. the duty-drawback scheme;
3. an export credit guarantee scheme;
4. establishment of the Export Development Fund to facilitate exporters' access to imported raw materials;
5. simplification of shipment procedures; and
6. facilitation of foreign-exchange allocations for business travel.

To reinforce these measures, a number of institutional arrangements for ensuring export credit flows and facilitating export promotion were also put in place.

Potential new export sectors

New industrial sectors with export potential identified in various studies include leather products (shoes), children's toys and electronic goods.

Trade-diversification approaches in the agricultural sector have focused on horticulture. In particular, the mango gardens of Rashahi are seen as a potential source of exports, for example, fruit products and cucumbers have been exported in recent years (Government of Bangladesh, BBS 1994b). There is also the potential, projected to be in the order of 0.5 to 1 million tons by the year 2000, for exporting food grains of both fine and medium varieties (World Bank 1994). Indeed, the current opening up of Japanese markets may provide specific opportunities.

Table 3.3 Direction of recorded trade, 1985–1993

	1985	1989	1990	1991	1992	1993
	(Exports as per cent of total exports)					
Industrial countries	48.2	65.0	71.4	75.8	78.8	78.7
of which						
Belgium-Luxembourg	4.5	2.6	3.2	4.3	3.4	3.8
France	0.5	2.2	3.7	5.4	5.2	5.6
Germany	1.9	4.3	6.5	10.4	8.2	9.9
Italy	3.5	6.8	6.4	6.6	6.7	5.3
Portugal	0.1	0.2	0.1	0.1	0.1	0.1
Spain	0.2	0.3	0.4	0.9	1.0	0.9
United Kingdom	5.1	5.8	7.1	8.5	7.4	8.6
United States	18.1	28.4	30.5	26.6	36.0	33.6
Developing countries	46.6	34.4	28.1	23.6	20.5	20.4
of which						
Africa	11.4	4.7	3.3	1.8	1.6	1.9
Côte d'Ivoire	0.2	0.1	0.1	0.1	0.2	0.2
Mozambique	1.5	1.0	0.3	0.3	0.4	0.1
Sudan	4.5	1.7	1.7	0.2	0.1	0.2
Tanzania	0.7	0.8	0.5	0.1	0.2	0.5
	(Imports as per cent of total imports)					
Industrial countries	44.1	39.6	42.9	36.5	33.2	35.5
of which						
Belgium-Luxembourg	0.2	0.4	0.3	0.4	0.4	0.4
France	1.0	0.7	1.4	1.1	0.8	0.8
Germany	3.5	2.9	3.4	3.7	3.2	2.9
Italy	0.3	0.5	0.5	0.7	0.6	0.9
Portugal	0.0	..	..	..	0.0	..
Spain	0.1	0.1	0.2	0.1	0.2	0.2
United Kingdom	3.5	2.5	3.2	2.9	3.5	3.1
United States	10.2	7.9	5.1	5.1	6.9	4.3
Developing countries	38.5	41.0	43.3	43.0	48.8	47.7
of which						
Africa	0.2	0.3	0.2	0.1	0.3	0.1
Côte d'Ivoire	..	..	..	..	..	..
Mozambique	..	..	..	..	..	..
Sudan	..	0.2	0.1	0.1	0.2	..
Tanzania	..	..	..	..	..	..

Sources: IMF, *Direction of Trade Statistics Yearbook*, 1991 and 1994.

2.2 Financing the Current-account Deficit

External-resource flows

Given its continued dependence on external resources for financing development, the volume, stability and security of the flow of such resources assume

critical importance for Bangladesh. An important source of foreign currency for the country is private unrequited transfers, most of which accrue from remittances by nationals working abroad. Although not fully reflected in the official statistics, such remittances increased consistently over recent years, but in 1990 they plunged to US$761 million, as Bangladeshi workers left Iraq and Kuwait. During FY 1992–93, however, these remittances surged to a record level of US$942 million (Government of Bangladesh, Planning Commission, 1991:Chapter 4).

In the case of official flows, aid commitments in 1989–90 were US$2.1 billion, with disbursements slightly above US$1.8 billion. Aid commitments for 1990–94 were low: for example, commitments for 1990–91 were about US$400 million less than those for the preceding year, although the rate of disbursement was much higher (Bangladesh Aid Group 1991). In nominal terms, per-capita aid disbursements fell to a low of just below US$14 in 1992–93. Considering increases in the cost of aid-related imports, it is evident that the flow of resources in real terms declined in recent years. Less than half of total aid disbursements is in the form of grants. The country has an Enhanced Structural Adjustment Facility (ESAF) agreed with the IMF in August 1990 for three years with a total ceiling of 258 million special drawing right (SDR) (UNCTAD 1991, 1994a).

External indebtedness and debt servicing

The external debt of Bangladesh reflects its medium- and long-term concessional borrowings. Between 1985 and 1991, the outstanding external debt doubled to US$13 billion with debt-service payments increasing from about US$400 million to US$620 million over the same period. The persistent debt burden of the country is attributable to low grant elements in total aid receipts and the gradual expiry of grace periods of earlier loans which outweigh the impact of GDP and export revenue growth. Loan-servicing liabilities have grown at an annual average rate of 8 per cent since 1985, but with export

Table 3.4 External debt, 1985–1991 ($ million)

	1985	1986	1987	1988	1989	1990	1991
Overall debt stock	6,783	7,945	9,972	10,897	10,657	12,066	12,747
Multilateral debt	3,321	3,993	5,013	5,417	5,843	7,036	8,032
Debt/GDP (%)	43	51	57	57	52	54	54
Debt service/exports (%)	31	42	39	34	35	33	28

Source: UNCTAD (1994a).

earnings (in nominal terms) growing at 11 per cent, the debt-service ratio declined by seven percentage points between 1989 and 1991 (see Table 3.4).

3   POLICIES FOR THE EXTERNAL SECTOR

3.1   The New Industrial Policy

In July 1991, the government of Bangladesh announced its new industrial policy (NIP), which explicitly recognizes export orientation of the industrial strategy, and the promotion of private-sector initiatives in industry as requirements for rapid industrialization. However it is not averse to 'appropriate' import-substitution industries.

The NIP maintains the 'reserve list' of seven categories of industrial activities which would be open for government investment only.[4] Private-sector investment would be permitted in all other subsectors of industry, although the scope for private initiative could be restricted in 'regulated industries' to be classified periodically by the government in the light of environmental, public health or national interest concerns.

Supportive policies and measures of the NIP aim at transforming the role of government from a regulatory to a promotional one, strengthening and expanding capital markets, and encouraging manufacturing activities with high value added. It also contains specific measures for the development of small, cottage and agro-based industries; balanced regional development; and protection of the environment.

The NIP provides priority treatment for export-oriented industries, defined as those directly exporting 70 per cent of output or using it as local inputs for export items. Wholly owner-financed export-oriented industrial units require no government approval, and are eligible for additional facilities such as duty rebate on capital equipment and spare parts; bonded warehouse facilities against back-to-back letters of credit; flat-rate refundable duties; and income tax rebates ranging from 30 per cent to 100 per cent depending on income earned from exports.

3.2   Foreign Investment Policies

The Foreign Private Investment (Promotion and Protection) Act of 1980 set forth a number of provisions in respect of foreign investment including non-discriminating treatment *vis-à-vis* domestic investment, protection from nationalization, repatriation of profit and proceeds from selling shares and so on. Under the NIP, the limitation on equity participation has been waived to allow foreign investors to invest with 100 per cent equity participation. The government intends to formulate appropriate laws for the protection of such intellectual property rights as patents, designs, trade marks, copyrights, and so on.

Foreign investment will also be encouraged in:

1. export-oriented industry;
2. industrial units in the export-processing zones;
3. manufacturing of goods based on higher technology for appropriate import substitution or export;
4. industries utilizing local natural resources, or mainly indigenous raw materials; and
5. areas enhancing the capacity of existing production units and improving the quality and marketing of goods produced.

Results

The policies have increased total FDI flows, estimated at $1.4 million in 1991 and $3.7 million in 1992, to Bangladesh (UNCTAD 1994b:66). Asian NICs have been primary investors, partly because they had reached their threshold levels in the preferential export markets in the developed world and graduated to production lines with higher value added (see Table 3.5).

Table 3.5 Approved foreign investment projects

	Asian NIEs	Japan	Other Asia	United States	EC–12	Others	Total
First FYP and Two- Year Plan 1973–80	3	1	5	0	7	1	17
Second FYP 1981–85	14	1	2	1	10	7	35
Third FYP 1986–90	23	4	14	14	27	4	84
First 3 years of 4th FYP 1991–93	29	10	13	3	12	8	75

Note: Asian NIEs comprise Hong Kong, Singapore, the Republic of Korea and Taiwan Province of China. Excludes projects in the export-processing zone of Chittagong.

Source: Government of Bangladesh, Planning Commission (1994).

Export-processing zones (EPZs)

In 1989, one EPZ was operating in Chittagong, another one was being set up near Dhaka, and two others were planned for Chittagong and Khulna. Manufacturing activities in EPZs could be fully foreign owned, joint ventures or fully locally owned. EPZ manufacturing units are also entitled to a number of other incentives such as income tax holiday for 10 years and income tax abatement of up to 100 per cent thereafter, depending on export sales; duty-free import of raw materials, capital equipment and other items used for production; three-year income tax abatement for the foreign executives and technicians, subject to certain conditions; tax abatement on foreign loans, royalties, fees on technical expertise and technical assistance and capital gains in the wake of transfer of shares; export of export-linked items produced in the EPZ to recognized domestic export-oriented industries; and offshore banking facilities.

3.3 Export-policy Objectives and Strategies

Export strategy
The government of Bangladesh has formulated an export policy (EP) on a biennial basis, starting from 1989, setting forth the objectives and strategies for trade expansion, export targets for individual categories of exportables, and the incentives to attain these targets. EP for the fiscal biennium 1991–93 aims at rapidly reducing the trade deficit, enhancing export values through improving product quality, increasing value added by creating conditions for backward-linkage manufacturing activities for the export sector, expanding and consolidating export markets, and intensifying production and marketing of export items.

The main elements of the current export strategy, in addition to the above, include 'rationalization' of the value of the taka; and promotional measures for individual export categories such as leather, prawns, electronics, computers and engineering services, and agricultural products.

Export incentives
Incentive schemes implemented here are in consonance with foreign investment policies discussed earlier, and do not differ much from those extended to exporters operating in the EPZs.

3.4 Exchange-rate Policies

The exchange-rate regime of Bangladesh has undergone few changes since the early 1980s. The Bangladesh taka is pegged to a 'basket' of currencies in which the dollar has a major share. The exchange rate has been adjusted to ensure that average nominal and real effective exchange rates depreciated during 1980–90 to maintain competitiveness abroad.[5]

Bangladesh maintained a dual exchange market involving multiple exchange arrangements. Preferential exchange rates, determined by the Bangladesh Bank, were available through the Wage Earner Scheme (WES) and the Export Performance Benefit Scheme (XPB). Since 1992, the exchange rate has been unified and foreign-account holdings liberalized.

4   TRADE-DIVERSIFICATION POSSIBILITIES

4.1   Leather Products: Opportunities and Constraints

The Bangladesh government, in consultation with the United Nations Industrial Development Organization (UNIDO) and the International Finance Corporation (IFC), identified that very considerable opportunities for Bangladeshi exports of leather footwear and goods exist during the 1990s and beyond. International production trends, which in the early 1960s favoured offshore production in Asia's newly industrializing economies (Hong Kong, Singapore, the Republic of Korea and Taiwan Province of China), recently show an increasing shift towards new low-cost locations such as Thailand, Indonesia, India and China. This reflects, among other indicators, the increased real-wage levels and appreciation of the currencies of the Asian NICs *vis-à-vis* the US dollar.

Apart from the steady growth of demand for leather goods and footwear on the international market, some characteristics of the industry also favour the low-wage economy of Bangladesh, for example, economies of scale in manufacturing are limited, and rapid changes of fashions and consumer preferences mitigate against capital-intensive automation. Thus, wage costs remain a key determinant of the production location decisions of manufacturers.

Production costs
A comparison of production costs in Bangladesh involves two components: comparing cost structures with those of other Asian producers, such as Thailand and China, and traditional US and European producers. Based on typical technical parameters for a medium-size footwear plant, it has been shown that the direct labour costs of Bangladesh compare favourably with other emerging producers, such as Thailand. This compensates for the lower labour productivity in Bangladesh, resulting in similar unit costs. For an OECD buyer, leather footwear production in Bangladesh, allowing for expatriate management and shipping costs, can result in a 35 to 40 per cent per unit cost saving. For a producer in the Republic of Korea, relocating production to Thailand or Bangladesh will reduce costs by about 15 to 20 per cent (Recovery Systems Inc. 1990). Considering the import content of leather footwear production, it is estimated that, in the first instance, the value added accruing to domestic labour and services is unlikely to exceed 20 per cent of the total operating costs of the industry.[6]

Sustainable import substitution
The government has, in recent years, banned the export of primary processed 'wet blue' leather, the third-largest export earner for Bangladesh in FY 1989–

90, and supported the upgrading of tanneries to enable secondary processing to crust and finish leather for export. The import content of leather footwear exports is substantial. However, if finished leather and soles could be procured locally, the value added to the Bangladesh economy, through its backward linkages to the leather-processing industry, could expand substantially. Earning opportunities in the leather-processing industry could also increase by about 35 to 45 per cent of the present export value. Moreover, the reduced transport costs could generate unit cost savings of some 7 per cent, increasing the competitive edge of Bangladeshi leather goods and footwear.

Domestic constraints
Although liberalization has improved the economic environment for the export sector in recent years, implementation and streamlining of procedures are yet to be concluded. Specifically, these include improving customs' performance, ensuring one-stop services for foreign investors, simplifying the holding of foreign-exchange accounts, and execution of duty-drawback and exemption schemes, all of which are important for the sector's expansion.

The basic advantage of Bangladesh, its production costs being equal to those of neighbouring countries, may not sway foreign buyers or investors. Investment in the tanneries to guarantee a cheaper supply of finished leather may be a precondition for winning the competitive battle *vis-à-vis* China, India, Indonesia or Thailand.[7]

International constraints to exports
Access to leather-product markets abroad is crucial, because of the protective tariff structures of OECD countries which erode potential gains to LDC producers as well as OECD consumers. The main importing countries, North America and the EC, also operate tariff and non-tariff restrictions.[8]

4.2   Energy-based Import Substitution: Natural Gas

The energy context
The per-capita energy consumption of Bangladesh at 56 kg of oil equivalent (kgOE) in 1990 is among the lowest in the world. Nearly two-thirds of total energy consumption in this year was met out of indigenous bio-mass supply. Agricultural residues, fuelwood and tree residues, and animal wastes accounted for about 40 per cent of overall energy supply. The power sector has been beset with numerous problems, including chronic 'system' loss. A notable development in power generation is the substitution of imported fuel. The share of petroleum in electricity generation for 1990 had been estimated at 5 per cent and that of natural gas at 85 per cent, as against 8 and 79 per cent, respectively, for 1989.

Domestic energy reserves

The fifteen gas fields of Bangladesh have a combined estimated reserve of 13 trillion cubic feet (TCF). The only oil field has a very low recoverable reserve estimated at about 1.6 million tons of crude oil. Of the five coal and peat deposits, exploitation of only two in north-western Bangladesh with a combined deposit of 685 million tons is thought to be economically viable.

Energy policy

The rapid increase in the supply of natural gas contributed to the rapid growth in fertilizer manufacturing and power generation. The government plans to diversify gas use from supplying to the fertilizer and power sectors towards a direct substitution of petroleum imports by liquified gas. An energy-sector reform programme, drawn up in 1987 by the government and the International Development Association (IDA), included energy investment planning, institutional development, energy pricing, and so on, to be implemented under an energy-sector adjustment credit which became effective in 1989.

Energy import substitution

During the 1980s, natural-gas production increased at the rate of more than 14 per cent per annum, reaching 165 billion cubic feet (BCF) in 1990. The total indigenous gas output of about 700 BCF during 1985–90 offset about 17 million tons of petroleum imports, resulting in an estimated saving of US$2.5 billion in foreign exchange. Production of natural gas is projected to grow at a rate of 10 per cent annually, raising the annual output to 275 BCF by 1995.

The development strategy in this sector, besides promoting the exploration and development of indigenous energy resources and maximizing the efficiency in energy use, also embraces the development of natural-gas liquids, including liquid petroleum gas (LPG). As a substitute for imported kerosene, the use of LPG could result in foreign-exchange savings. A World Bank (1991b) report on LPG indicates that completion of the project, which involves downstream transportation and distribution of LPG from two storage facilities, would enable annual production of some 140,000 metric tons per year by the mid-1990s. Given the ratio of per unit cost of recovery of domestic LPG to the import costs of LPG and the kerosene equivalent at 0.34 per cent and 0.46 per cent, respectively (World Bank 1991b), the switch to domestic LPG could lead to significant savings of foreign exchange for the economy.

The indirect benefits of the project, with an estimated rate of return of 20 per cent, include the bridging of the energy consumption imbalance between the country's more developed eastern region, and the western region, reducing pressure from biomass-based energy and promoting private-sector initiatives in the transportation and distribution of LPG.

Limits to energy-based import substitution

Energy-related import substitution in Bangladesh is constrained by the country's gas reserves and deposits of coal. With almost one-tenth of known gas deposits already extracted, future exploitation will need to proceed cautiously. The extraction strategy should not only reflect present needs and foreign-exchange savings, but also the non-renewability of gas. It will be necessary to continue to explore new sources of energy, particularly of hydrocarbons, although there are constraints, such as lack of donor funds, shortage of qualified manpower, delays by government ministries and agencies in the process of procurement and appointment of contractors.

5   TRADE DIVERSIFICATION AND GOVERNANCE

Integrating 'governance' into the analysis of trade diversification is important for a variety of reasons:

1. the discretionary use of government instruments in the external sector throughout the 1980s accommodated rent seeking, for example, with regard to the imports of sugar, edible oils and other commodities;
2. pervasive government controls over the external sector through customs, duty and tariffs, and other fiscal instruments in the past constrained the scope for development and realization of new trading opportunities and trade diversification; and
3. the strategy for trade diversification in the 1990s, and thereafter, will have to extend beyond 'export illusion' to a value-added approach, which requires improved targeting of incentives, the success of which depends on administrative transparency and accountability.

5.1   Objectives

The objectives of government in the context of trade liberalization are to:

1. enhance efficiency in the public sector by improving the quality of decision making;
2. reduce opportunities for rent seeking through simplification and streamlining of tariff structures, customs procedures and the reduction of quantitative restrictions;
3. move from a 'control' approach in the executive institutions of the government, such as the Board of Investment and the Export Promotion Board, to a surveillance and promotional one; and
4. institute a 'minimalist' government which only engages in activities for which it has the financial and managerial resources and expertise.

5.2   Preconditions for Improved Governance

Responsible private-sector behaviour is a *sine qua non* for improved governance, and a necessary counterpart to adopting institutional changes in government culture and operations. In particular, private-sector entrepreneurs will
need to endorse and perform various forms of self-assessment which aim at
eliminating tax evasion, rent seeking and maintenance of quality standards.

Adherence to product standards for exportables should be of interest to all
exporters, as failures to meet set standards may result in a universal rejection of
exported goods from the source country. Similarly, disregarding legal obligations, labour laws and standards, environmental regulations, and so on, may
jeopardize further expansion of particular (sub)sectors. Self-assessment may
have to be enforced through discretionary rather than random checks and
penalties.

5.3   Instruments of Improved Governance

In general, the structure of government intervention will need to move from
'positive' regulation, describing a complex set of obligations and restrictions, to
'negative' regulation banning only specific, well-defined activities. The creation of promotional and surveillance institutions, started in the mid-1980s, has
to be concluded, and control institutions will need to be demobilized, including
possible partial redeployment of staff in newly-formed surveillance institutions.
Criteria for improved accountability for the civil service, including a customs
ombudsman and one-stop appeal procedures, have to be developed. Finally, the
elaboration of the supporting legal framework should be a priority.

5.4   Interministerial Demarcation

One problem, closely related to the question of governance, and much debated
in Bangladesh, is the imprecise definition of mandates and responsibilities
between governmental institutions dealing with the external sector. The setup
costs for an entrepreneur wanting to manufacture for exports are very much
increased, if contacts and approvals are to be obtained at many different
ministries and levels. The lack of demarcation and coordination, and the absence of a single window for export-oriented industrialization, have contributed
to rent-seeking behaviour within the economy.

6   CONCLUSIONS

6.1   Strategic Considerations for Economic and Trade Diversification in Bangladesh

Export illusion

One important issue arising from this study is that, in appraising the 'success' of trade diversification the emphasis should be on value added rather than foreign-exchange earnings from exports or savings from reduction in imports. Bangladesh's 'successful' export diversification, measured by the increase in export earnings and the widening of the export product range, does not adequately capture the high import content of much of the 'new' non-traditional exports. Informal estimates for the ready-made garment sector indicate that the value added per dollar export earning is less than 25 per cent, while for the leather footwear sector, using imported inputs, it may be as low as 20 per cent. Against this background, it is important that the priorities of the export (sub)sectors are reviewed. As a simple example may show, if the import content[9] of traditional and non-traditional export is, respectively, 20 and 80 per cent of export value, one dollar of 'traditional' exports generates as much foreign exchange as four dollars of non-traditional exports.[10]

This observation tempers the optimistic accounts of the increased earnings of non-traditional exports. But more importantly for policy, it leads one to question the focus and the effectiveness of the export incentives, which are, at present, based on gross foreign-exchange value of exports, rather than net earnings to the Bangladesh economy.

This evaluation of the earning potential of the traditional sectors, however, should be seen in the light of the upper limits of import demand in the major importing countries, and the long-term downward trend of prices of traditional exports. Moreover, the stability of export earnings needs to be considered – fluctuations of prices for traditional exports (raw jute, jute goods and tea) have been considerably greater than those for non-traditional items.

Limits to the import substitution

The export of urea fertilizer, using natural gas, seems to be based on a valuation of this natural resource below its current opportunity cost in the international market. However, the intertemporal aspect needs to be taken into account: natural gas, Bangladesh's only significant natural resource, is non-renewable. Thus an analysis of its economic viability has to take into account both foreign-exchange savings and its non-renewability.

Subnational balance

Investment incentives designed to promote less-developed regions in the country proved ineffective, and were prone to misuse. However, the issue of regional balance in export industrialization remains important and needs to be addressed. Incentives need to go hand in hand with development of infrastructural facilities opening up remote areas. In this context, the emphasis on horticultural development and export, for example, seems appropriate.

Considering the gradual elimination of the MFA under the Uruguay Round which may intensify the competition for market outlets for RMGs, the sector's competitiveness will need to be enhanced by developing its backward linkages. In the absence of quotas, these suppliers might evolve into producing for final markets.

6.2   Lessons for other Least Developed Countries

Macro-policy context
Bangladesh's non-traditional export growth has been among the highest within the LDC group. One lesson could be drawn regarding the macroeconomic management context of trade policy. A 'sensible' set of macro policies, including exchange-rate policies, appear to be a necessary requirement for diversification and development of exports.

Sequencing of trade reforms
Second, Bangladesh did not follow the 'classical' path of phased trade reform. Instead of moving from quantitative restrictions (QRs), to tariffication, liberalization and value-added taxation, elements of all these phases were put in operation simultaneously. Moreover, some QRs are instruments used to promote trade diversification and enhance value added, as in the leather sector.

The deepening of liberalization
Liberalization at the policy level itself will not suffice, unless it is followed quickly by institutional reform directed at deregulating and decontrolling institutions in favour of promotion, facilitation and information activities.

Governance
At least two phenomena stand out which need to be avoided:

1. indiscriminate lending to projects and entrepreneurs without appropriate evaluation of repayment ability; and
2. proliferation of centres of decision making at the micro level in response to institutional weaknesses.

Development of skills
The experience gained from the successful export of Bangladesh garments points to the importance of international marketing skills, assured access to markets, quick generation of a semi-skilled workforce and export incentives provided by government.

NOTES

1. For an account of Bangladesh's trade policies and practices by measure and by sector, see GATT (1992).
2. The export sector was estimated to have lost a total of US$258 million, more than half ($148 million) of which was suffered by some 38 companies in the export-processing zone (EPZ) of Chittagong, and the frozen foods sector in the south-eastern coastal belt (Communication of the Bangladesh Export Development Bureau (1990) to the UNCTAD mission).
3. See UNDP (1993).
4. Reserved sectors are arms, ammunition and defence equipment; nuclear energy, security printing and minting, afforestation in reserved areas and mechanical extraction thereof; airways and railways and electricity (except private generators).
5. A similar pegged system was adopted by 36 other member states of the IMF, twelve of which are classified as LDCs, as at January 1991.
6. The Indian leather industry, for example, which has been dramatically transformed over the last twenty years, only began experiencing fast growth of local value added (from 37 per cent in 1984 to 57 per cent in 1988) in the mid-1980s, when vertical integration between tanneries and final producers was achieved.
7. However, US and European firms are investing only hesitantly in this sector. Throughout the 1980s, only three joint ventures were initiated, two from Europe upgrading tanneries, and one from Canada, vertically integrating leather processing and footwear production. During the 1990s some four new projects have been approved, three for processing, and a fourth for shoe production. In India, for example, manufacturers for export markets are experiencing difficulties obtaining sufficient quantities of local leather of international standards.
8. As of May 1990, the tariff rate (*ad valorem*) was 7.5–10.5 per cent in the US, 4.8–20 per cent in the EC, and 35–40 per cent in Canada which also had preferential access rates of 21.3–32.1 per cent for countries with most-favoured nation (MFN) status, and 15–18 per cent for Commonwealth countries. In addition, all three operate different types of non-tariff restrictions: for example, voluntary export restrictions of large East Asian suppliers, and quantitative restrictions (US Department of Commerce 1990).
9. This includes direct and indirect imports of sectors supplying material inputs.
10. A comprehensive evaluation would include an analysis of the labour and capital intensity of the production process.

REFERENCES

Bangladesh Aid Group (1991), 'Memorandum 1991–1992', mimeo, Dhaka.

Export Development Bureau (1990), 'Estimates of Exports 1990/1991', mimeo, Dhaka.

General Agreement on Tariffs and Trade (GATT) (1992), *Trade Policy Review: Bangladesh*, vol. 1, Geneva: GATT.

Government of Bangladesh, Bangladesh Bureau of Statistics (BBS) (1993), *Yearbook of Agricultural Statistics 1992*, Dhaka: Government of Bangladesh.

Government of Bangladesh, Bangladesh Bureau of Statistics (BBS) (1994a), *Monthly Statistical Bulletin of Bangladesh December 1993*, Dhaka: Government of Bangladesh.

Government of Bangladesh, Bangladesh Bureau of Statistics (BBS) (1994b), *Statistical Pocketbook 1993*, Dhaka: Government of Bangladesh.

Government of Bangladesh, Board of Investment (BOI) (1994), *Bangladesh, a New Horizon for Investment*, Dhaka: Government of Bangladesh.

Government of Bangladesh, Planning Commission (1991), *Fourth Five Year Plan 1990–1995*, Dhaka: Government of Bangladesh.

Government of Bangladesh, Planning Commission (1994), *Bangladesh Economic Survey (1993–94)*, Dhaka: Government of Bangladesh.

International Monetary Fund (IMF), *International Financial Statistics*, various years, Washington, DC: IMF.

International Monetary Fund (IMF), *Direction of Trade Statistics Yearbook, 1991 and 1994,* Washington, DC: IMF.

Rahman et al. (1991), 'Trade and Industrialization in Bangladesh Reconsidered', mimeo, Paris: OECD Development Centre.

Recovery Systems Inc. (1990), *Leather Products and Shoe Industry in Bangladesh*, Washington, DC: Recovery Systems Inc.

UNCTAD (1991), *Least Developed Countries 1990 Report*, New York: United Nations.

UNCTAD (1992), *1991 Trade and Development Report*, New York: United Nations.

UNCTAD (1994a), *Least Developed Countries 1993–94 Report*, New York: United Nations.

UNCTAD (1994b), *World Investment Report 1994, Transnational Corporations, Employment and the Workplace*, New York and Geneva: United Nations.

UNDP (1991), *Human Development Report 1991*, New York: United Nations.

United Nations (1991), *The 1991 Cyclone in Bangladesh: Impact, Recovery and Reconstruction*, SG/CONF/6.1, Geneva: United Nations.

UNDP (1993), *Human Development Report 1993*, New York and Oxford: UNDP.

US Department of Commerce (1990), *Footwear Tariff and Trade Regulation*, Washington, DC: Department of Commerce, Government of USA.

World Bank (1991a), *Bangladesh: Managing the Adjustment Process – An Appraisal*, Report 8344–BD, Washington, DC: World Bank.

World Bank (1991b), *Liquified Petroleum Gas Transport and Distribution Project*, Report 9398–BD, Washington, DC: World Bank.

World Bank (1993), *Bangladesh: Implementing Structural Reform*, Report No. 11569–BD, Washington, DC: World Bank.

World Bank (1994), *Bangladesh: From Stabilization to Growth*, Report No. 12774–BD, Washington, DC: World Bank.

World Bank, *World Development Report*, various years, Washington, DC/Oxford: World Bank.

4. Trade diversification in Benin: prospects and constraints[1]

Lena Chia with Samuel Gayi

1 OVERVIEW OF ECONOMIC AND POLITICAL CONTEXT

Benin, situated on the coast of West Africa, has a population of 4.5 million people. Its per-capita income averaged US$397 in 1989–92, but in real terms per-capita growth over the last two decades was negative (UNCTAD 1994). Growth in the 1980s fluctuated enormously: the boom at the beginning, capped by a 9 per cent growth rate in 1981, gave way to alternating negative and positive growth rates for the rest of the decade. Real GDP growth rate averaged about 2.7 per cent per annum between 1980 and 1993. Generally, growth rates have fluctuated in line with Nigeria's oil booms and slumps. Benin's trade with Nigeria is an important activity, estimated to provide about a quarter of GDP, though much of this trade is unrecorded.

The country was under a totalitarian regime for 17 years until 1990. The military government of Kerekou which came to power in 1972, after a decade marked by a series of *coups d'état*, adopted Marxism-Leninism as the official national ideology in November 1974. Increasing economic and financial difficulties from 1985 led to civil unrest which culminated in the adoption of a multiparty system in March 1990, and with it a change in the style of economic management.

Benin's economy is geared mostly towards agriculture. Cash crops cultivated include cocoa, coconuts, coffee, karité (sheanuts), oil palm and cotton, and among the food crops produced are maize, millet, sorghum, cassava and yams. The *agricultural sector* employed about two-thirds of the active population, and accounted for about 36 per cent of GDP in 1991–93 (Table 4.1) and one-third of foreign-exchange earnings. This sector performed relatively well in the 1980s with palm oil and cotton accounting for about 50 per cent of the country's total exports. Food-crop production has been favourable after the drought of 1982 to 1984 and the country has since attained overall food self-

Table 4.1 GDP by activity and by expenditure (percentage)

	1980	1985	1989	1990	1991	1992	1993
By activity							
Agriculture	35.4	31.9	35.6	34.1	36.2	36.7	35.8
Industry	12.3	16.7	14.0	14.6	14.2	12.7	12.9
of which							
Manufacturing	8.0	7.6	8.5	8.5	8.5	7.8	7.8
Services	52.3	51.4	50.4	51.3	49.6	50.6	51.4
By expenditure							
Exports	23.0	33.3	22.0	28.0	26.9	23.3	22.1
Imports	43.3	45.1	30.0	36.3	37.7	33.2	32.9
Private consumption	96.5	83.5	82.8	80.7	83.9	84.2	84.9
Government consumption	8.6	12.5	13.0	12.4	11.7	11.9	11.6
Gross domestic investment	15.2	15.8	12.2	15.2	15.2	13.8	14.3
Memo item							
Gross domestic savings	–5.1	7.8	5.2	5.7	5.6	3.9	3.5

Source: UNCTAD database.

sufficiency. It is estimated that approximately 20 per cent of the food output is traded informally to Nigeria. Cotton, the major export crop, benefited from international assistance and its production increased by six-and-a-half times in 1989 as compared to 1980 and 1981. Stockraising (cattle, small ruminants and hogs) represents about a fifth of agricultural production and 9 per cent of GDP.

Industry's contribution to GDP in the last decade has remained fairly stable at about 14 per cent, providing employment to about 6 per cent of the population. The only major extractive industry is the oil exploited at Sémé. Manufacturing consists mainly of processing agricultural products, and production for import substitution, in the consumer goods sector, in particular, flour, soaps, beverages, processed palm-oil products, sugar and cement. The sector's sharp growth in 1982 reflected the investments in petroleum exploitation and in a cement plant and a sugar complex.

The performance of the *service sector*, especially of the important entrepôt and transit trade, influences the economy directly through its contribution to GDP (just over 40 per cent) and fiscal receipts (about 55 per cent). Its growth, however, weakened, at negative 1.7 per cent, during 1985 to 1990, reflecting the sector's vulnerability to the changing economic conditions in neighbouring countries, Nigeria and Niger, to which the Cotonou port is linked by road (Nigeria), and by road and rail (Niger).

The fragile growth in Benin's economy in the 1980s was exacerbated by the sluggish development in the region, which included the recession in Nigeria from 1983: falling world demand for oil and uranium curtailed economic activity in Nigeria and Niger, the major markets of Benin's re-exports, and led to a reduced demand for the country's transit services.

Benin's external debt almost doubled from $644 million (1982–87) to $1,243 million at the end of 1990 (UNCTAD 1994): the settlement of arrears alone would have absorbed more than 100 per cent of domestic export earnings in 1989. In June 1989, the country obtained a rescheduling of its bilateral debt on Toronto terms at the Paris Club.[2] Despite this, total debt service payments increased by $12 million in 1989–90 before falling by $6 million to $42 million in 1991. The debt service ratio improved from 14 to 10 per cent in 1989–91 (UNCTAD 1994:Tables 30 and 31).

Under the second medium-term plan (1983–87) the government adopted a policy of reducing its direct involvement in productive activities, according private capital a greater role in the development process and easing the budgetary deficit by reducing personnel expenditure in the public sector by 10 per cent. These reforms, however, did not arrest the deterioration in the economic situation. In 1989 the government embarked on a structural adjustment programme (SAP), (1989–92) supported by conditional finance from the World Bank and IMF. Emphasis was placed on reducing the size and role of the public sector; reforming trade policy; deregulating economic activity and actively promoting the growth of the private sector; and restructuring the banking sector, including establishing new commercial banks with private participation, to enable it to resume effective financial intermediation in the economy. The programme also contained measures to address the social dimensions of structural adjustment. At a donors' meeting held by the World Bank in June 1991, loans totalling $93 million were agreed for 1991 and 1992 to support the SAP.

2   RESOURCE ENDOWMENT

2.1   Natural-resource Base

Benin has known reserves of iron ore, marble, phosphate and oil. So far only the oil deposits at Sémé, offshore from Cotonou, are exploited. Exploitation began in 1982 and production was about 300,000–400,000 tonnes during 1984 to 1986 but fell subsequently because of technical, managerial and financial difficulties which prevented additional investments needed to maintain output.[3] Potential oil reserves which have been found at greater depth, could offer a new source of growth for Benin. The second SAP (1991–92) includes an energy-sector strategy under which the government is to initiate economic surveys, exploit the main fields, diversify business partners and design appropriate exploitation contracts to attract oil companies to take part in the exploitation

(World Bank 1991). In the Sémé field, a multilaterally-funded project to improve recovery rates has begun (EIU 1993b:35).

Quarrying activities are carried out on limestone deposits which supply a cement plant set up in the early 1980s. In 1988, the construction of a hydroelectric dam on the Mono River between Benin and Togo was completed. Prior to this, about 90 per cent of Benin's electricity needs were imported from Akosombo hydroelectric dam in Ghana. A second dam with a 20 MW. installation has been planned for Adjarala.

Agronomic conditions in Benin, favourable for growing a variety of crops, are not fully exploited because of the lack of knowledge of the production possibilities of specific crops and their technical requirements (see section on trade diversification).

The country's fish resources, mainly from inland waters, rivers and lagoons, are exploited by small-scale operators using traditional methods. The resource base is estimated to be limited, but some species are already exploited by national and foreign companies. Fish exports comprise mainly prawns. Benin is a net importer of fresh fish as annual production levels of about 9,000 tons cover less than half of domestic requirements (EIU 1994:31).

2.2 Human-resource Development

Benin's adult literacy rate in 1990 was 23 per cent. Its net primary school enrolment ratio was 52 per cent, and the gross secondary school enrolment ratio was 11 per cent in 1988–90 (UNDP 1993).

The country faces a major unemployment problem following the liquidation of several public enterprises and reduction in the number of civil servants under SAP. Graduates from tertiary institutes are also unable to find jobs. To optimize the use of human resources, the Centre for the Promotion of Employment in Small and Medium-sized Enterprises (CEPEPE), was created in March 1990 with financing from the World Bank, to train unemployed workers, school leavers and graduates in new skills which would meet the needs of the industrial sector.

3   EXTERNAL TRADE PERFORMANCE

3.1   Trend and Structure of Trade Flows

Benin's imports includes processed-food products, textiles, refined petroleum and industrial machinery. France remains Benin's largest supplier, contributing an average of 20 per cent of all imports between 1985 and 1993 (see Table 4.3).

Over the last two decades, Benin's exports were primarily processed agricultural products. In the 1970s, palm kernel oil, cotton fibre and cocoa were the major 'official' exports, comprising about 60 per cent of total domestic exports. By 1987, cotton emerged as the leading official export as its share of export earnings rose to 50 per cent (UNCTAD 1993:Table 9), largely as a result of government support to the cotton sector, in the form of inputs, extension services and guaranteed producers' prices.

Although Benin produces some cocoa, much of its cocoa exports constitute re-exports of cocoa imported, mainly informally, from Nigeria. The volume 'imported' from Nigeria and exported 'officially' has fluctuated, and during 1970–90 constituted about 25–33 per cent of total export earnings (Igue 1991).

A spectacular increase in exports and a change in their structure was recorded in 1984, following the first petroleum exports of significant value. The total value of exports of goods (domestic exports and re-exports) reached 118 billion CFA francs in 1984, an increase of 62 per cent over the previous year. When operational problems in petroleum exploitation occurred in 1986, exports fell by about 44 per cent from 1985 levels. Total exports of goods fell as a consequence, but sustained growth of re-exports, which started from 1985, helped to reduce the effect; and continued to dominate Benin's export profile in 1990 and 1991, contributing to more than half of total exports of 81.5 billion CFA francs ($289 million) in 1991 (EIU 1994:41).

The export of manufactured goods was limited during the last two decades. There has been some export of textiles; its share of domestic export earnings peaked at 28 per cent in 1982, but during 1984-87 this share varied between 2 and 6 per cent.

The 1994 devaluation of the CFA franc will make the prices of Benin's exports more competitive, but its effects on the volume of exports and foreign-exchange earnings may take some time to register.

In the future, enhancement of the country's export earnings from petroleum, and exploitation and processing of other mineral resources, will depend on the commitments of additional investments, especially for oil reserves.

Any assessment of Benin's trade needs to take into account the preponderance of unrecorded re-exports. Goods re-exported from Benin, via informal cross-border trade, comprised three major groups, namely, cereals, tobacco and cigarettes, and textiles and textile products (Table 4.2).[4] Rice was the major unrecorded re-export to Nigeria from 1987.[5] Benin's informal-sector traders who re-export these goods to Nigeria receive payments in naira, the Nigerian currency, which is not officially convertible. Often the naira equivalent is recycled to purchase manufactured goods from Nigeria. These goods are comparatively cheap, either because of the high subsidies (such as for petroleum) or because the rate of exchange makes prices competitive.[6]

Table 4.2 Composition of re-exports, 1985-1988 (CFA franc billions)

	1985	1986	1987	1988
Vegetables	17.2	15.3	0.9	0.0
Cereals	3.1	8.7	27.0	23.9
Tobacco, cigarettes	20.7	10.2	17.2	22.0
Textiles	22.0	30.8	29.8	25.6
Industrial machinery	0.3	1.1	0.5	10.1
Others	15.7	16.1	6.1	10.5
Total	79.0	82.2	81.5	92.1

Source: INSAE (1991).

Nigerian goods are sold in Benin not only to the local population, but also to traders coming from the West African Monetary Union (WAMU), and from countries in the CFA franc zone in Central Africa, namely, Cameroon, Central Africa, Congo, Gabon, Equatorial Guinea and Chad. The amount of money which circulated in this parallel market was estimated to have averaged about 70 billion CFA francs in 1980–90, peaking at 93 billion CFA francs in 1985–87 (Igue 1991). Thus, informal cross-border trade helps to keep Benin's economy buoyant. While the 50 per cent devaluation of the CFA franc in January 1994 may undermine the price competitiveness of manufactured goods from Nigeria, the net effect on informal cross-border trade flows between the two countries may be difficult to predict for some time yet.

The main destination for Benin's recorded exports in the early 1980s was the EEC, but its share of exports declined from about 95 per cent to an average of about 50 per cent between 1989 and 1993. Exports to developing countries, particularly outside Africa, increased correspondingly (Table 4.3).

Balance of trade
Benin's trade balance is persistently in deficit. The dominant informal re-export trade, estimated to average about 70 per cent of total exports during 1986–88, keeps imports at a high level. When domestic exports of crude petroleum became significant in 1984 and 1985, the trade deficit was immediately trimmed by half from about 70 billion CFA francs in 1983 to 34 billion CFA francs in 1984, which was about 7.6 per cent of GDP. It increased thereafter to an average of 10.7 per cent of GDP during 1986–88. Recorded exports covered only some 20 per cent of the cost of imports in 1992 (EIU 1994:37).

Table 4.3 Direction of recorded trade, 1985–1993

	1985	1989	1990	1991	1992	1993
	(Exports as per cent of total exports)					
Industrial countries	94.5	44.0	61.4	50.0	49.7	44.7
of which						
Belgium-Luxembourg	3.2	3.5	1.8	5.1	5.1	1.4
France	10.4	5.3	0.9	4.4	7.3	4.1
Germany	21.7	1.8	0.9	0.7	1.4	0.7
Italy	7.3	8.0	8.8	8.0	9.4	7.6
Portugal	10.1	12.4	16.8	11.0	12.3	13.8
Spain	26.9	1.8	9.7	..	2.9	2.1
United Kingdom	5.1	0.9	1.8	0.7	2.2	1.4
United States	0.1	6.2	17.7	16.8	6.5	10.3
Developing countries	5.5	55.9	37.7	49.1	49.5	54.5
of which						
Africa	4.4	18.9	15.7	22.3	25.0	27.3
Côte d'Ivoire	0.3	4.4	4.4	0.7	0.7	1.4
Nigeria	0.1	0.9	..	1.5	1.4	1.4
Senegal	0.0	..	..	..	..	..
Togo	0.6	4.4	4.4	4.4	4.4	4.8
	(Imports as per cent of total imports)					
Industrial countries	72.0	53.5	53.2	54.7	53.9	49.8
of which						
Belgium-Luxembourg	2.1	2.2	2.6	2.9	2.6	2.6
France	20.1	20.7	21.1	20.3	22.5	19.8
Germany	2.6	4.3	3.9	4.8	3.2	2.9
Italy	5.0	4.1	3.5	3.4	2.6	2.8
Portugal	0.0	0.2	0.2	0.2	..	..
Spain	2.4	1.0	1.1	1.4	1.2	1.8
United Kingdom	2.7	3.1	2.2	3.4	4.4	5.9
United States	15.9	4.6	4.8	4.6	4.2	2.8
Developing countries	26.9	45.7	46.1	44.6	45.4	49.5
of which						
Africa	6.2	9.0	7.7	6.6	6.6	6.4
Côte d'Ivoire	3.4	3.9	3.5	2.9	2.8	2.7
Nigeria	0.4	0.2	0.2	0.2	0.3	0.2
Senegal	1.1	1.2	0.9	0.8	0.8	0.8
Togo	0.3	1.9	1.1	1.1	1.1	1.0

Sources: IMF (1991 and 1994).

4 TRADE-POLICY REGIME

During 1974–88, Benin's external trade policies were heavily oriented towards state control, and the policy regime was biased against exports. The country's major exports were controlled by state-owned marketing boards. Protection for domestic industries through quantitative import restrictions undermined efficiency and productivity, thereby making them uncompetitive. Furthermore, the tariff system was seriously distorted as taxes on some imported raw materials were equal to, or higher than, the tariff protection afforded to the finished product. The unfavourable cost structure of the sector inhibited industrial exports.

Under the 1989 SAP, Benin's macroeconomic policies emphasized liberalization, deregulation to introduce greater competition, and export expansion to improve the country's balance-of-payments position. The state-owned enterprises were to be reformed, liquidated or privatized; the taxation system was completely overhauled to promote economic efficiency and enhance government revenue, and the investment code was revised to encourage private investment. As crucial components of trade policy, the foreign-exchange, trade and investment regimes will be discussed in turn, with a view to assessing their potential impact on diversification efforts.

4.1 Foreign-exchange Regime

Benin, as a member of the WAMU, has no autonomy to use the exchange rate as an instrument of trade policy, as its currency was on a fixed parity with the French franc until early 1994. The exchange rate of 50 CFA francs to 1 French franc had remained fixed for about fifty years. In the second half of the 1980s, the CFA Franc appreciated against the US dollar,[7] which resulted in a worsening of the country's balance-of-payments position. To counteract the problems caused by the overvaluation of the CFA currency, the CFA franc was devalued by 50 per cent in January 1994 after protracted negotiations between France and these countries.[8]

4.2 Trade Regime

Import policies
The liberalization of imports in 1988 took the form of the removal of all quantitative restrictions and the gradual abolition of import licensing. The latter in respect of the EC, ACP countries and member states of the West African Monetary Zone was completed in 1990, and for other countries in July 1991.

In 1990, a major reform was carried out to simplify, rationalize and harmonize the import taxation system, which was cumbersome for traders and encouraged tax evasion, resulting in substantial revenue losses. Taxes and duties have now been integrated with tariffs applied on a value-added basis. Under the revised structure, tax is levied on domestic goods and services as well as imports. Tariffs on products for re-export and consumption goods have been harmonized and reduced. At the insistence of the IMF, an independent company was appointed to verify all imports to strengthen tax collection.

Export policies
Until 1988, there was no clear strategy relating to export development. In a move to correct the chronic external imbalance, institutional arrangements to coordinate and promote export development were formulated, and two bodies were created: Centre Béninois du Commerce Extérieur, CBCE (Benin Centre of External Trade) in 1988, and Conseil National des Exportations, CNEX (National Council of Exporters), in 1990. The CBCE is to assist exporters by providing advice on trade possibilities under regional trading arrangements; the use of trade preference schemes; trade and finance-related training; the organization of local trade fairs; and coordination of participation in overseas trade fairs with a view to prospecting for markets for both imports and exports.[9] The CNEX has as its purview the provision of assistance to exporters on marketing, negotiating contracts and rules governing trading practices, and training, particularly in trading rules and practices. It also makes representations to government authorities on problems of exporters and proposes measures to facilitate their exports.

The administrative hindrances to exports have been minimized; and from May 1990, export licensing was abolished. Export taxes, which ranged from 10 to 55 per cent prior to 1988, have now been reduced to a uniform rate of 3.15 per cent.

The marketing of cotton exports continues to be handled by the government marketing board, Société Nationale pour la Promotion Agricole (SONAPRA). Since 1987, SONAPRA has sold cotton to seven official international buyers through a tender system which has increased efficiency: first, because prices are determined on a competitive basis and; second, because the officially-appointed buyers, who have a better knowledge of the international markets for cotton, can act as intermediaries for Benin and its trading partners.

Export financing
Benin's banking sector is being rehabilitated after the banking crisis of 1989–90.[10] Three new banks were established (Bank of Africa, ECOBANK and the International Bank of Benin) in 1990 and 1991 and together with the Financial Bank which has been operating since 1988, they are in the process of recreating a system of financial intermediation capable of offering a full range of financial services. In January 1993, the first major international bank, Crédit Lyonnais,

opened a branch in Cotonou, reinforcing banking confidence in the country (EIU 1994:36) and bringing the total number of new banks to five.

There is no special scheme for export financing; exporters who need commercial credit obtain it from the banks against letters of credit furnished by their foreign buyers. The BCEAO (Central Bank of West African States) provides a refinancing facility of up to 90 per cent for the purchase of agricultural produce to traders against a forecast of receipts and the balance of operations lodged with the Central Bank. To ensure that foreign-exchange receipts enter the banking system, the BCEAO requires exporters with an annual turnover of more than 500,000 CFA francs to appoint an agent to keep records of exports and to transfer the receipts to an account with the BCEAO under the name of the exporter once the sales transaction is completed.

4.3 Investment Regime

The investment code of 1982 was revised in 1990 to reduce the bias in favour of public enterprises and capital-intensive investments, and to limit tax exemptions. The new legal framework is designed to promote private initiatives to develop small and medium-size enterprises, and favour investments in areas outside Cotonou, where at present more than half Benin's industries are located. It provides fiscal and customs incentives to local and foreign enterprises of different sizes under three different regimes.[11] It guarantees free conduct of businesses, protection from nationalization, entry and movement of expatriate staff, and repatriation of capital and dividends, as well as of any assets arising from business cessation. The provisions will apply equally to enterprises already established in Benin which extend their businesses to meet the criteria set.

All three regimes grant exemption from income and export tax during a specified period, depending on the specific location of the industries.[12] Imported machines, materials and tools used in production are also exempt from customs duties. Spare parts used in imported equipment are exempt from duties up to 15 per cent of the value of the equipment.

Benin's liberalized trade regime is expected to contribute to efficiency in the long term, but the short-term indications are that its trade deficit, financed by international aid, debt relief and debt rescheduling, widened by about 55 per cent between 1990 and 1991 (EIU 1994:38ff.). By the first half of 1993 the trade gap had widened by about 26 per cent (EIU 1993b:36). The rate of expansion of exports was limited by the country's inability to depreciate its currency to boost exports while imports surged in response to liberalization. One objective of the CFA devaluation was to bolster exports and compress imports with a view to containing the trade deficit. To what extent this succeeds depends, essentially, on enhanced production capacity. This, however, would entail increased imports of capital goods and intermediaries, which would again put pressure on the balances of trade and payments. Under these circumstances, reliance on export incentives becomes even more important.

5   TRADE-DIVERSIFICATION PROSPECTS

The medium-term objectives of improving the country's balance-of-payments position, and stabilizing and increasing foreign-exchange availability for economic development makes trade diversification imperative. The external balance in the short and medium term will depend on the export performance of the two major export products, cotton and crude petroleum, both of which exhibit considerable fluctuations in volume of output and international prices. However, the prospects for diversifying production, and subsequently external trade, in Benin are fairly restricted in the short run considering its small domestic market and the protectionist trade measures, of other West African countries producing competing goods, which hamper Benin's ability to benefit from economies of scale in expanding production.

Infrastructure as well as productive capacity development require capital inflows which had not been forthcoming in sufficient volume and reliability in the past. Indeed, Benin's previous attempts at diversification yielded little result: the manufacturing sector's contribution to GDP has remained almost unchanged over the last decade. Thus, diversification will require a multipronged effort in terms of both domestic policy and capital formation via concessional and commercial international finance.

Nevertheless, the potential for trade diversification in the following sectors deserves some consideration:

1. the agricultural sector offers a favourable base for developing agro-based industries;
2. the industrial sector's contribution to value added could be improved, as much of the existing capacity remains either idle or underutilized, and the exploitation of the country's mineral resources stands to be enhanced;
3. in the services sector, Benin's transit-transport services are well placed to serve its land-locked neighbours. The country has several interesting tourist sites and a rich cultural heritage but the tourism sector's potential has not yet been tapped.

The prospects and constraints of developing these sectors are examined below.

5.1   Agricultural Diversification

A feasibility study on agricultural diversification (FAO 1989) pointed to the possibility of increasing the production of a number of crops. The production levels of various crops, including palm nuts (for palm oil), coconuts, karité (sheanuts) and cashew nuts, had declined because of poor producers' prices, inefficient management and lack of support policies. Introducing new crops and enhancing traditional crops, thus widening the product mix, would improve the stability of agricultural incomes and export revenues.

Reviving palm kernel oil production on an industrial scale would require major investments in replanting oil palm trees. The quantity which would be produced would be marginal in the world market, and would have to compete with more efficient producers, such as Malaysia which provides roughly 45 per cent of the world supplies.

Exporting processed cassava for animal feed to the EU market is another possibility. In the late 1980s, average production costs of the cassava variety grown in Benin exceeded that from Asia (FAO 1989). Thus for Benin to compete in the EU market, it would need to use high-yielding varieties and optimal farming methods.

The potential for horizontal diversification exists for horticultural products like pineapples, mangoes, papayas and vegetables which could be exported to the EU market. Benin has started exporting pineapples to France and Belgium but on a very small scale. The returns tend to be curtailed by air freight costs. If Benin is to penetrate these markets, exporters must be aware of the norms of foreign markets, for example, being able to meet quality standards and delivery schedules.

Other areas with export potential in the longer term include commercial cattle raising in northern Benin. Improving stockraising looks promising in terms of pastures, but may be jeopardized by poor management of surface-water resources, the traditional production systems currently used, and increasing competition from crops. New investment in this sector may have to be scrutinized to limit problems of environmental degradation.

In general, vertical diversification possibilities in agriculture are constrained by the low level of technology, a small internal market, competition from imports of similar goods and the lack of knowledge of international markets. Also, the lack of capital contributes to underutilization of existing capacity, and constrains modernization and expansion of processing plants.

5.2 Increasing Manufactured Exports

The industrial sector is characterized by a myriad of small and medium-scale establishments engaged in agricultural and natural-resource-based manufacturing (UNIDO 1990).[13] Most of the major branches of industries, reportedly, operated at a loss (UNIDO 1990). They suffered from low productivity and capacity underutilization due to obsolete equipment which rendered their production costs uncompetitive: adaptation to new technologies has been constrained by a lack of credit and skills.

The problems of the industries are partly attributable to protectionist policies pursued in the past which acted as hindrances to production in so far as industries ignored factors that enhance international competitiveness, for example, comparative advantage and efficiency of technology employed. Trade-liberalization measures implemented are envisaged to increase the sector's profitability through improved efficiency. They would be augmented by the rehabilitation of existing industries (UNIDO 1990), and the privatization of some 25 enterprises.

5.3 Developing Tourism

In recognition of the foreign-exchange earnings potential of international tourism, the Benin government drew up a national tourism plan in 1993: hotel capacity is to be increased by constructing small-scale hostels and establishing holiday villages, and beach facilities will be improved (EIU 1993a:41). In addition to diversifying foreign earnings, tourism could confer considerable economic benefits on Benin through its forward and backward linkages. It would provide employment in the service sector, including hotels, transport, travel agencies and restaurants, and promote the development of cottage industries. This would, however, require promotional activities locally and abroad, and the training of services-sector staff on a large scale. Given the large initial investment involved in the provision of infrastructural support, success will depend on the response of foreign and private investors to the plan. In the short term, however, possibilities of Benin and Togo cooperating in joint tourist packages could be explored since the Togolese capital is only a two-hour drive away from Benin.[14]

5.4 Enhancing Transit Services

Benin is a transit country for goods destined for Niger, Burkina Faso and Mali, and could expand its transit services, with benefits accruing to transport operators and cargo-handling companies, if it rationalizes its operations and tax schemes to enhance the international competitiveness of these services, especially with reference to Nigeria and Togo. Cotonou is the nearest seaport for eastern Mali, and Burkina Faso is well developed to handle the transit trade. Niger, Mali and Burkina Faso are granted the use of Benin's free-trade-zone facilities; and agreements have been entered into with Niger regarding the use of the Cotonou port and the sharing of freight by the transport operators of the two countries.

Out of the total general cargo handled in 1984 and 1985 at the port, about a third was transit cargo to Niger. However, transit cargoes to Niger have been falling since 1986, because of competition from Togo.[15] Revenues from transit services could fall steeply if Nigeria liberalizes trade in rice and wheat which had been prohibited since 1987 (EIU 1993a:42), as some 80 per cent of rice imports unloaded at the port in 1992 were destined for Nigeria.

6   CONCLUSIONS AND RECOMMENDATIONS

Measures to promote both traditional and non-traditional exports as part of the strategy for development were initiated in 1990 by the new government. The set of laws which have been passed providing for trade liberalization, privatization of enterprises, revision of the Private Investment Code and export promotion by special export bodies, attempt to inject a new dynamism into the economy. Benin's success in meeting this challenge is predicated on its ability to overcome the main constraints in the following key areas:

- competitiveness;
- access to external markets;
- raising capital and tapping technology;
- strengthening and sustaining export promotion efforts; and
- meeting training needs.

Studies have shown that a congenial macroeconomic environment and institutional infrastructure are a necessary, but not sufficient, condition for export development to succeed (ITC 1990). Both need to be underpinned by strong direction from the government, with a clearly-defined export-promotion strategy and targets, and a firm commitment by government and business sectors, including the banks. As partners in export development efforts, banks can mobilize finance and provide export credit facilities for export projects. The experience of countries with a high export growth rate indicates that recognition by the banking sector of government priorities for export development has influenced their financing policies (ITC 1990). Firm commitment by the government will entail coordination, for example, among the various ministries responsible for:

- product policy and development (agriculture, industry, tourism, transit-transport development);
- services (finance, customs, information, investment and trade promotion, technical education); and
- infrastructure (main road network and feeder road links to production areas, storage and conservation facilities, telecommunications, railways, ports and airport).

In the case of Benin, the government's involvement in export development has so far been limited to providing an appropriate economic policy framework and meeting minimum institutional requirements. The bodies in charge of export promotion do not have adequate financial resources and trained person-nel; and a positive concerted effort is lacking: there was no single body to coordinate intersectoral policies on export development and establish linkages with the business sector, at the time of the mission in 1991.

The revised investment code seemed to have been designed as a stop-gap measure to mobilize private investment by small and medium-sized enterprises to replace the government as a main source of productive activity. Conse-quently, it may have to be revised further to serve the long-term objective of attracting private investment, particularly to export-oriented projects.

The country's labour development programme is geared to meeting the medium-term objectives of the structural adjustment programme. The CEPEPE provides essential retraining for redundant workers displaced from the civil service and liquidated parastatals, and trains unemployed graduates for jobs with the small and medium-sized enterprises promoted by the government. However, if trade-diversification efforts are to be successful, skills develop-ment in line with the new orientation needs to be addressed more systematically. This may take the form of on-the-job training, seminars, and formal training in such areas as agricultural research, management and business administration, finance, market research and marketing, and in hotel management and catering. In particular, a combination of national and international measures need to be considered.

6.1 National Measures

The fiscal, legal and institutional framework to promote trade diversification should be further strengthened. The following recommendations could help address weaknesses in existing arrangements:

1. Measures should be designed to promote the import substitution of identified products. Increasing the production of food crops, in particular those subject to supply fluctuations, may require special programmes to improve exten-sion services, supply credit at affordable rates, ensure a steady supply of fertilizer and other inputs, and facilitate access to markets by constructing feeder roads and providing storage or preservation facilities.[16]
2. A focal point, or body, may need to be established to coordinate the activities of CBCE and CNEX. This body should have executive powers and financial resources, and be staffed by experts in trade-promotion strategies and meas-ures to undertake market research on product and market possibilities, and assess the production potential for selected exportable products. It should also take the lead in coordinating, with the various ministries, intersectoral policies to promote exports in consonance with an export development plan which clearly defines the strategies and time frame for attaining objectives.
3. A specialized autonomous body, such as an investment board, is a prerequi-site if specific issues relating to investment policies are to be given proper

attention and thrust. Such a body can also help to provide some technical support services: initiate measures to attract investment, such as proposals for conducting preinvestment studies, compilation of product profiles based on local resources, identifying potential investors with access to marketing channels in target markets, attracting joint ventures to produce and market exportable goods, and providing direct assistance to selected enterprises to facilitate both the development and export potential of their products.[17] Foreign companies can provide financial participation, technical know-how, market contacts and training.

4. The merits of developing an export-processing zone to attract export-oriented industries and those engaged in international contracting could also be examined.

5. Unlike the bigger businesses with considerable resources of their own and easy access to credit, a large number of the small and medium-sized enterprises lack access to funds. They need not only financial support but also technical assistance such as project feasibility studies, management and quality-control assistance.

These measures may have to be carefully examined within the context of the overwhelming economic influence of the neighbouring economies which may restrict the investment and market potential of Benin in the short run.

6.2 International Measures

Benin has to overcome numerous constraints in various areas before it can realize its potential fully. International financial and technical assistance in the following areas are of paramount importance: institution strengthening and building, improving the government's capabilities in policy formulation and implementation, developing infrastructural facilities, and providing training and advisory services in financing, marketing and export promotion.

Benin's utilization of GSP schemes is very low and limited mainly to unprocessed agricultural products, namely, cocoa and coffee, because of the lack of knowledge of non-traditional markets, and of the availability and use of GSP schemes.[18] Seminars could be organized to make exporters aware of these schemes and to assist them to increase their participation in them. Assistance can also be provided to ensure that potential exports meet the rules-of-origin requirements.

NOTES

1. Data was compiled during a field mission to Cotonou in 1991. Simeon Fagnisse, national consultant, and Basile Awassi, Department of External Trade, provided assistance. The chapter draws upon government policy statements and legislation, results of previous studies as well as

interviews with officials in the public and private sectors. UNCTAD would also like to thank the UNDP office in Cotonou for sponsoring the national consultant and for the excellent preparations and support given during the mission.

2. The total debt rescheduled under Toronto terms was estimated at $193 million (June 1989); $160 million (December 1991), and $25 million (June 1993) under the enhanced concessional terms (UNCTAD 1994:35).

3. During 1984 to 1985 oil extraction was operated by a Norwegian company (Saga Petroleum) under a service contract. In September 1985, Saga's contract was abruptly terminated, and Pan Ocean Oil (Panoco), a Swiss-based company, took over. However, Panoco's plan to launch a $2 billion development programme did not materialize, and in 1988 the contract was taken over by Ashland Exploration, an American company, to manage the field for two years.

4. Wide discrepancies exist in the trade data on Benin because of the large amount of informal unrecorded trade with its neighbouring countries, chiefly with Nigeria. A more accurate assessment of the implications for Benin in terms of revenue contribution/loss and the country's balance-of-payments position is derived from estimates which take account of the significant informal import and re-export trade. Estimates for the years 1982 to 1988 are now made available by the Institute national de la statistique et de l'analyse économique (INSAE 1991). This information has been complemented by IMF (1993).

5. Igue (1991) estimated that re-exports of rice and cereals were primarily to the Nigerian market, and the amount involved was in the region of 12 billion CFA francs in 1987 and 19 billion CFA francs in 1988. Import restrictions placed by Nigeria on rice and other cereals had led to a flourishing of unrecorded cross-border trade with Benin for these products. Cereals became an important item of re-export only in the second half of the 1980s.

6. In the case of petroleum, for example, at the time of the UNCTAD Mission in August 1991, a litre of 'super' cost 17.50 CFA francs; but it traded for about 100 CFA francs across the frontier where the pump price was about 150 CFA francs.

7. In 1980, the exchange rate of the CFA franc to the dollar stood at 211.3, increasing to 449 in 1985 before falling to 265 CFA francs to the dollar in 1992.

8. For a cautiously optimistic evaluation of economic performance in the franc zone, in comparison to other Sub-Saharan African countries, see Lane and Page (1991).

9. At the time of the Mission in 1991, the CBCE had, however, been able to organize only one local trade fair, and participated in two overseas fairs, at Marseille and Berlin, supported by external financing. Because of financial constraints only two subregional trips, to Dakar and Guinea, had been possible.

10. Three state banks went into liquidation in 1989–90: La Banque Beninoise pour le développement (BBD) in May 1989, La Banque Commerciale du Benin (BCB) in June 1990 and La Caisse nationale credit agricole (CNCA) at the end of 1990. The government has taken over the debt obligations of these three banks to BCEAO (amounting to 57 billion CFA francs) as well as the medium and long-term loans which were guaranteed by the state.

11. The three regimes (A), (B) and (C) apply to different sizes of enterprise: the first applies to small and medium-sized enterprises with investments between 20 and 500 million CFA francs employing at least 5 permanent salaried staff of Benin nationality; the second to large enterprises with total investments of between 500 million CFA francs and 3 billion CFA francs; and the third to big enterprises with investments exceeding 3 billion CFA francs. The last two categories must employ at least 20 permanent salaried staff of Benin nationality.

12. In a cascading system, these fiscal incentives are granted for five years for investment in Cotonou and areas within a radius of 25 km. (Zone 1), 7 years in urban districts of Porto Novo, Parakou, Abomey and Bohicon (Zone 2), and 9 years in the remaining territories (Zone 3).

13. These establishments comprised 3 subgroups: (a) a 'modern' sector which makes up about 47.6 per cent of total investments in the economy; (b) the 'artisanal' sector with businesses of less than 10 million CFA francs turnover; (c) the 'informal' sector comprising small, family businesses estimated to involve about 100,000 persons.

14. At present, Togo organizes trips on a large scale to various tourist sites; these are reported to cost less than those organized from Cotonou.

15. A host of taxes and fees are payable to port operators in Benin; the transit trade chain is handled by various operators who have monopolistic control; and inefficient operations have led to higher operating and administrative costs, delays and losses (UNCTAD 1989). Consequently,

although rail transport costs through Lomé may be higher than through Cotonou, cargoes are routed through the former because of efficiency considerations. This could probably have been reversed after 1992 because of Togo's political crisis which made its competing routes unsafe.

16. The Regional Action and Rural Development Centres (CARDERs) which were successful in providing support and technical assistance to farmers in the 1970s could be asked to concentrate these tasks. But they should be supplied with the necessary resources.

17. For example, the provision of an authoritative investment pre-feasibility study by such a board, for petroleum exploration which requires heavy investment, could help to mobilize prospective investors.

18. As the major exports are to the EC, Benin could benefit from two schemes if it is able to take full advantage of them, namely, the EC GSP scheme and the tariff concessions offered under the Lomé IV Convention for ACP countries. The degree of preferential market access is, however, likely to be frustrated when the recently concluded Uruguay Round agreement comes into effect.

REFERENCES

Economist Intelligence Unit (EIU) (1993a), *Benin Country Report*, no. 4, London: EIU.

Economist Intelligence Unit (EIU) (1993b), *Benin Country Profile*, no. 1, London: EIU.

Economist Intelligence Unit (EIU) (1994), *Benin Country Profile*, London: EIU.

FAO, UNDP (1989), *Diversification Agricole*, no. 76/89.

Government of Benin, Decree no. 91–23, 1 February 1991.

Government of Benin, Decree no. 90–005 of 15 May 1990.

Igue, J. (1991), 'Le rôle du secteur informel et des tontines dans la relance économique', mimeo, Cotonou.

IMF (1991), *Direction of Trade Statistics Yearbook 1986–1990*, Washington, DC: IMF.

IMF (1993a), *Direction of Trade Statistics Yearbook 1986–1992*, Washington, DC: IMF.

IMF (1993b), *International Financial Statistics*, Washington, DC: IMF.

IMF (1994), *Direction of Trade Statistics Yearbook 1987–1993*, Washington, DC: IMF.

Institut National de la Statistique et de l'Analyse Economique (INSAE) (1991), 'L'évolution récente de l'économie du Benin', *Compte Economique 1982–1988*, Estimation 1989, Paris: INSAE.

ITC (1990), *Trade Development – Support for Structural Adjustment*, ITC/121/AI/90-VIII, Geneva: ITC.

Lane, C.E. and S. Page (1991), *Differences in economic performance between the Franc zone and other sub-Saharan African countries*, Working Paper no. 43, London: Overseas Development Institute.

UNCTAD (1989), Rapport Préliminaire, *Appui du secteur transport de la république du Benin*, Project BEN/87/018, New York: United Nations.

UNCTAD (1993), *The Least Developed Countries 1992 Report*, New York: United Nations.

UNCTAD (1994), *The Least Developed Countries 1993–1994 Report*, New York: United Nations.

UNDP (1993), *Human Development Report 1993*, New York: United Nations.

UNIDO (1990), 'Mission approfondie strategies et politiques industrielles du Benin' (draft), mimeo, Vienna.

World Bank (1991), *Mission de post-évaluation de deuxième crédit d'ajustement structurel et des négociations du deuxième document cadre de politique, économique et financière*, Washington, DC: World Bank.

5. Trade diversification in Cape Verde: prospects and constraints

Willem van der Geest

1 GENERAL BACKGROUND

The Republic of Cape Verde is an archipelago of islands some 500 km. west off the coast of Sénégal, West Africa. It consists of four leeward islands Brava, Fogo, São Tiago and Maio (*'sotavento'*) and six windward islands Sal, Boa Vista, São Nicolau, Santa Luzia, São Vicente and Santo Antão (*'barlavento'*) scattered over 58,000 sq. km. of the Atlantic Ocean. Cape Verde has a Sahelian climate with a low and unreliable rainfall averaging less than 300 mm. per year; water shortages and drought are a persistent feature. Once the rain arrives, the islands appear temporarily transformed, and only then does its name – the green cape – seem befitting. Notwithstanding Cape Verde's natural-resource paucity – with the exception of its large fishing zone – socioeconomic indicators are well above the average for LDCs. This reflects the adaptive ability of its people as well as the commitment of Cape Verdean emigrants to support the country through considerable remittances.

1.1 Political Developments

Cape Verde's political regime changed towards a multiparty system in January 1991: the Movement for Democracy (MPD), founded only eight months earlier, scored a victory gaining 56 seats, whereas the African Independence Party (PAICV), the single party which had been in power during 15 years of Independence, managed to retain only 23 seats. The presidential elections, one month later, confirmed popular support for the MPD. The full impact of this peaceful transition, popularly known as *A mudança* (change), cannot yet be evaluated comprehensively. What is clear is that the new government has initiated a sequence of adjustment policies designed to make Cape Verde's economy more outward oriented (see Section 2 below).

1.2 Social Development

An interesting feature of Cape Verde is the ratio of resident to migrant population. The population was estimated at 365,000 in 1992, but the overseas Cape Verdean population might be twice as high: in 1983 there were more than 700,000 Cape Verdean emigrants.[1]

A 1983 study of children under 6 years found that about a quarter of them experienced a moderate degree of malnutrition, with some 2 per cent classified as suffering from severe deficiency; moderate malnutrition among infants ranged from 16 to 20 per cent, with approximately 4 per cent of them severely malnourished. Infant mortality has been reduced significantly since Independence, from 85.6 per thousand live births during 1975–78 to 54 during 1985–90 (see UNICEF 1989 and Comité National Préparatoire de la Conférence Internationale sur la Nutrition 1991). Differences among the islands, closely correlated to the availability of fresh drinking water,[2] are significant: for example 'moderate' malnutrition reached a level of 30 per cent in the islands of São Tiago and Fogo. Nevertheless, the average life expectancy at birth of 66 years is among the highest in Africa (UNICEF 1989 and Table 5.1).

The slow creation of employment and the persistence of un- and underemployment is Cape Verde's most pressing problem. The estimated level of employment in 1990 stood at 88.3 thousand whereas unemployment stood at 30.9 thousand, or approximately 26 per cent of the labour force. The net creation of new employment opportunities during the period 1985–90 has been estimated at only 2,000 per year. Even under optimistic assumptions, the five-year period 1990–95 is projected to create only 3,100 additional jobs each year and, given demographic trends, the unemployment rate cannot be expected to fall (see Ministère des Finances et de la Planification 1992b:24). Given this context, any measures which reduce public-sector employment are likely to have a direct and severe negative social impact.

Table 5.1 Selected social indicators, 1990

Indicators	
Population density (per sq. km.)	95
Urban population (% of total)	30
Infant mortality* (per 1,000 live births)	54
Life expectancy at birth (years)*	66
Crude birth rate*	37
Crude death rate*	8
Percentage of children immunized against DPT	88

Note: * 1985–90 average.

Source: UNCTAD (1994).

1.3   Characteristics of Small Island States

Constraints which characterize least developed island micro-states such as Cape
Verde are manifold; some reflect the natural- and human-resource endowments,
whereas others are an expression of structural 'economic' constraints. The
endowments demonstrate the viability of the micro-state as a sovereign economic system, whereas the structural constraints need to be addressed through
longer-term human and economic development policies. Endowment-related
constraints include, *inter alia*:

1. the inability to reap economies of scale in production and distribution of
   goods and services;
2. limited availability of natural-resource inputs, such as drinking water;
3. long distances to import and export markets;
4. proneness to various types of natural disaster; and
5. a fragile natural ecology.

Positive features of the endowment include the 'exclusive economic zone'
which reserves rights to living and non-living ocean resources under the Law of
the Sea.

Structural economic constraints for small island states include:

1. the dependence on a narrow range of tropical agricultural export products;
2. a narrow range of local skills;
3. inarticulate market structures with monopolistic or oligopsonistic features;
   and
4. restricted, if any, access to international capital markets.

In consequence, least developed small island countries typically face serious
balance-of-payments problems, coupled with a strong dependence on
concessional aid to finance these (see Dolman 1985). The dependence on
imports and financial inflows complicates the setting of domestic economic
targets because the key determinants of aggregate demand and investment are
exogenous to the economic system: often private- or public-sector institutions
cannot influence them (Dommen and Hein 1985:Chapter 7). Two common
responses to this dependence include:

1. to 'buffer' the economy through relatively large public-sector enterprises in
   selected sectors; and
2. to opt for an export strategy of 'extreme' specialization in an attempt to find
   a unique market niche.[3]

Even when compared to other LDC island micro-states, Cape Verde presents
a special case. It has been labelled a 'recycling economy' – an economy with
large financial inflows, which are used primarily for imports and hence large
financial outflows. The high level of imports reflects the limited domestic

production capability underscored by the inability to realize economies of scale, given the small domestic market. Cape Verde's exports of goods and services cover only a small percentage of the import-resource requirements. The dependence on private foreign remittances as well as foreign aid is persistent. The financial inflows cover not merely domestic investment but partly finance consumption as well.

Other features of Cape Verde's economy include, up to 1992, a 'monobank' system which combined central, commercial and investment banking functions. Institutional changes, implemented during 1993, were intended to relinquish commercial and investment banking to separate financial institutions.

The structure of the balance of payments of Cape Verde reflects these unusual features of the 'recycling' economy. The trade deficit remains large. Exports, including the resale of fuel for maritime use through a transnational company, merely covers some 35 to 40 per cent of the imports of goods and services, if re-export of fuel is included, and just 7 to 8 per cent excluding such re-export. Imports were approximately $326 per capita in 1992, equivalent to just over 40 per cent of GDP. During 1986–91, Cape Verde's debt service payments as a percentage of the (low) exports of goods and non-factor services, varied only between 13 and 25 per cent. Unlike other small island economies, Cape Verde has a net inflow of private remittances covering some 55 per cent of the trade deficit. While private transfers provided a strong underpinning of the economy, the level of official transfers to Cape Verde declined steadily, from 29 per cent of GDP in 1986 to approximately 10 per cent in 1991. Inflows on account of direct foreign investment have been negligible throughout the 1980s (see Chattrabhuti 1993b; see also Table 5.2).

Table 5.2 Selected economic indicators, 1991

GDP ($ millions)	325.2
Per-capita GDP ($)	813
External debt ($ millions)	150
Growth of GDP 1980-85 p.a.	6.4
Growth of GDP 1985-90 p.a.	5.6
As percentage of GDP	
Agriculture*	13
Manufacturing*	9
Export value	2
Import value	45
External debt*	46

Note: * Data for 1989.

Source: UNCTAD (1994).

The predicament is also clearly expressed in terms of the expenditure of available resources. The level of private and public consumption within Cape Verde (disregarding investment) exceeds the total value added from domestic production (GDP) – domestic savings are negative. The whole of public and private investment is covered through foreign official and private transfers. Investment as a share of GDP has fallen sharply during the period 1986–91. Private investment fluctuated about the 10 per cent level of GDP, but public investment fell sharply from a level above 30 per cent of GDP to below 20 per cent. The persistent dependence for investable resources on sources outside the economy limits the scope for remedial action.

2 MACROECONOMIC OVERVIEW

2.1 Macroeconomic Objectives

The overall macroeconomic objectives of Cape Verde are fourfold:

- to maintain internal and external balance;
- to fight against poverty and un- and underemployment;
- to balance development between the various islands; and
- to roll back the structural constraints on economic development facing the islands: weak infrastructure between and within each of the islands; the low productivity and high factor costs, and the absence of a modern production system guided by efficiency and profitability.

The institutional conditions for a market-oriented economy are to be created or consolidated and the domain of government intervention in the economy redefined. The long-term objective is to create a more competitive economy with a reduced dependence on aid and remittances through:

1. an improved ability to export goods and services; and
2. attracting foreign risk-bearing investment resources.

One key component of the adjustment programme being implemented by the newly-elected government is liberalization, in the sense of exposing economic agents to the stimulus of competition, as well as 'debureaucratization' of the economic environment. Specific policy measures include a rapid liberalization of the price and wage controls regarding the domestic markets for goods, labour and capital, a gradual and controlled liberalization of trade, especially of imports, and a simplification of the fiscal system (see Ministère des Finances et de la Planification (1992a:30–31)). The central question addressed, but not decisively answered in the country's Third National Development Plan 1992–95 (henceforth Third Plan), is how to initiate and sequence the transition.

The process of import liberalization is intended to be gradual, and aims to expand the list of 'free' goods for which no specific foreign-exchange allocation will be made. For these goods 'own finance' needs to be available (or suppliers' credit to be obtained). At the end of 1992 the list of 'free' goods covered some 46 per cent of total imports.

The second major initiative to increase competitiveness in the Cape Verde economy is a programme of privatization, aimed at reducing the size and number of state monopolies in many subsectors of the economy. In tandem with the privatization programme, the number of civil servants will be reduced by half from the present level of 12,000 (approximately one out of every seven Cape Verdeans in employment). The scale of the privatization and civil service reform, relative to the size of the economy, will require that objectives are well articulated, and that the methods and techniques of privatization and retrenchment are commensurate both with economic and with social objectives.

In the design and implementation of privatization, two key characteristics of the Cape Verde economy need to be borne in mind: first, the monopolistic and oligopsonistic market structures; and second, the limited availability of domestic liquidity and thin capital markets. The first renders product markets *noncontestable*, whereas the second restricts the scope for creating broad ownership through shares. The objectives of any privatization programme will inevitably be wide ranging and, at times, contradictory. Such objectives will include:

1. increasing enterprise efficiency and private-sector growth;
2. relieving fiscal pressure on the government arising from underwriting loss-making enterprises;
3. stimulating domestic savings and capital market development;
4. attracting foreign risk-bearing capital; and
5. broadening share ownership.

Once privatization objectives are clarified and the valuation of state-owned enterprises (SOEs) has been completed, the selection of privatization methods becomes a strategic decision. As the national objectives are likely to focus primarily on efficiency and attracting foreign risk-bearing capital, appropriate privatization methods might include management contracts, leasing arrangements as well as build–operate and transfer (BOT) arrangements (see Price Waterhouse 1992).

2.2 Traded and Non-traded Sectors

Cape Verde's primary sector accounts for only 12.6 per cent of the total value added. The industry and energy sectors grew slowly, though their share of value added averaged a mere 6.5 per cent between 1980 and 1990. Hence, more than 80 per cent of domestic production focused on non-traded goods and services, with unusually large shares for the commerce and public services sectors.

Indeed, the value added in the commerce sector alone, at an average of 22.1 per cent in 1980–90 (disregarding import taxes), exceeded that of the entire traded-goods sectors.

Structural adjustment in Cape Verde is not a matter of balancing the public and trade deficits, as elsewhere in Sub-Saharan Africa. The issue is one of transformation, that is, a continued reallocation of investable resources away · from import and import-substituting production towards activities which create opportunities for trade and export of goods and services. For this reallocation to succeed, the expected profits in the export sector would need to be much above their present level.

2.3 Legal and Institutional Framework

A recent review of the legal and institutional framework for encouraging industrial investment by UNIDO reemphasized the pivotal role of industry for Cape Verde's economic development in view of both the high level of un- and underemployment, as well as the large deficit on the balance of trade. The review noted that the Institute of Promotion of Industry (UPI), created to promote domestic entrepreneurship and serve as an entry point to foreign parties interested in making industrial investment in Cape Verde, has not yet succeeded in transforming any such interest into significant export-oriented investment. This partly reflects UPI's own institutional weakness during the political transition in the early 1990s, but also the absence of a legal framework and Cape Verde's high factor costs.

A new legislation drawn up in 1991 has improved the legal framework regarding foreign investment. First, by defining 'foreign' investment on the basis of the external source of finance, it has opened up opportunities for Cape Verdean emigrants. Second, it has cancelled restrictions or requirements on the sector or type of investment, except those regarding the financial sector. Third, the legal basis of duty-exempted enterprises has been clarified.

The review notes that in Cape Verde an 'export culture' still needs to be promoted, that a one-stop shop for foreign investment urgently needs to be created and that potential foreign investors lack the necessary information. Moreover, the national capacity for preparing feasibility and pre-feasibility studies needs to be strengthened.[4]

2.4 Medium- and Long-term Outlook

The efficiency of Cape Verde's industry and services sectors is low, their markets are small and fragmented across different consumption centres and factor costs are high by international comparison. Moreover, the rapidly-growing labour lacks training: about 40 per cent of the labour force, 75 per cent of whom are female, is unskilled and is unlikely to enter the formal sector without some initial training.

The overall growth targets for the Third Plan 1992–95 are 5 to 6 per cent per annum, but these are conditional upon two key issues of contention between the Third Plan and the one prepared by the World Bank for the 1992 Round Table conference (see World Bank 1992). The first is a significant increase in official transfers, and the allocation of these resources to investment. Second, is increasing the share of capital goods in total imports.

3   EXTERNAL-SECTOR DEVELOPMENTS

3.1   Indicators of Trade Diversification

The geographical diversification of imports by country of origin is very limited as is borne out by area-wide import and export statistics. Approximately two-thirds of the total imported goods (c.i.f.) for 1989 originated from the European Community (EC), with two countries, Portugal and the Netherlands, accounting for nearly 40 per cent of Cape Verde's total import bill. In particular, the position of Portugal has remained dominant: during the five-year period, 1989–93, the value of total imports originating from this country alone averaged 36 per cent. In Africa, Côte d'Ivoire is the major import supplier.

In 1985, more than two-thirds of Cape Verde's total exports went to Africa, but since 1990, Europe has become the major export market for the country, taking more than four-fifths of total exports, more than 50 per cent of which went to Portugal alone between 1991 and 1993 (Table 5.3).

3.2   The Import Sector

For most LDCs, imports are positively correlated with the level of domestic production: intermediate inputs comprise a large share of imports. In the case of Cape Verde, changes in imports are negatively correlated to the level of domestic production. Imports tend to replace for domestic production; hence any increase of production may be expected to change the composition of imports from final towards intermediate and capital goods. A detailed account of the structure of imports by economic purpose prepared for 1986 and 1987, illustrated the importance of consumer goods in the total import bill: for 1986 household goods (food, consumer durables and so on) comprised about half of the imports, whereas for 1987 it was considerably less at approximately 28 per cent (Ministère de la Planification et de la Coopération 1989:95). However, the estimates of imports of consumer goods are bound to be biased downwards, because of inadequate registration and under-reporting for reasons related to the evasion of import duties.

Table 5.3 Direction of recorded trade, 1985–1993

	1985	1989	1990	1991	1992	1993
	(Exports as per cent of total exports)					
Industrial countries	26.5	41.8	93.1	84.8	85.9	82.0
of which						
Belgium-Luxembourg	..	..	..	..	..	..
France	4.1	..	..	..	..	..
Germany	..	..	..	..	..	..
Italy	6.1	..	..	..	16.7	..
Portugal	14.3	28.6	28.6	60.0	50.0	50.0
Spain	..	..	50.0	..	..	16.7
United Kingdom	..	..	14.3	..	16.7	..
United States	..	..	..	..	..	..
Developing countries	71.4	55.3	3.6	10.5	9.9	12.3
of which						
Africa	71.4	55.3	2.9	9.9	8.9	12.1
Algeria	..	55.3	..	..	..	..
	(Imports as per cent of total imports)					
Industrial countries	76.4	77.2	84.3	79.2	78.7	76.2
of which						
Belgium-Luxembourg	1.4	2.7	2.8	4.7	2.9	4.2
France	3.4	3.6	4.9	3.3	3.5	5.3
Germany	5.9	4.5	6.9	3.3	8.1	5.3
Italy	4.2	4.5	5.6	3.3	4.1	1.1
Portugal	30.3	30.4	37.5	37.3	36.6	39.7
Spain	4.4	2.7	2.1	7.3	1.7	1.1
United Kingdom	3.8	2.7	2.1	2.7	3.5	3.2
United States	1.8	4.5	4.2	3.3	2.9	3.2
Developing countries	21.8	16.5	10.1	14.9	15.6	17.7
of which						
Africa	4.1	3.0	4.1	8.6	7.6	8.2
Algeria	..	..	..	..	..	..
Angola	..	0.9	0.7	0.7	0.6	1.1
Côte d'Ivoire	1.0	1.8	2.8	6.0	5.8	6.4
Togo	..	..	0.7	0.7	0.6	0.5

Sources: IMF, *Direction of Trade Statistics Yearbook*, 1991 and 1994.

Although the need to diversify the sources of imports is pressing, the following factors mitigate against this:

- historical colonial relations, including the linguistic factor, imply continued close relations between Cape Verde and Portugal;
- the importing firms need secure agreements and the search costs involved in establishing new relationships deters the Cape Verdean firms from switching away from their traditional suppliers;
- current information about the terms and conditions on the international market is limited and costly to gather.

The Ministry of Commerce and Tourism has built up two information centres – one in the capital Praia and another in the industrial port town Mindelo, and an importers' guide has been prepared, in an attempt to redress some of these problems. Despite this and the partial import liberalization, importing companies still face some key constraints including, *inter alia*, difficulties in access to import-financing credits and in obtaining assurance facilities; high costs of transportation, both maritime as well as inter-island; and regulatory delays.

To reduce the unit costs of imports at the enterprise level would be a first step towards making the economy more outward oriented. It requires improved scheduling, obtaining competitive quotes, wider sourcing and, in general, negotiating better terms.

3.3 The Export Sector

Three main export growth sectors have been identified in the Third Plan: fisheries, industries, including its backward linkages to industrial freezing and processing of fish, and hotels and tourism. The industrial sector is projected to grow at nearly 40 per cent per annum, the fisheries, and hotels and tourism sectors, at about 26 and 22 per cent per annum, respectively. The key assumptions underlying the projected export development and growth are:

- introduction of improved equipment and technology in the fisheries sector;
- increased capacity utilization in existing industries and the starting up of new industries in ready-made garments, shoe making, pharmaceuticals and the conservation of fish;
- provision of varied tourist facilities on the islands of Sal, Boa Vista and São Vincente, including maritime and air transport services.

To achieve the growth targets will, however, prove a formidable challenge for policy making in Cape Verde. As argued by private-sector representatives, exporting goods, other than a few primary products such as fish and bananas, is not feasible under present conditions. They observed that most of the consumables in Cape Verde are imported, and that the very limited industrialization of the country focuses nearly entirely on import substitution.[5]

It is widely recognized that even in the long term, the earnings from exports of goods, such as fishery products and services, including tourism, maritime services, refuelling and port facilities, cannot be expected to fully cover the bill for imported goods and services. Hence, any long-term strategy to meet the trade deficit, other than relying on private remittances from Cape Verdeans abroad, would include foreign direct investment (FDI). However, progress on the process of creating conditions to facilitate FDI is slow, with only one significant result in 1993, when some Hong Kong businessmen took a lease on a Cape Verdean garment factory with a view to producing for the EC market (see Chattrabhuti 1993b).

Attracting investment funds from Cape Verdeans abroad is actively pursued through investment promotion among emigrants in Europe and the United States; but this is hampered by the fact that Cape Verdeans abroad are, in general, wage and salary earners without a tradition of investing in productive activities which only generate income in the medium and long run.

3.4 Preferential Access to Markets

Cape Verde's arrangements for access to OECD markets are not less favourable than those of other LDCs whose preferential market access tends to be restricted by specific criteria related to, for example, the rules of origin and/or the percentage of value added generated within the LDC (UNCTAD 1992a).

The US–GSP and the US Harmonized Tariff Schedule provision (HTS 9802) control the access of Cape Verdean exports to the United States market.[6] Under the Economic Community of West African States (ECOWAS) treaty on the free movements of goods, persons and capital within its Community, two leather products from Cape Verde qualify as priority industrial products, and are thus eligible for lower import duties.

Cape Verde is a beneficiary of the African, Caribbean and Pacific (ACP) Convention with the EC, usually referred to as the Lomé Convention, which allows duty and quota-free access to materials originating in Cape Verde, or materials which have a mixed-country origin, provided that: (i) processing has been done in Cape Verde, and (ii) non-ACP or non-EC sourced materials do not constitute more than 5 per cent of the total material cost. Further to the ACP, the European generalized system of preferences (EC GSP) is applicable, though of limited relevance as the terms of the Lomé Convention (Lomé IV) are more favourable (Ernst and Young 1991).

The conclusion of the Uruguay Round and the intended phasing out of the Multi-fibre Arrangement, however, means that Cape Verde may, in the medium term, not retain its attractiveness as a country with an unencumbered garment quota.

3.5 External Dependence

Reducing aid dependence of Cape Verde is a medium- and long-term issue – the share of the total import bill financed from abroad through official and private transfers can be expected to remain high in the foreseeable future. Nevertheless, Cape Verde did not need to borrow from the IMF and the World Bank through structural adjustment facilities. The EC is a large donor of Cape Verde: the grant allocation under Lomé IV stands at 23 million ecu, while another 4 million ecu has been earmarked through the European Investment Bank (EIB) for investment purposes as risk-bearing capital. The foreign assistance obtained from the Community under Lomé Conventions I to III up to 1991 amounted to 117 million ecu. Some 35 per cent was programme aid, 40 per cent was food aid and the remaining 16 per cent divided over emergency aid, exceptional aid, and regional aid. Another 7 per cent was through the EIB, and the remaining 2 per cent was for export earnings stabilization (STABEX)[7] and cofinancing of non-governmental organizations (NGOs). Projects included urban development in Praia focusing on water and electricity, vocational education and training, as well as country-wide multiannual food aid schemes, import programmes for building materials, emergency programmes and investment through the EIB.

4   PROSPECTS FOR TRADE DIVERSIFICATION: SECTORAL PERSPECTIVES

The trade-diversification problem facing Cape Verde, like other small island micro-states, is how to identify 'market niches' which:

1. generate sufficient additional employment to reduce current and projected unemployment; and
2. do not merely create value added within a protected economic environment, but attract sustainable financial inflows and/or expand the export value of goods and services.

4.1 Agriculture

The evolution of Cape Verde's agriculture has been analysed by Moran (1982). He observed that the pattern of unequal ownership and the prevalent system of land tenure, introduced at the time of colonial settlement, have reduced incentives to improve the land, and thus to realize even its limited potential. The virtual absence of sweet water further limits the scope for sustained agricultural production. When the meagre seasonal rains, which vary between 150 and 250 mm. for much of the country per annum, do not materialize, the limited domestic production may cause transitory food insecurity. The major famines which have struck the islands throughout the centuries have generated a risk-averse attitude about the food stocks and import policy.[8]

The production of food items, including export crops like banana, displays an extraordinary degree of variability which is primarily determined by climatic conditions. Peak production occurred in the years 1987–88 for most of the agricultural food items (maize, beans, potato and sweet potato, and manioc), meat and milk, whereas the drought years 1982–85 scored the worst production levels for most of agriculture. The present regime of import liberalization has meant moving from a food security system with state-sanctioned public monopoly for importing essential food items to a 'hybrid system'. In principle, the aim of the policy is to protect those sectors where local production is possible (or taking place) on the basis of an infant industry argument. Other imports are no longer prohibited. However, in some cases the hybrid system appears to have failed to create a level playing field. For example, potatoes were not authorized for free import in 1992 even though domestic production is very limited. Similar questions can be raised regarding import restrictions on poultry, green beans, sugar, maize, rice and edible oils.

4.2 Fisheries Exports

There is little doubt that Cape Verde's potential to expand fishery earnings is significant; currently only a small fraction of the potential catch is achieved. The exclusive economic zone covers more than 600,000 square kilometres and marine resources are abundant. The potential sustainable catch is estimated to be 40 to 45 thousand metric tons (mt) per year, whereas the reported catch ranges between 10 to 11 thousand mt, of which about 1.5 to 1.8 thousand mt are exported. A recent FAO technical report notes that the total catch could be three times its present size 'without danger of over-exploitation of the resources' (FAO 1992:Section 4). Revitalization of the fisheries sector would permit a growth of export volume to three times its present level within five years.

4.3 Tourism

The natural assets conducive to tourism development include exceptional climatic conditions (an average temperature of 25 degrees and a fresh breeze throughout the year). Moreover, the differences between the islands in terms of scenic beauty and quality beaches makes the Cape Verde Islands a unique and attractive micro-cosmos: Isle de Fogo boasts of a volcanic landscape while others are hilly and green or feature sandy beaches and nautical excursions including yachting.

Despite these attractive features, the estimated number of tourists visiting Cape Verde Islands each year is a mere 19,000. To improve this, tourism has been made a priority sector in the Third Plan, ending the ambiguity which hitherto had characterized the government's attitude to it. Improvements in lodging and hotel facilities are scheduled to move ahead, and a 3 per cent surcharge on tourist bills to finance tourism development has been introduced. In addition, the government has initiated a move to privatize the Hotel Praia Mar, one of the few four star hotels in the country, aiming to attract funds for its upgrading and expansion. Market and tourist development feasibility studies are under way, and the World Tourism Organization is providing assistance in the preparation of a tourism-sector strategy.

In order to attract a larger share of the international tourism market, the wholly state-owned national airline Transportes Aereos de Cabo Verde (TACV) has introduced special tourist airfares. Negotiations with German, Portuguese and South African tour operators to attract group and package tourism were concluded in 1993, and have already attracted increased such tourism from Germany, facilitated by a stop-over in Frankfurt on the flights between Sal and Amsterdam.

The environmental impact of tourism has received considerable attention, not least in view of a popular campaign to protect rare species, in particular the large sea turtles. This would suggest that tourism development will need to be gradual, and that significant net economic contribution from it may only be realized in the medium to long term.

4.4 Air Transport Services

At the end of 1992, the TACV operated a fleet of seven planes for its domestic operations. Four of these are aged between 16 and 18 years whereas three were purchased in 1990. The aircraft are of different makes, which increases the cost of maintenance and spare-part management and has reduced TACV's financial viability. Preliminary figures for the fiscal year 1991–92 reveal a comparatively high load factor on domestic flights of 60 per cent. This was, however, below the break-even point, because most of the aircraft complete only about three flying hours per day, compared to four to five hours per day before the fleet's expansion. On international flights, the load factor of 68 per cent rendered the operations profitable; the break-even point is between 47 and 50 per cent. To reduce costs and increase utilization rates of aircraft, and restore TACV's profitability, three aircraft were sold in 1993. Some problems, however, persist: first, TACV is overstaffed, for example, staffing levels were estimated, in 1991, to be 35 to 40 per cent higher than needed to run an airline of this size (Ernst and Young 1991); and second, poor-quality airports, except the international airport on Sal, hamper the TACV's operations.

The cost of air freight is an important factor in the development of trade, for example for fresh fish. The 1992 rate for cargo from Sal to Amsterdam was

$1.12 per kilogram, which appeared competitive by international comparison. Nevertheless, the total transport costs for an exporting company may be considerable higher as additional costs for inter-island transport to Sal (by boat or air) need to be added.

4.5   Trade in Financial Services

Regulatory changes might allow offshore company formation, in ways comparable to the Cayman Islands or the British Virgin Islands. Incorporation of a company in, for example, the British Virgin Islands costs upwards from $500 with subsequent annual fees starting from $250 per year, depending on the volume of transactions and so on. Under present regulations, the formation of an importing company in Cape Verde requires complying with a complex set of conditions which demands the assistance of business consultants. For Cape Verde to participate in the international market for offshore company formation, simplification of these requirements would seem essential.

The regulatory framework could be reviewed for the following offshore services: international banking, and accounting services; registration of patents, trade marks and ships; and offshore trusts for individuals and corporations. The possibility could also be explored for a fee-based granting of nationality for dual citizenship.

The key physical investments required for these activities would be in the area of telecommunications. The institutional requirements would include legislative and taxation changes which are enforceable, and can be recognized by the main trading partners, including Portugal.

5   CONSTRAINTS TO TRADE DIVERSIFICATION

The Third Plan recognizes that reducing factor costs to a level which is internationally competitive is a *sine qua non* for exporting goods and services from Cape Verde (Ministère des Finances et de la Planification 1992b:56). The scope for export-oriented industry is limited because of infrastructural, regulatory and institutional constraints, reflected in high costs of factors of production as well as those of material inputs and services such as water and electricity, and telecommunication. However, telecommunication charges are decreasing, partly reflecting the technological changes taking place in the industry. Infrastructural constraints include:

1. the difficulties in obtaining land for industrial buildings;
2. high frequency of power disruptions;
3. an underdeveloped telecommunication network;

4. limited air freight capacity among the islands and to West Africa; and
5. inefficient port services.

Insurance services are expensive on account of a monopolistic national insurance agency with a relatively high return on capital;[9] and transport is costly, partly reflecting the distance to final export markets (Europe and the United States) as well as to the source of intermediate goods (for example, South-east Asia for garments), and the high ton/kilometre charges in maritime transport.

As part of the revision of labour legislation, it has been identified that labour laws would need to be revised to keep wages at a competitive level in order to attract export-oriented industries, considering capital-intensity and labour efficiency.[10]

More generally, the ongoing economic liberalization can be expected to result in the provision of services at increasingly competitive rates.

5.1 Tourism

The problems of encouraging tourism include: the high level of investment, and its associated risks; and the bottleneck of travel to and from the country, compounded by the complexity of transport between the country's islands.

These limit the choice of possible types of tourism: it has been argued that the country should target the exclusive, high-expenditure type of tourism, comparable to that of some of the small Caribbean Islands. However, the quality of supporting infrastructure required for this is very high, and present facilities are inadequate. Currently only two islands can be reached directly from international destinations; the other islands can only be reached by domestic air links or by boat. Indeed, some of the islands do not have port facilities.

5.2 Financial Services

The BCV combines three banking functions: monetary and exchange rate policy formulation; banking supervision and control; and provision of risk-bearing capital for the short or long term.

However, its primary focus on the first two functions has created a situation where risk-bearing capital for private investment is in short supply; and banking information to facilitate private investment is limited. The Banco de Cabo Verde (BCV) does not finance any large-scale projects, and although it may furnish public guarantees, these have not usually been forthcoming (see Chattrabhuti 1993a). Methods of credit risk assessment need to be modernized, as delays, of six months to one year, which may occur in project evaluation and approval, are too long.

New entrants into the financial sector should help ease some of these problems: a new commercial bank, the Banco Commercial Atlantico, became operational in 1991, providing financial services for commerce; and the Caixa Economica, a savings bank, provides loans for any kind of economic activity at competitive rates.

5.3 Food Imports and Exports

The relation between food security and import liberalization needs to be carefully examined in order to clarify the case for a continued public monopoly. The system of restrictions tends to create scarcity premia and rents for the public exchequer and the public company in the food sector (EMPA). The government of Cape Verde considers EMPA essential for food security (and also for ensuring the availability of construction material such as cement, iron and wood at reasonable prices). It is doubtful if the current system is the best for attaining the objectives of ensuring availability at low costs, considering the cost of preferential access to foreign exchange and aid-financed storage facilities.

5.4 Fisheries

The dismal state of the fisheries sector can partly be explained by the limited priority it received in the past in economic planning and policy. The four-year programme for the development of the fisheries sector, under the Third Plan, intends to address this. Its long-term objectives are to 'optimize the economic and social benefits which may be obtained from the exploitation of the resources', while the short- and medium-term objectives include, *inter alia*, increasing production and improving the contribution of the sector to the country's economic development.

Constraints on the development of this sector relate to regulatory and planning measures as well as to the cost structure (see FAO 1992). Regulatory constraints include the concentration of decision-making authority in Praia on Santiago, whereas the industrial fleet has its base in Mindelo on San Vincente. The low efficiency of the wholly state-owned enterprises Interbase (the export agency) and Pescave (the owner of the industrial fleet) reflects the impact of regulation. Interbase has installations in Sal and Mindelo for refrigeration and storage, but does not have fish-processing facilities. Its capacity utilization is low at 30 per cent, but it reports small positive returns on assets and equity. Pescave sells fish at fixed prices to Interbase; the level of prices results in a negative net profit margin as well as negative (accounting) returns on assets and equity. Low capacity utilization, lack of investment in modern facilities, price fixation in trade between the companies and overstaffing within the companies have created persistent financial losses.

Modern trawlers, equipped with fish-freezing facilities, are fishing in Cape Verde's zone under international agreements; they process and package directly for auctions close to the final consumption centres.

6   CONCLUSIONS

Two important and closely-related steps towards 'opening up' Cape Verde's economy, in the sense of transformation towards a more competitive economy, would include: (i) lowering entry barriers to encourage import diversification, including geographical diversification of imports towards greater shares of goods and services obtained from non-traditional suppliers; and (ii) accelerating institutional reform of the banking system.

Both import diversification and banking development aim to decrease the costs of factors and material inputs to levels which are comparable to that of other countries, in order to attract FDI. Efficiency increases through the privatization programme are unlikely to be realized without substantial progress in these two areas.

Cape Verde's comparatively high factor costs would, in accordance with classical economic theory, recommend a capital-intensive semi-industrialized production technology. This would require a relatively highly-skilled labour force. However, as indicated above, more than 50 per cent of the labour force are unskilled. To absorb this large unskilled labour, it has been emphasized that labour-intensive, low-skill production, and service activities such as the garment and apparel industries and tourism, would be a suitable approach.[11]

Attracting foreign investors to these sectors in Cape Verde will require further specific steps to improve the country's international competitiveness, including:

1. implementing the Labour Code in such a way as to ensure that the low-skill, low-wage segments of the labour market can be effectively tapped by domestic and foreign investors;
2. increasing competition in the telecommunications field to ensure upgraded installation as well as lower prices for services;
3. improving transport connection both by air as well as sea through, *inter alia*, transport-users' groups; and
4. ensuring that land offered on long lease is priced competitively *vis-à-vis* other potential industrial locations.

NOTES

1. They were, at that time, primarily settled in the US (500,000), Portuguese-speaking countries in Africa (68,000), the European Community (81,000, of whom 50,000 in Portugal) and Brazil (25,000). These estimates are indicative only and may be subject to large errors. More recent data are not available.
2. General problems include the lack of hygiene at the supply point, polluted water as well as high prices: the high percentage of diarrhoeal diseases relates to these. Reports about specific locations describe the need to queue from 2 am onwards, without a guarantee of actually obtaining water that morning.
3. Such specialization may be related to the export of invisible services. Cayman Islands, for example, function as a tax haven; the number of registered companies exceed the adult population. Its insurance licensing yields considerable income (see Dommen and Hein 1985).
4. By the end of 1993 various projects were operative which attempted to address these weaknesses including, *inter alia*, the institutional support programme to the Institut d'Aide au Développement Entrepreneurial (IADE) (financed by the Fonds Africain de Développement), the Project d'Etudes Prospectives (financed by the Directorate General for International Cooperation of the Netherlands Government) and the Economic Management Project (financed by the World Bank).
5. Interview with a representative of one of Cape Verde's business associations.
6. The US GSP offers duty-free access for Cape Verdean exports, provided the cost of inputs and processing within the country constitutes at least 35 per cent of the ex-factory value, and the article is imported directly to the US. The HTS 9802 exempts inputs sourced from the US from duty.
7. Thus, Cape Verde received 1.3 million ecu in 1977–84 to make up for losses of banana export triggered by drought (see Traore 1991a).
8. Famines were a recurrent phenomena during the colonial period: major famines occurred in 1773, 1830–32, 1863–65, 1900–1903, 1920–21, 1960–62 and 1976–78. In the post-colonial period the determination to avoid famine by ensuring availability through public stock and import management has been the central objective of food security policy.
9. A study conducted by national consultants (UNCTAD 1991) analyses the profitability of Cape Verde's insurance industry. The ratio between indemnities paid and the premium receipts within the same year indicates that the pay-out varied between 45 and 90 per cent with an (unweighted) average of just below 70 per cent. The return to liquid capital varied between 31 and 43 per cent with an unweighted average at 39 per cent over the same period. With the opening of a second insurance company in 1991, the return to capital would have reduced to some extent.
10. Communication of the UNDP Resident Representative.
11. See, for example, the export development study conducted by Hein and Queyrane in 1987.

REFERENCES

Chattrabhuti, A. (1993a), 'Trade Financing in Cape Verde', mimeo/draft, UNCTAD, LDC Division, Geneva.

Chattrabhuti, A. (1993b), 'Exchange Rate Policies in Cape Verde', mimeo, UNCTAD, LDC Division, Geneva.

Comité National pour l'évaluation de l'année agricole (1989), *Direction générale des pêches*, Praia: Government of Cape Verde.

Comité National Préparatoire de la Conférence Internationale sur la Nutrition (1991), *Document National du Cap Vert*, Praia: Government of Cape Verde.

Dolman, A. (1985), 'Paradise Lost: The past performance and future prospects of small island developing economies', in Dommen and Hein (eds).

Dommen, E. and P. Hein (eds) (1985), *States, Micro States and Islands*, London: Croom Helm.

Duarte, C. and D. Almeida (1991), 'Estudio Sectorial dos Transportes', mimeo, Estudio Nacional do Sector de Servicos de Cabo Verde, Directorate General for Trade, Praia: Government of Cape Verde.

Economist Intelligence Unit (EIU) (1992), *Cape Verde Country Report*, no. 3, London: EIU.

Economist Intelligence Unit (EIU) (1993), *Cape Verde Country Report*, no. 1, London: EIU.

Ernst and Young/The Services Group (1991), *Prefeasibility Study for the Establishment of Commercial Free Zones and Industrial Free Zones in Cape Verde*, Praia: PROMEX for USAID.

Food and Agriculture Organization (FAO) (1992), *Programme Cadre de développement des Pêches pour la Période 1991–1995*, Rapport Technique Ministère des Pêches, de l'Agriculture et de l'Animation Rurale.

Fortes, Rui (1991), 'Estudio Sectorial, Telecommunicacoes', mimeo, Directorate General of Trade, Praia: Government of Cape Verde.

Foy, C. (1993), *Cape Verde: Politics, Economics and Society*, London, New York:

Hein, Ph. and Ph. Queyrane (1987), *République du Cap-Vert: Politique et Programme pour le développement des exportations*, UNCTAD ST/LDC/8, Geneva: UNCTAD.

International Monetary Fund (IMF), *Direction of Trade Statistics Yearbook* (various years), Washington, DC: IMF.

Ministère de la Planification et de la Coopération (1989), *Boletim Anual de Estatistica*, Praia: DG de Estatistica.

Ministère des Finances et de la Planification (1992a), *République du Cap-Vert*, Conference de Table Ronde des Partenaires du Développement, Praia and Geneva: Government of Cape Verde.

Ministère des Finances et de la Planification (1992b), 'Third National Development Plan, 1992–1995', draft, Praia: Government of Cape Verde.

Moran, E.F. (1982), 'The Evolution of Cape Verde's Agriculture', *African Economic History*, pp. 63–86.

Price Waterhouse/International Privatization Group (1992), *Privatization in the Republique of Cape Verde – A Preliminary Assessment*, Praia: USAID.

Rodney, W. (1965), 'Portuguese attempts at monopoly on the Upper Guinea Coast, 1580–1650', *Journal of African History*, vol. 6, no. 3.

Shaw, C.S. (1991), *Cape Verde: World Bibliographical Series*, Oxford: Cleo Press.

Transportes Aereos de Cabo Verde (1992), *Plano Operativo*, Internal Report, Praia: TACV.

Traore, A. (1991a), 'A Mudança – Change', *The Courier*, no. 127, May–June, pp. 10–11.

Traore, A. (1991b), 'Leaders must not behave like rich men', *The Courier*, no. 127, May–June, pp. 14–16.

UNCTAD (1991), *Estudio Nacional do Sector de Servicos de Cabo Verde: Sector de Seguros*, Praia: UNCTAD/Directorate General for Trade.

UNCTAD (1992a), *The Least Developed Countries 1991 Report*, New York: United Nations.

UNCTAD (1992b), 'Diversification of Trade in the Least Developed Countries', mimeo, UNCTAD/LDC/2, Geneva: UNCTAD.

UNCTAD (1993a), *Trade and Development Report 1993*, New York: United Nations.

UNCTAD (1993b), *Handbook of International Trade and Development Statistics*, New York: United Nations.

UNCTAD (1994), *The Least Developed Countries 1993–94 Report*, New York: United Nations.

UNICEF/Gouvernement du Cap Vert (1989), *Analyse de la Situation de l'Enfant et de la Femme en Republique du Cap Vert*, Praia: UNICEF.

UNIDO (1989), *Coût des Facteur de Production*, UNIDO Report, Praia: UNIDO.

UNIDO (1993), *Réflexion sur l'encadrement légal et institutionnel et les conditions du développement industriel au Cap Vert*, Project Report DP/CVI/90/001, prepared by M. Renato Feitor, Praia: UNIDO.

United Nations (1992), *International Trade Statistics Yearbook*, New York: United Nations.

United Nations (1993), *International Trade Statistics Yearbook*, New York: United Nations.

World Bank (1992), *Republic of Cape Verde, Updating Economic Note, Opening Up A Small Economy: An Agenda for the 1990s*, Africa Region, Sahelian Department, Report no. 10594 CV, Washington, DC: World Bank.

6. Trade diversification in Haiti: prospects and constraints

Gérard Fischer with Samuel Gayi

1 ECONOMIC OVERVIEW

1.1 Social, Political and Macroeconomic Context

Haiti occupies some 28,000 square kilometres of the western part of the island of Hispaniola, the Dominican Republic occupying the other part of the island. With more than 6.4 million inhabitants, it is densely populated (more than 200 per sq. km.). With a GDP per capita estimated at $399 (1991), Haiti is, next to Guyana, the poorest country in the western hemisphere. Social indicators reflect a high level of poverty in the country: three out of four Haitians live below the World Bank poverty line, and adult literacy rate was 53 per cent in 1990.

During the 1970s, per-capita agricultural production fell sharply as population pressure forced farmers to cultivate the hillsides: the contribution of agriculture to GDP sharply declined by half, but it has since then recovered to about a third of GDP from the mid-1980s to the early 1990s. The overall shortage of land and the increased demand for wood as a source of energy have entailed severe deforestation, land erosion and soil exhaustion.

The interaction of private-sector initiatives in agricultural and industrial exports, and simultaneous public-sector investment in infrastructure, tourism and other services resulted in modicum of economic development during the late 1970s. However, this relative economic prosperity was short lived as the government increasingly intervened by introducing fiscal and trade policies that were biased against exports and discouraged private-sector investment. This was exacerbated by other constraints within the economy: a small domestic market which resulted in the creation of a number of private monopolies in cement, oil and sugar, barriers in the export sector, especially in coffee, and the low productivity of monopolistic public enterprises supported with substantial public funds increased the budget deficit.

During the first half of the 1980s, all the sectors of the economy showed a marked decline while domestic savings and private investment diminished. This caused internal and external imbalances which resulted in higher inflation, exchange-rate misalignment and the drawing down of international reserves.

Following the expulsion of the Duvalier government, wide-ranging economic reforms were introduced in 1986–87. These included a review of taxes, public expenditure and investment, the introduction of industrial incentives, and the revision of trade and agricultural pricing. These measures assisted in stabilizing the economy even though improvements in real GDP growth were modest. Inflation was reduced as monetary financing of the fiscal deficit was minimal, and employment grew by 1.6 per cent per annum. The reforms were supported by significant commitments of external assistance.

After mid-1987, when the political situation had further deteriorated, the effects of the reform programmes were quickly lost. Frequent work stoppages occurred and private investors became cautious in view of uncertainties. Shortfalls in public revenue caused many project activities to close down. External assistance was either significantly cut back or suspended, while the public debt increased with a rapid deterioration in the macroeconomic situation.

In 1989, the government introduced a stabilization programme to strengthen public finance, stabilize the balance of payments, and reverse the decline in investment and overall economic activity, but the objectives of the programme could not be achieved: the fiscal deficit widened because of revenue shortfalls, and domestic credit expanded more rapidly than expected. Gross domestic investment decreased from about 17 per cent of GDP in 1980 to about 12 per cent 1990, reflecting both the curtailment of external assistance and a fall in gross domestic savings (Table 6.1).

The newly-elected Aristide government in December 1990 took some measures to improve the fiscal revenue situation, capture informal cross-border trade flows, promote tourism and encourage the private sector. It committed itself to implementing a development strategy that would increase the quality of life in Haiti. This strategy called for complementary roles for the private and public sectors, a stable macroeconomic environment, trade liberalization, and the promotion of domestic and international competition. Monetary and exchange-rate policies were to be enhanced, and distortions in agricultural and industrial sectors eliminated. The emphasis was to be on fiscal discipline, and public savings were to be raised to finance domestic investment in critical areas.

Overall, the government intended to focus its efforts on three key areas: investment in its people through school and health facilities; developing the physical infrastructure with emphasis on the maintenance and rehabilitation of roads and transport, water, power and irrigation systems; as well as restructuring public utilities and improving the quality of the civil service.

Table 6.1   GDP by economic activity and by expenditure, 1980-1993
(percentage)

	1980	1985	1988	1990	1991	1992	1993
By activity							
Agriculture	..	..	31.0	31.8	32.4	38.6	38.6
Industry	..	..	37.6	37.6	20.8	18.7	15.3
of which							
Manufacturing	..	..	16.2	15.0	12.6	11.9	10.4
Services	..	..	30.4	47.4	48.9	46.1	45.9
By expenditure							
Exports	21.6	29.4	15.4	10.0	11.5	6.0	7.4
Imports	30.5	15.9	24.1	18.0	26.8	16.1	22.6
Private consumption	81.9	85.3	85.7	87.9	96.9	99.4	104.2
Government consumption	10.1	11.5	9.6	8.0	7.4	7.0	7.3
Gross domestic investment	16.9	16.7	13.4	12.1	11.1	3.7	3.7
Gross domestic savings	8.1	3.2	4.7	4.0	-4.2	-6.4	-11.5

Source: UNCTAD database.

After the anti-Aristide coup in September 1991, fiscal discipline and the gradual widening of the general sales and property tax base have been spurned. As such, resources available to the public investment programme are likely to remain scarce even after the political impasse has been settled.

1.2   Foreign Exchange and Monetary Policy

Haiti's banking network consists of a Central Bank (Banque de la République d'Haiti (BRH)), development finance institutions, Haitian and foreign commercial banks and governmental financial institutions. The country's monetary policy is characterized by the absence of domestic bond financing, hence, by the problem of financing the public-sector deficit after external financing has been taken into account. The sharp decline in external assistance since 1987 encouraged inflationary financing of the public deficit (through the Central Bank), and contributed to inflation (30 per cent at the end of 1990), which has increased sharply since the coup.

The official exchange rate of five gourdes to one US dollar has remained fixed since 1919. However, a free foreign-exchange market exists, and almost all transactions were transferred to this market in August 1991. Subsequently, the export surrender requirement at the official exchange rate of five gourdes per US dollar was reduced to 40 per cent of gross export earnings. In August 1993 the exchange rate in the free market was G11.8 to US$1 (EIU 1994:35).

1.3 Balance of Payments

Balance-of-payments surpluses were recorded in 1985–90. In 1991, a balance-of-payments deficit of a little over $21 million, attributable to a 21 per cent increase in the value of imports that year, was recorded. Although the marginal recovery in the value of exports in 1989 continued to 1990, the trade deficit increased by about 58 per cent, to $138 million in 1991.

Coffee exports and assembly industries are the most important sources of income, even though the predominance of coffee declined in recent years. Many secondary agricultural export products such as cocoa, sisal and essential oils also became less important.

Food imports increased by two percentage points between 1980 and 1989 and accounted for approximately 18 per cent of import payments in 1989. Machinery, fuel and manufactured products, which represented more than 57 per cent of all payments in 1980, were down to 30 per cent by the end of the 1980s.

Emigration, affecting 0.5 per cent of the population every year, generated significant remittances from workers abroad. These transfers have offset trade imbalances and gained importance over time. In contrast, receipts from tourism have declined rapidly: since 1986, the number of tourists has decreased by about 8 per cent per year in reaction to civil unrest and the AIDS pandemic. During 1988–89, tourism generated some $46 million, a significantly lower figure than the average for 1980–87. Given the country's political crisis, receipts from tourism are likely to have collapsed since the last quarter of 1991.

1.4 External-resource Flows

Foreign assistance to Haiti grew from $75 million in 1977 to about $258 million in 1987. Average annual commitments amounted to $160 million during the 1980s. Following the donors' disappointment with the election of 1987, aid declined to less than $150 million per annum.

Of the $174 million in total assistance to Haiti in 1990, 63 per cent was in the form of bilateral aid with the United States, France and Canada remaining the largest donors. The US suspended its $100 million annual aid package on several occasions from 1987 because of Haiti's political instability. When the democratically-elected government of Aristide assumed power in February 1991, many multilateral technical assistance programmes were resuscitated or initiated. Most of these were, however, cancelled or suspended in the wake of the military coup which overthrew the new government in September 1991.

Bilateral donors, increasingly aware of the risk of implementing their assistance with government departments of doubtful reliability, have been using NGOs as major channels for their funds. It is estimated that more than 300 NGOs were active in Haiti before the coup, and that the largest part of their assistance was destined for community development.

1.5   External Indebtedness

The stock of publicly-guaranteed foreign debt rose sharply during the 1985–87 period, and amounted to $830 million by 1989. Approximately 75 per cent of the total debt is on concessional terms. Debt service accounted for 14 per cent of total export earnings in 1990, but it fell to 9 per cent in 1991, when Haiti also cleared its arrears to the IMF. Arrears of about $20 million, recorded in early 1991, were mostly to bilateral agencies.

2   INDUSTRY AND EXTERNAL TRADE

2.1   General Background

The traded sector includes import-substitution industries serving the local market, and an export assembly sector. While import-substitution industries were highly protected from external competition up to 1986, the assembly sector has been operating, since its inception more than 20 years ago, under a relatively free-trade regime. Three major industries account for approximately 70 per cent of the industrial value added: food production (35 per cent); electrical and electronic equipment (22 per cent); and textiles, leather and clothing (13 per cent).

Haiti's export configuration changed dramatically in the 1980s. The share of agricultural exports in total exports fell from 42 per cent in 1975 to about 13 per cent in 1990 while that of manufactured goods more than doubled from almost 38 per cent to about 83 per cent over the same period (UNCTAD 1992:148).[1]

The direction of Haiti's external trade has not undergone any major changes over time. The US remains the most important trade partner, accounting for about three-quarters of total exports since 1985. European Community countries are the second most important destination. The geographical composition of imports is similar, with the US as the largest source of Haiti's imports (Table 6.2).

It is commonly acknowledged that the analysis of only recorded trade flows is misleading as it represents less than half of the actual trade value: according to government estimates, more than US$60 million worth of rice, flour and sugar, corresponding to a value of about 50 per cent of recorded agricultural

Table 6.2 Direction of recorded trade, 1985–1993

	1985	1989	1990	1991	1992	1993
	(Exports as per cent of total exports)					
Industrial countries	97.4	97.4	98.4	99.4	98.5	98.7
of which						
Belgium-Luxembourg	3.9	4.2	2.0	0.6	1.5	1.1
France	8.8	9.0	4.8	2.5	6.8	4.0
Germany	2.7	2.8	2.4	2.2	4.5	2.3
Italy	5.0	4.9	4.0	2.5	5.3	2.8
Portugal	..	..	..	..	..	..
Spain	0.0	..	..	0.3	0.8	..
United Kingdom	0.6	0.7	0.4	0.6	0.8	0.6
United States	73.5	73.6	80.2	85.4	75.9	84.0
Developing Countries	2.5	2.5	1.5	0.5	1.4	1.1
of which						
Africa	..	..	..	..	..	..
	(Imports as per cent of total imports)					
Industrial countries	85.2	77.8	77.5	78.2	74.2	72.5
of which						
Belgium-Luxembourg	0.4	0.3	0.8	0.6	1.4	2.1
France	3.6	2.7	2.9	2.2	3.6	3.3
Germany	2.0	2.1	2.1	1.9	2.5	2.3
Italy	2.1	0.3	0.4	0.4	1.1	0.6
Portugal	0.0	..	..	..	..	..
Spain	0.3	0.3	0.6	0.6	0.9	0.6
United Kingdom	1.0	1.0	1.7	2.0	3.2	3.5
United States	62.0	52.2	58.1	61.9	54.2	50.4
Developing Countries	14.8	22.2	22.5	21.8	25.8	27.5
of which						
Africa	..	0.2	0.1	..	..	..

Sources: IMF (1991 and 1994).

imports, enters the country informally every year.[2] Thus, tariffs and import licences have provided only limited protection for domestic producers of these commodities and have created an environment where informal trade flourishes despite the risks of confiscation and fines involved (see Table 6.3).

Consequently, in order to improve government control over trade patterns, and to address the issue of informal cross-border trade, efforts were made in 1991 to reduce tariff levels and to simplify the existing tariff structure. However, these attempts to remedy the problem backfired, notably after the anti-

Table 6.3 Estimates of unreported trade, 1986–1989

		1986	1987	1988	1989
Exports ($ millions)					
Source:	BRH*	191	210	180	159
	OECD	494	472	..	..
	United States	371	379	394	367
Imports ($ millions)					
Source:	BRH	303	311	284	256
	United States	376	433	436	479
Unreported exports (%)					
Source:	OECD	61.3	55.5	..	..
	United States	48.5	44.6	54.3	56.7
Unreported imports (%)					
Source:	United States	19.4	28.2	34.9	45.9

Note: * Banque de la République d'Haiti.

Source: World Bank (1991).

Aristide coup: under the military regime this trade has proved an invaluable route for circumventing and undermining the US trade embargo.[3]

2.2 Trade Reforms

Until 1986, the trade system of Haiti was highly distorted: only the export-oriented assembly industries were able to develop in the second half of the 1970s, taking advantage of the opportunities offered by the US market. During Jean-Claude Duvalier's period of office (1971–86), the nominal tariff on luxury goods was 200 per cent and the average rate of effective protection for all goods was more than 100 per cent. Import quotas, licences and prohibitions affected 111 commodities. The prices of most consumer goods were 60 per cent higher than border prices. Because of high export taxes, farmers received farm gate prices equivalent to about half of border prices. For example, the 22 per cent export tax on coffee during 1980–85 (reduced to 10 per cent in 1986) caused great distortions in coffee production, discouraged investment in the sector and eventually reduced export capacity.

The first post-Duvalier government (1986–87) reduced the number of commodities subject to quotas and licensing to 35 and abrogated the import licensing and quota law. A new import licensing law was introduced for seven agricultural commodities. Quantity restrictions were eliminated and replaced by *ad valorem* tariffs averaging 20 per cent. Direct export taxes were eliminated.

An attempt was also made to revise the entire tariff structure, although customs officers still found the new one complex and difficult to apply.

With the exception of cereals and gasoline, which attracted 50 and 57.8 per cent tariffs, respectively, tariff rates varied between 0 and 40 per cent. Effective protection rates for consumer goods were reduced to 30 per cent, and for equipment to 10 per cent; tariffs on raw materials and some other inputs were assessed at 20 per cent. In addition, customs procedures were streamlined and petty taxes on trade were rationalized or eliminated. Import notifications for recording purposes were automatically processed at the Ministry of Commerce and Industry. An administrative charge of 1 per cent of the c.i.f. value applied to all imports except pharmaceuticals and petroleum products.

The trade-reform package supported the objective of realigning domestic prices towards world prices of agricultural commodities to the extent that export taxes were eliminated, although major agricultural commodities were still protected by licence requirements and tariffs of up to 50 per cent on competing imports. Exportable goods were implicitly taxed through the protection of import-substituting agricultural commodities; and by the 40 per cent export surrendering requirement at the official exchange rate (see above), which many exporters perceived as a serious impediment to export expansion.

One possible option for consideration in further tariff-reform efforts would be the introduction of a uniform tariff structure which would simplify the work of customs officers. It is believed that the introduction of a general tariff of 5 per cent on most goods would curb the informal trading pattern and make enforcement easier for the Customs Department. Considering that actual imports may represent as much as twice the amounts officially reported, revenue earnings are likely to remain about the same. A low uniform tariff should overcome the cumbersome process of selective import-duty exemptions, and, in the longer term, generate gains in revenue and administrative efficiency. There is, moreover, a need for complementary reforms, such as the introduction of an Investment Code, the elimination of exemptions for public enterprises and the availability of credit facilities for farmers.

2.3 Sectoral Performance

Under the impetus of tariff preferences such as the generalized system of preferences (GSP) for imports into the US, many private enterprises were established, particularly in the assembly sector. As a result, more than 40,000 jobs were created during the 1970s. In the early 1980s the development of the Caribbean Basin Initiative (CBI) stimulated competition in assembly production between Caribbean countries. At the same time, there was a decrease in the demand for the electronics assembly sector. Haiti continued to retain its export workforce and its relative position in export earnings, but export earnings levelled off during the 1980s after the rapid export expansion of the 1970s.

Considering export values, Haiti was outperformed by several countries which increased their exports to the US. For example, exports from the neighbouring Dominican Republic to the US doubled between 1984 and 1990,[4] while Haiti experienced a 9 per cent decline causing considerable unemployment, especially in the export assembly sector.[5] One contributing factor may have been the (small) rise in the daily minimum wage to 24 gourdes, which according to some private-sector associations might have cost Haiti its comparative advantage over other countries in the region:[6] certainly political factors would have played a more important role in Haiti's deteriorating position as an exporter.

2.4 Private-sector Associations

Before the development of the export-oriented assembly sector, the only important business organization in Haiti was the Chamber of Commerce and Industry. Its main function was to act as a channel and lobbyist for commerce and matters concerning legislation and taxes. In the 1970s and 1980s, a number of more specialized trade and industry associations were founded with varying levels of resources and types of activities. The Association des Industries d'Haiti (ADIH), with more than 150 members, strongly supports assembly industries, dealing with internal regulations, legal issues, infrastructure, feasibility studies and market information/surveys. Other associations such as the Inter-American Businessman's Organization (AIHE) and the Haitian–American Chamber of Commerce (HAMCHAM) have strongly lobbied against US sanctions and defended Haiti's preferential access to the US market. The Centre de Promotion des Investissements et des Exportations Haitiennes (PROMINEX), an agency of the government partially financed by USAID from 1986, was responsible for informing and assisting domestic and foreign investors. PROMINEX was closed down when cofinancing from USAID was suspended. A replacement agency, PROBE, was to be launched later to operate on a smaller scale, using the services of private consultants to save on personnel costs. It is generally agreed that the mandate of PROMINEX should be maintained more or less unchanged.

A major channel liaising between the private and public sector is the Comité Mixte de Consultation pour le Développement Industriel (CMCID) which is composed of leading representatives of the private and public sectors. As a private-sector group, and the primary forum for debate on economic policy between the public and private sector, the CMCID has been successful in maintaining an open dialogue on major economic issues. Several other associations with fewer members are supportive of particular local interests. Further efforts should be made to encourage dialogue among private-sector associations. One organization that could become the umbrella for this purpose is the Fédération Haitienne des Associations du Secteur Privé (FHASEP).

3   POST-COUP ECONOMIC SITUATION

The sketchy information available since the overthrow of the Aristide government indicates that the economy has continually declined. A little over two years after usurping power, the government is in disarray with some government ministers reportedly denied access to the Treasury, or even information on the state of public finance. The economy is all but ravaged by its new rulers, and reduced to 'structural insolvency' by a poorly-enforced, but nevertheless impairing, embargo. Haiti's central bank quarterly bulletin reported a government budget deficit of G87.6 million for the quarter, April–June 1992, compared with a G128.4 million surplus in the same quarter of 1991. Budgetary receipts fell by almost 56 per cent to G189.5 million, and customs receipts by about 69 per cent to G26.7 million over the same period (EIU 1993a:24). Balance-of-payments figures for October 1992–March 1993 depicted the continuing decline in the volume of trade and the prominence of transfers from abroad in compensating for the trade and services deficits (EIU 1993b:29).

4   CONSTRAINTS TO TRADE DIVERSIFICATION

4.1   Basic Constraints

One of Haiti's strengths is the existence of a class of entrepreneurs. Labour is available at relatively low-wage rates for labour-intensive manufacturing activities, although they may require training in some specific skills. In addition, there are opportunities in agriculture and agribusiness which do not immediately require standardization, expensive infrastructure or new marketing channels. The geographical proximity to US markets has made Haiti reasonably competitive among non-US manufacturers because of short shipping times and low transport costs. This competitive edge, however, has been destroyed for the time being by political strife. Once political normalcy is restored, the government will need to tackle the many serious weaknesses inhibiting private-sector development, including:

1. *Weak physical infrastructure*   Inadequate physical infrastructure is one of the most severe obstacles to further industrial development. Electricity is expensive, unreliably supplied and available only in certain areas. Water for industrial use is scarce and expensive. The road network is badly maintained,

both in urban centres and in the rest of the country. While the overall situation in the ports improved in 1991, port facilities are still outdated and need to be upgraded. The quality and reliability of telecommunications was rapidly improving at the time of the UNCTAD mission in 1991. However, it was still difficult to obtain new fax or telephone lines as waiting periods were lengthy.

2. *Lack of credit and capital*   A serious obstacle to investment seems to be the lack of capital for small entrepreneurs, most of whom are forced to obtain credit from the informal sector at a high cost, varying from 10 per cent per month to 10 per cent per day. Formal lending institutions, operating under conservative assumptions, cater only to the established business community, rather than to new enterprises exposed to risks, even if the latter expect high returns.

3. *Inadequate land management and tenure policies*   Problems of land management have led to under-registration of land titles, the lack of zoning and land-use planning, high costs of land, construction, rent and utilities. Competition for available land, particularly land with access to services, is intense, raising costs and encouraging haphazard development.

4. *Insufficient access to market information*   The lack of accurate, accessible and timely market information frequently inhibits investors who are considering new investment or the expansion of existing enterprises. The business community lacks contacts for assistance in project identification, access to information on alternative foreign markets, specific technical knowledge and reliable financial data.

5. *Shortage of skilled personnel*   Whereas it is relatively easy to engage local unskilled or semi-skilled labourers, there are chronic shortages of skilled labourers, supervisors and managers who tend to emigrate, mainly to the US. The paucity of middle- and upper-level personnel is a serious obstacle to further development of the industrial sector. Trained personnel, for managerial positions when available, expect salaries comparable to those obtaining in the US.

4.2 Legislative Inadequacies

The policy and regulatory environment, despite some reforms, remains complex, muddled and frustrating to investors. The administration of import and export flows, tax collection assignments, investment code procedures, for example, need to be streamlined and made transparent. The present investment legislation provides for different types of special status for industrial or craft-related investment: the privileged status A, B and C, or a special status[7] individually negotiated between the government and an enterprise. Enterprises outside the metropolitan area and in industrial parks have the benefit of tax and duty exemptions, but eligibility requirements are complex and often difficult to interpret.[8]

4.3 Political Constraints

As a consequence of political instability after September 1991, domestic and foreign private investors have lost confidence in Haiti's economy, and many have withdrawn their capital or cancelled contracts. The current political instability is not conducive to attracting new domestic and foreign investments, or indeed for maintaining established investments. Lack of effective governance, breakdown of law and order, and the inability to reach a quick and unambiguous political settlement with the military cum civilian rulers on restoring a democratic government continue to have ruinous effects on the economy.

5 PROSPECTS FOR TRADE DIVERSIFICATION

Although the export sector has been contracting in recent years for political reasons, it has remained reasonably competitive. Prospects for growth and further diversification, particularly in agribusiness, assembly industries, tourism and mining, were seen as promising by private entrepreneurs and representatives of banks interviewed in 1991.

Agribusiness shows some promise for both vertical and horizontal diversification. Processed food and feed producers, and exporters of processed and fresh agricultural products have demonstrated their commitment to small farmers' associations, for example, the Agricultural Producers' Association (APA), which have been instrumental in advising producers on broadening the agricultural production base.

Vertical diversification, based on sugar derivatives, could be achieved in rum and liquor production, which have a considerable export potential. There are also opportunities for processing cassava or manioc roots into flour which could be mixed with imported wheat flour to provide bakery products for the local market; in addition, a substantial export market exists in the US and Canada, for starch, paste and caramel derived from cassava.

Opportunities also exist for diversifying into specialised horticultural products (cut flowers, mushrooms, macadamia nuts, mangoes) and essential oils. Some diversification efforts had by 1991 allowed sales of cut flowers to the US, a market with potential for expansion. The APA was specially successful in supporting an expanding mango export sector, which, however, needs new capital injections for continued growth.

Private production of essential oils for the preparation of perfumes and soaps, once a significant source of income, suffered a serious setback when direct sales were stopped and a monopolistic market, controlled by a few families, was created.[9] Considering the worldwide demand for essential oils, and the fact that Haiti's market share does not seem to have been taken over by any other country, there are good prospects for Haiti's return into this market, if the necessary investment to upgrade technical installations for the extraction of oils are procured.

Coffee remains Haiti's main export. However, since 1985 the volume exported had fluctuated and generally declined with volume exported in 1990 less than 60 per cent of that exported in 1985 (EIU 1994:45). The possibility of improving coffee production could be examined. Reviving this crop could have a positive effect on the environment if it contributes to reducing the production of import-substituting agricultural commodities:[10] the latter are mostly annual crops which have exacerbated soil erosion on the hillsides where they are planted, while coffee cultivation is considered to be more environmentally friendly. Substantial new investment in replanting and pruning would be necessary in the first instance.

The assembly sector could also be further diversified. Existing electrical and electronics factories were supplying mainly the US defence industry and the consumer market with relatively advanced items such as transformers, conductors, switches and motors/starters.

The apparel industry almost tripled its export earnings to the US from $71 million in 1982 to more than $185 million in 1989, and offers good prospects for further growth. Producers have special access to the US market.

International tourism to Haiti was negatively affected by the AIDS pandemic as well as by recurrent political and social instability. Haiti's attractive environment (including beaches), and existing hotel infrastructure make tourism development possible. Important linkages with the local economy (agriculture, handicraft, and so on) could benefit the whole economy.

The handicraft sector, which is already active in Haiti's economy, could be diversified if certain constraints were alleviated. These include the lack of institutional infrastructure at the national level, the absence of regulation and financial support for artists, and the lack of a coordinated approach to marketing handicraft in spite of the existence of the National Office of Handicraft. The creation of a well-functioning central organization to provide assistance to craftsmen and women could enhance handicraft exports. Art and souvenirs such as paintings, sculpture, marble objects, pottery, ceramics and straw products, designed and produced by local artists, could be produced specially for the export market.

Since the closure of the bauxite mines in the mid-1980s, virtually no mining activities have taken place in Haiti. There are at least six sites of good quality marble with promising business prospects. A major constraint is the lack of management experience in this field. Considering the high demand for marble abroad and its favourable price structure in Haiti compared with Canada and the US, a marble industry could earn significant foreign exchange for the Haitian economy. However, an environmental impact analysis must be undertaken as part of the cost–benefit analysis of such a project.

Haiti's exports have privileged access to the markets of developed countries because of its participation in non-reciprocal trade arrangements offering opportunities for Haitian or foreign private investors. Under the following arrangements, products of Haitian origin enjoy tariff concessions to foreign markets: tariff position 806.3 and tariff position 807 (US markets[11]); generalized system of preferences (GSP) (US markets); Caribbean Basin Initiative (CBI) II (US markets); EC Preference System (EC markets); GATT Multi-fibre Arrangement (US markets); Lomé IV Convention (EC markets).[12] The recently concluded Uruguay Round agreement may erode these preferential terms and dampen their effects as it becomes fully operational. Thus, in the long term, access of Haitian exports to international markets will depend on their international competitiveness.

6   RECOMMENDATIONS AND CONCLUSION

The present political situation, ensuing from the overthrow of an elected government, does not provide any positive signals to the national or international business community. In spite of this drawback, the longer-term objective of trade diversification could be achieved provided action is taken in a number of areas:

1. updating and improvement of the legal, regulatory and institutional environment which has been under way since 1987 should be continued;
2. public institutions responsible for trade, agriculture, industry and banking should be strengthened; and
3. investment should be promoted through initiatives which recognize the role of the domestic private sector and the comparative advantages of the Haitian economy.

The existence of an appropriate legal and regulatory environment is a major prerequisite for the creation of a business climate conducive to domestic and foreign investment. Legal texts creating a regulatory framework on labour, trade and investment have been issued since 1986. While this new legislation may be generally favourable to trade diversification, some aspects require improvements.[13]

Both the new investment code and the commercial code have to be continuously reviewed. One objective of such a review should be to facilitate decentralization of commercial and industrial activities to reduce the danger of high concentration of industries, with its concomitant problems of excessive urbanization and environmental degeneration that may be associated with the current privileged investment status of Port-au-Prince.

While some of the recent reforms had began showing desired effects until the resurgence of political turmoil, further changes will be needed in the policy and regulatory environment. Examples of desirable regulatory changes concern the administration of imports and exports, and streamlining of tax collection and duties:

- The government may have to devise and implement policies to discourage informal imports which bypass normal import formalities and avoid payment of duties, thereby undercutting domestic private-sector competition.
- There is a need to redirect existing cash assets into credit availability by revising the credit code (for example, permitting the use of insurance company pension funds for mortgage loans).
- The development of an agribusiness investment code to clearly define investment procedures and protect agribusiness entrepreneurs is also required.
- The existing labour code requires revision to facilitate worker representation through unions, and to outlaw repressive labour practices of some entrepreneurs.
- Finally, government ministries and specialized departments have to be strengthened to allow the preparation of appropriate macroeconomic policy guidelines and the realization of the policy framework through efficient implementation mechanisms.

It is doubtful whether the present bureaucracy has the capability to carry out regulatory and legislative changes without external assistance. The necessity of cutting back the civil service[14] has created a human-resources problem, as some key civil servants chose to leave because of deteriorating working conditions. Consequently, the government machinery is now even more handicapped than before. One way of easing the problem may be to review the remunerative system with the aim of maintaining highly-skilled staff and attracting newly-qualified staff into the service.

Promotion of private-sector investment should be activated. In the past, the responsible agents (for example PROMINEX) and private associations had only limited success in such an effort, mainly because of a lack of funds and skilled staff, and political and economic instability.

Domestic entrepreneurship is often fragile. Many small enterprises are inefficient, have obsolete equipment, suffer from low levels of skills, and are financially insecure. Among potential indigenous entrepreneur groups are unemployed young people with qualifications, former civil servants and employees of public enterprises. Few individuals in these groups have management or sufficient business experience, and/or knowledge, and their financial resources are meagre. There is the need to train practising, or aspiring, business persons, in areas such as launching, and/or seeking financial support for, new small-scale enterprises; and in the management of such enterprises in order to improve the management culture in the small-scale sector. The provision of training opportunities or internships for school leavers in well-established enterprises should enable them to gain invaluable practical experience in their vocations. Easily accessible data banks on markets and international fairs are important to facilitate the access of new businesses to international markets.

Once political stability is reinstituted, bilateral assistance, most of which was channelled through NGOs prior to the 1991 coup, could be enlarged to support other programmes beyond community development, for example, entrepreneurship training which could benefit the indigenous sector. Large numbers of NGOs already operate in Haiti so there may be the need to coordinate their operations, without unnecessarily fettering their activities, to avert the proliferation of an 'NGO jungle', and to avoid duplication and waste of resources.

A restructuring of the banking sector should be considered in order to enhance financial intermediation, for example, improve financing to productive enterprises and to attract specialists in project analysis. While bank financing of projects is relatively easy for well-established clients, small-scale and first-time entrepreneurs find it extremely difficult to obtain financial support as they are considered high-risk customers. A rationalization of informal-sector lending, based on the outcome of a diagnostic study, could thus benefit new private business initiative. Such a study could address itself to the following issues:

- socioeconomic characteristics of borrowers and lenders in the informal sector;
- sources of funds for informal lenders;
- possibility of channelling official funds to improve the supply of loanable funds to reduce high interest rates;
- recommendations for improving the efficiency of informal-sector lending; and
- creating links between the formal and informal financial sectors.

Establishing a system of recording land ownership, in addition to resolving the problems noted earlier, would also facilitate mortgage lending, and perhaps, the use of land as collateral for bank credit by new entrepreneurs.

If Haiti's business environment is to promote foreign investment, specialized institutions need to be established to that effect. At present, there is no organization responsible for promoting the Haiti economy abroad. The favourable geographic position of the country and its large low-cost labour force, should facilitate the creation of an export-processing zone, if feasibility studies confirm the viability of such a venture.

NOTES

1. Because of persistent political instability and uncertainties in the investment climate, a number of industries have since closed down. Some of these have reportedly moved to the Dominican Republic and elsewhere in the region (EIU 1994:35).
2. For example, a fall in recorded imports and exports between 1985 and 1989 was partly explained by an increase in informal cross-border trade (not captured by official statistics) and a sharp rise in underinvoicing of exports.
3. Well-to-do groups are reported to have benefited hugely from the flourishing contraband trade. For example, between November 1991 and March 1992, 'ships from Latin America, Europe and Africa supplied Haiti with goods ranging from Argentine steel to French perfume ... [and] tankers from half a dozen countries delivered almost a million barrels of oil' (Constable 1993:183). See also Griffin (1992:671) for how wealthy élite Haitians are deriving business opportunities from the trade embargo.
4. The Dominican Republic became the world's fourth largest export-processing zone during the 1980s, based on a policy of orienting its productive capacity to US markets, especially for textiles and shoes. A detailed discussion of this strategy is presented by Kaplinsky (1993).
5. Available figures on job losses are contradictory. According to one source, by 1992 about 150,000 had been lost mostly in the export assembly sector (see Constable 1993:182). Another source estimated that a total of 130 factories, out of 180, had been closed, eliminating an estimated 32,000 jobs, out of which 4,000 were restored when 12 factories reopened after July 1992 (EIU 1994:41).
6. This argument is weak, though, since the real wage index (1980=100) deteriorated to 88.3 in 1989, and, in 1990 dollar terms, stood at only $0.58 per hour compared with $0.57 per hour in neighbouring Dominican Republic. Only two other countries had hourly rates less than this in the region, Honduras ($0.48), and Guatamala ($0.45); and Puerto Rico paid as high as $5.40 per hour (Association des Industries d'Haiti, March 1995).
7. The highest status (A), applicable only to investment within the Port-au-Prince metropolitan area, provides for income tax exemption for a period of five years and eliminates all customs duties for the life of the business.
8. For example, the applications are dealt with by four different ministries/committees, excluding the Appeals Committee: Ministry of Commerce and Industry, Consultative Committee for Preferential Investments, Inter-ministerial Consultative Commission for privileged investment, and the Ministry of Finance with which the nature and the size of any rebate must be negotiated in advance.
9. The value of export earnings fell from an average of 15.4 million gourdes (1987–88) to 3.8 million gourdes (1989–90) before recovering slightly to an estimated 9 million gourdes (US$1.8 million) in 1991 (EIU 1994:45).
10. That is, if enough foreign exchange is earned from coffee exports to import them. However, food security implications of reviving coffee cultivation may have to be analysed, particularly as the shift away from coffee and other traditional cash crops has been explained by a shift to subsistence crops (rice, maize, sorghum, millet and beans) because of population pressure (see EIU 1994:38).
11. Of these, TSUS 807A is the incentive tariff which has been most widely used in Haiti.
12. The list of eligible products under this excludes certain agricultural products which are subject to import quotas or must comply with specific import regulations. Primary producers, however, benefit from an export earnings insurance system, STABEX, which provides compensation for losses due to fluctuations in export receipts for designated products.
13. All new legislation need to be accompanied by implementing decrees, as in the past certain pieces of legislation had remained on the shelves not only as a consequence of lack of publicity, but also because they could not be enforced.

14. At the beginning of 1991 more than 8,000 public servants were laid off to bring the total number of civil servants to about 37,000.

REFERENCES

Constable, P. (1993), 'Dateline Haiti: Caribbean Stalemate', *Foreign Policy*, no. 89, pp. 175–90.
Economist Intelligence Unit (EIU) (1993a), *Country Report: Haiti*, 2nd quarter, London: EIU.
Economist Intelligence Unit (EIU) (1993b), *Country Report: Haiti*, 4th quarter, London: EIU.
Economist Intelligence Unit (EIU) (1994), *Country Profile: Haiti*, London: EIU.
Griffin, C.E. (1992), 'Haiti's Democratic Challenge', *Third World Quarterly*, vol. 13, no. 4, pp. 663–73.
IMF (1991), *Direction of Trade Statistics Yearbook*, Washington, DC: IMF.
IMF (1994), *Direction of Trade Statistics Yearbook*, Washington, DC: IMF.
Kaplinsky, R. (1993), 'Export Processing Zones in the Dominican Republic: Transforming Manufactures into Commodities', *World Development*, vol. 21, no. 11, pp. 1851–65.
UNCTAD (1992), *Handbook of International Trade and Development Statistics*, New York: United Nations.
UNCTAD (1994), *The Least Developed Countries 1993–1994 Report*, New York: United Nations.
World Bank (1991), *Haiti: Restoration of Growth and Development*, Country Economic Memorandum, Washington, DC: World Bank.

7. Trade diversification in the Lao PDR: prospects and constraints

Gabriele Köhler with Willem van der Geest

1 GENERAL BACKGROUND

The economy of the Lao PDR is characterized by a set of complex features which may either benefit the country or shackle its development: the very low per-capita income, underdeveloped formal productive and financial sector and the lack of infrastructural facilities jeopardize rapid socioeconomic progress (UNCTAD 1994). On the other hand, the country is endowed with abundant natural resources, and is situated in the centre of several actual or potential 'growth poles' which could enable it to gain from transit trade as well as investment linkages with the surrounding 'second-tier NIEs' such as Thailand and China, and with reforming economies such as Vietnam. The potential of the Lao economy to expand and diversify international trade needs to be analysed in the context of these opportunities and constraints, as they will determine the scope for its trade expansion and diversification.[1]

The Lao PDR has a total land area of 236,000 sq. km. – twice as large as Bangladesh and nearly half the size of neighbouring Thailand. Approximately 8,000 km. of borders with five countries render control of informal cross-border trade difficult, especially along the Thai and Vietnamese borders.

Its natural resources include hydropower, minerals and timber. With the exception of forest products, most of the potential remains to be surveyed and explored. However, any exploitation of natural resources would need to take account of environmental sustainability because of the country's fragile ecological balance.[2]

The population and terrain are fragmented: of the total population, estimated at 4.3 million for mid-1991, only about one-third inhabit the fertile Mekong valley strip while the majority of the population lives in dispersed and inaccessible areas, with population densities as low as 6 persons per square kilometre in the northern mountainous areas. Approximately 85 per cent of the population are involved in subsistence agriculture, but given the low population density, there is less pressure on arable lands than in other parts of South-east Asia.

The total GDP of approximately US$1 billion comprises about 59 per cent agriculture, 13 per cent industry, and 28 per cent services, with industry as the most expansive sector in official GDP statistics (UNCTAD 1994). Per-capita income averaged $237 (1991).[3]

1.1 Human Development and the Skills Profile

Social indicators such as longevity and literacy rates are low, and mortality is high: female and male life expectancy are at 52 and 49 years, respectively, and the infant mortality rates are 100/1,000 live births (UNCTAD 1994).

A web of gender, ethnic and subnational disparities serves to marginalize segments of the population. For example, average under-five mortality is 145/1,000, but in some mountainous areas it may rise to as much as double that ratio. Educational statistics for the early 1990s indicate overall literacy rates of 92 per cent for males, but only 76 per cent for females. The respective subnational female/male literacy rates were even more disparate when disaggregated by regions (UNCTAD 1994). The Mekong valley strip enjoys a privileged access to social services, while the highland areas are underserved: primary school enrolment ranged from 100 per cent in the greater Vientiane area and the riverine provinces, to as low as 14 per cent in Sekong.

The Lao PDR faces a severe paucity of skilled personnel. According to the 1986 census, not more than 25,000 persons had post-secondary schooling or training. Among these were 500 engineers and 1,500 high-level technicians. Another dimension to the skill problem is the 'incompatibility' of these professionals: trained in different educational and political contexts they find it difficult to interface with one another, as their reference systems and communication styles are often very different.[4]

Prospects for improving the skills profile through in-country higher education are limited in the short term: approximately 1,200 students graduate annually from the country's 14 vocational schools; there are only 4 higher-level technical institutions (UNCTAD 1992a), and the university of Vientiane is limited to teacher training.

Trained professionals were predominantly based in the government sector, but in the course of the current retrenchment programme to reduce government-sector employment by 25 per cent by 1995, many of the more dynamic civil servants are joining the private sector. In the urban areas, a class of small and medium enterprise (SME) entrepreneurs are engaged in petty production and trade. Though probably never exposed to formal entrepreneurial or managerial training, they have succeeded in establishing themselves rapidly in response to new business opportunities. This 'informal' sector may prove an important source of growth for the Lao economy in the process of opening up.

2   MACROECONOMIC REFORMS AND PERFORMANCE

2.1   The New Economic Mechanism of 1988

From 1975 until the mid-1980s, the government pursued an inward-looking policy. Trade ties were limited almost exclusively to the COMECON countries, and the Lao PDR was isolated from its South-east Asian neighbours. A process of change began in 1986, marked by the adoption of the New Economic Mechanism (NEM)[5] which introduced some degree of privatization into the economy. Specifically, the NEM was to facilitate technical change and capital intensification through the reemergence of private-sector enterprises and the transfer of technology through joint ventures, and to foster diversification of economic activities.

Since the late 1980s, some key policies have been implemented to liberalize, and enhance the external orientation of the economy, including: exchange-rate liberalization, tax and financial sector reforms, divestiture of state-owned enterprises (SOEs), and retrenchment of staff in the government service to cut down public expenditure.

The debate on overall economic policy is, however, far from over. Two contrasting development strategies are under consideration in the Lao PDR. One strategy represented by one group of government officials, representatives of the private sector and external donors, is that of creating a 'resource-based economy' pivoted on the primary and tertiary sectors – similar to Australia or Canada; and benefiting from expansionary processes in neighbouring countries by emerging as a hub of transport and financial services, by exploiting its transit position between China, Myanmar, Vietnam and Thailand. The alternative, a 'diversification' approach, advocated by other dominant groups within government, favours attracting foreign capital into the manufacturing sector so as to diversify production, leasing out, rather than selling off, SOEs, and designing a series of measures to protect the natural-resource base, in particular forestry.

The informal sector is very important in the Lao economy: the centrally-planned economy covers only the comparatively small, urban and formal economy while the subsistence sector remains largely unaffected, and the informal trading sector follows a rationale of its own. The dynamic process of monetization and increasing linkages among the productive sectors appears to emanate from the informal, rather than the formal, services sector, in particular commerce.

To date, the growth demonstrated, albeit on a small scale, in the emerging manufacturing and services' sectors, indicates that the aspired diversification of the economy is feasible.

2.2　Macroeconomic Reform and Performance in the 1990s

Real GDP growth rates averaged about 8 per cent per annum between 1989 and
1992 (see Table 7.1). However, considering the drought of 1987–88, which
depressed agricultural output as well as hydropower production, these high
growth rates are probably exaggerated. The macroeconomic performance in the
post-reform period is discussed through a review of the three main interrelated
components of the programme: (i) financial-sector reform; (ii) tax reform; and
(iii) industry/enterprise policy reform and privatization.

*Table 7.1　GDP at factor cost and growth rates, 1985–1993 (1990 constant
market prices)*

	1985	1989	1990	1991	1992[a]	1993[b]
Billions of kips	497	566	607	628	671	717
Percentage	..	14	7	4	7	7

Notes:
a. Estimation.
b. Projected.

Sources: State Statistical Centre and IMF Resident Office, Bank of Lao PDR, December 1992.

Financial-sector reform

Until the mid-1980s, the financial system in the Lao PDR was organized along
the lines typical of centrally-planned economies: the State Bank of the Lao PDR
covered all treasury, monetary as well as financial functions. In 1988, a new
banking law was promulgated, essentially introducing a banking system based
on commercial principles. The State Bank is now responsible solely for central
bank functions; and its branch offices have been converted into four regional
banks. A number of private banks nationalized in 1975 have been re-commer-
cialized, but retained in 100 per cent public-sector ownership (Vilaihongse
1992:73). The Banque du Commerce Extérieur du Lao PDR has lost its monopoly for foreign-exchange transactions and export finance. A joint venture, the
Joint Development Bank, was founded in 1989 as one of the country's first
mixed enterprises.[6]

　　The banking-sector reforms have had two major results. First, by 1991, real
interest rates turned positive for the first time since the late 1970s, resulting in
increases in the savings-to-GDP ratio.[7] Gross domestic investment averaged 14
per cent between 1988 and 1992 and is likely to increase in the course of
liberalization. Second, the financial system regained stability, and consumer
price inflation was reduced to 10 per cent in 1992 (Table 7.2). A floating

Table 7.2 Selected economic indicators, 1988–1992

	1988	1989	1990	1991	1992
Gross domestic saving (% of GDP)	2.2	1.1	0.8	2.1	3.6
Gross domestic investment (% of GDP)	14.9	15.1	14.8	13.1	14.5
Changes in consumer prices (% p.a.)	14.8	59.5	35.7	13.4	9.8
Changes in money supply (% p.a.)	37.1	89.3	14.0	9.5	49.0
Growth rate of merchandise exports (% p.a.)	..	9.5	24.3	22.7	37.3
Growth rate of merchandise imports (% p.a.)	..	29.7	–4.3	13.1	16.5
Balance of payments on current account (% of GDP)	–14.5	–16.2	–9.2	–4.7	–3.6
Debt service ratio (% of exports)	15.5	15.9	10.3	11.2	6.3

Source: Asian Development Bank (1993b).

exchange rate was introduced in 1988, and the official and parallel market premium rates were unified. The exchange rate has remained stable at 695–720 kips per US dollar since 1989, but the parallel market premium disappeared in 1993.

For business transactions in the Lao PDR, cash payments as well as bank drafts in Thai and US currencies are accepted, and accounts in foreign exchange are available for licensed export–import traders and other authorized individuals/enterprises. Authorization is required and commission charges range from 0.3 to 3 per cent (BCEL 1993). Despite this, there is still a flourishing informal financial sector dealing in foreign exchange because of the significance of informal cross-border trade in the overall economy.

Tax reform

Another key component of the reform process was the transition from a centrally-planned system where revenues of SOEs were transferred to the government budget and constituted the major source of public revenue, to reliance on public taxation. The tax reform of 1988 introduced a six-pronged system comprising an agricultural tax, a land tax, a set of resource-exploitation related taxes, an import–export tax, a turnover and an income tax. Import taxes are levied at the rates of the domestic turnover tax, that is, at 5 to 10 per cent *ad valorem*. The decree provides for tax exemption on raw materials, intermediates and means of production; provision is also made for a certain, unspecified degree of protectionist tariffs (see Council of Ministers, Decree No. 47, Annex, Article 21).

Tax revenue increased fourfold, in current terms, since the introduction of the reform. Import-duty revenue more than doubled in 1991 due, *inter alia*, to improved enforcement of import regulations (UNDP 1993). After a slump in 1988 and 1989, non-tax revenues also increased considerably. The projected revenue increases for the medium-term programme, 1990–95, assume that non-tax revenues will improve from approximately 12 per cent of GDP in 1992 to 17 per cent by 1995 (Ministry of Economy, Planning and Finance 1992:6).

Trade taxes comprise import duties and an intricate system of export licence fees. The abolition of export tariffs is in line with the government's commitment to external trade expansion and diversification. At the same time, the introduction of a specified system of royalties or export fees on non-renewable as well as specific renewable resource-based products corresponds to the need to limit environmental degradation.

Despite these new developments, in particular the positive impact of the banking-sector reform, in the short to medium term, the government will be dependent on the timely release of ESAF tranches to cover the gap in current and capital expenditure. Moreover, capital formation will require a further improvement in domestic savings performance, as well as an increase in foreign investment.

Industry/enterprise policy reform and privatization

There are currently more than 9,100 registered enterprises in the greater Vientiane area alone. Among these are 370 private-sector enterprises, which have reemerged since the introduction of the NEM in 1986, of which the majority engage in trade and services.[8] In terms of sectoral composition, the tertiary sector is predominant, followed by banking and marketing services. Since the inception of the NEM, investment has been accelerating both in the formal and the informal sectors. However, the privatization of SOEs has stalled for a combination of reasons:

1. divergent views on privatization are held by different political groups in the party and government;
2. unattractiveness of the Lao domestic market for private investors because of its small size;
3. problems inherent in economies in transition, previously dominated by SOEs with 'soft' budget constraints are reflected in difficulties in the appropriate valuation of the SOEs; and
4. the nature, and countries of origin, of the tentative offers received has reinforced the reservations Laotians have had on the issue of conserving national ownership.

In 1991, the government created a Foreign Investment Authority under the auspices of the Ministry of Economy and Planning. Foreign direct investment (FDI), whether mixed public enterprises, private-sector joint ventures, or fully foreign owned, is regulated by the Foreign Investment Code adopted in 1988 (ESCAP 1989:45).

Licensing requests have been impressive, but do not necessarily lead to actual investment disbursements. Thailand is the major source country of FDI, accounting for 39 per cent (112) of the total number, representing 38 per cent (US$159.5 million) of total value, of projects approved in 1988–92 (Ministry of Economy, Planning and Finance 1993). Many of the investment proposals from the US and France actually originate from expatriate Laotians.

Thailand-sourced investment in the Lao PDR is concentrated in natural-resources extraction (in particular wood processing) and the services sector. Investment which could result in vertical diversification has not yet material-ized, with the exception of some garment manufacturing, which, in its current operations, lacks backward linkages within the domestic economy. Although it would be conceivable to promote the use of textile inputs (cotton and silk) produced in the Lao PDR, enterprises currently engaged in garment production seem to be attracted solely by the considerable wage differentials[9] and the opportunity for quota jumping.

Foreign investment in the Lao PDR remains cautious because of perceived or actual legal uncertainties, and constraints in financial as well as economic infrastructure. Also, many contracts have collapsed, either because Lao author-ities decided to put them on hold, or because investors failed to procure capital, or reconsidered their investment projects after a scrutiny of prevailing infra-structure or skill levels (Mugione 1993:9ff.).[10]

2.3 External Assistance for Transition

External assistance to the Lao PDR has undergone considerable changes since the mid-1980s. Aid flows from the former Soviet Union and CMEA countries which virtually disappeared after 1989[11] created considerable friction, both in terms of volume of aid flows and technical cooperation modalities, in particular with regard to technical personnel. Moreover, given the interdependence be-tween aid flows and trade patterns established among CMEA and affiliated countries, the transition away from this bloc created problems in the SOE sector.

Traditional convertible currency area bilateral donors such as Sweden and Australia have remained active in the Lao PDR, and new bi- and multilateral donors have emerged, including Japan. Nevertheless, their total bilateral contri-butions have not been able to compensate for the losses in non-convertible aid flows. Instead, the Asian Development Bank and the World Bank have evolved as the largest donors, and by 1991 multilateral flows were more than double bilateral flows (OECD 1993:171). This may become problematic in as far as multilateral loans are non-reschedulable.

In assessing assistance flows to the Lao PDR, several caveats are called for. First, the size of multilateral loans in relation to total GDP or to the balance of payments is all but overwhelming; there is a danger of the Lao government overextending itself in terms of future loan-servicing obligations. Second, the disbursement ratio has fluctuated widely; although this is in part due to the 'lumpiness' in financing large-scale infrastructure development schemes,[12] and thus inevitable, it may, nevertheless, create additional instability in the economy. Third, the low disbursement ratio (in some years) is indicative of problems of absorptive capacity both in terms of the managers, skilled and unskilled personnel required to implement projects, and in terms of the sheer physical accommodation of development assistance schemes. Fourth, the over-emphasis on physical infrastructure will generate high maintenance/recurrent costs for which insufficient provision has been made in project documents. The government may find it difficult to service this debt if expected revenues from projects and from the overall development of the economy should fail to materialize (see also Lam 1994). Better coordination among ministries and among regional governments is called for to prioritize, synthesize and coordinate development projects.[13]

3   THE EXTERNAL TRADE FRAMEWORK

3.1 Trade Policies

With the exception of the Mekong river valley, as much as two-thirds of the country are only partially integrated into the urban cash economy, given the rugged terrain, prevalence of subsistence agriculture, and the lack of transport and communications infrastructure. Formal trade was, until the late 1980s, the prerogative of the state which regulated domestic trade flows and had a monopoly on export and import transactions.

Although an explicit trade-policy statement has not yet been formulated, the government's Policy Framework Paper outlined the objectives of external trade promotion as:

- the creation of a legal framework for private-sector trade and commerce;
- removing the remaining restrictions on trade and decontrolling prices;
- elimination of taxes which discriminate against exports or are to the advantage of SOEs;
- clarification of FDI guidelines and maintaining a favourable attitude towards foreign investors;
- concluding banking sector reforms;
- acceleration of SOE divestiture; and

- the development of a strategic trade policy covering major exports such as electricity and timber as well as transit rights by air and land (Ministry of Economy, Planning and Finance 1992:1).

In this context, the government is pursuing policies to foster agricultural diversification into cash crops, horticulture and livestock (particularly cattle). Selective import and export restrictions, however, remain, especially for environmental reasons.

With regard to formal-sector foreign trade, the Lao PDR is currently in the process of 'switching' export markets: minerals such as gypsum, tin, copper and anthracite which were formerly exported mainly to the Soviet Union, generally in barter for petroleum, need to be redirected. Trade with the major trading partner, Thailand, is regulated through the 1991 Trade Agreement, and is based on the MFN principle; and, preferential import tariff rates are applied to Lao products in acknowledgement of its landlocked and LDC status. In switching direction of trade, the Lao PDR will need to aim at attaining greater geographical diversification of its exports, particularly in view of large-scale hydropower development schemes targeting Thailand as the sole user (see below).

3.2 Trade Performance

A discussion of the Lao PDR's international trade performance is hampered by the inconsistency of data provided by different sources, such as the IMF, the ADB, the EIU, the UN Statistical Office, and Lao authorities themselves. Nevertheless, the various sources are consistent in registering a steady increase in official exports (in current prices) between 1985 and 1992 accompanied by a significant increase in the trade deficit.

The share of total exports to developing country markets averaged almost 90 per cent between 1985 and 1990, but fell sharply to 50 per cent in 1992–93. On the other hand, the share of total imports from developing countries increased from about two-thirds to three-quarters over the same period (Table 7.3).

It needs to be emphasized that recorded trade flows reflect only a portion of total trade flows; cross-border trade and informal trade are major factors in the Lao trade picture. Notably, there is significant unrecorded cross border trade in agricultural produce and inputs and consumer goods with Thailand. At the borders with China and Vietnam, barter trade as well as transit trade in Thai goods is becoming increasingly significant.

3.3 Trade-enhancing Transport Infrastructure

The development of geographically-diversified trading patterns hinges crucially on upgrading the country's transport infrastructure and on improving cross-border and transit trade conditions. The road network is underdeveloped,

Table 7.3 Direction of recorded trade, 1985–1993

	1985	1989	1990	1991	1992	1993
	(Exports as per cent of total exports)					
Industrial countries	4.0	12.6	20.4	37.1	50.9	48.7
of which						
Belgium-Luxembourg	..	..	..	1.3	..	..
France	0.2	..	3.3	10.1	12.4	12.5
Germany	..	..	3.3	11.4	5.2	8.8
Italy	..	..	..	1.3	1.0	2.2
Portugal	..	..	..	..	..	..
Spain	..	..	..	..	1.0	..
United Kingdom	..	2.2	..	..	..	..
United States	..	1.1	..	2.5	6.2	5.9
Developing countries	95.2	87.0	79.6	62.9	49.1	51.3
of which						
Africa	..	0.7	1.1	1.3	1.2	1.0
Thailand	72.8	43.0	65.6	54.4	38.1	41.9
Other						
Russian Federation*	37.5	21.2	31.5	4.8	..	..
	(Imports as per cent of total imports)					
Industrial countries	42.5	30.8	29.2	26.3	24.1	23.7
of which						
Belgium-Luxembourg	..	0.8	0.8	..	0.4	..
France	7.4	1.6	2.3	2.0	1.2	1.2
Germany	7.2	1.6	0.8	0.7	0.4	1.2
Italy	2.3	..	0.8	4.6	0.4	0.6
Portugal	..	..	..	..	..	..
Spain	..	..	..	..	..	..
United Kingdom	0.7	0.8	1.5	1.3	0.4	0.6
United States	4.8	..	0.8	0.7	0.4	1.8
Developing countries	55.1	67.3	70.0	73.0	75.4	75.9
of which						
Africa	0.6	0.1	0.1	0.1	..	..
Thailand	48.6	55.6	55.0	55.6	55.0	57.1
Other						
Russian Federation*	77.9	48.1	42.0	5.0	..	..

Note: * Former USSR.

Sources: IMF, *Direction of Trade Statistics Yearbook*, 1991 and 1994.

and the northern and southern provinces are not easily accessible by road. There is no railway system and it will be difficult to develop given engineering problems as well as the issue of finance.[14] Domestic air transport suffers from a lack of economies of scale and air freight is not yet a commercially viable alternative to road or river transport.

River transport is the major mode of transport, in particular for goods. Although the Mekong river runs the length of the country and has several tributaries, its full potential to conduct traffic is hampered by low water levels in the dry season. Domestic water transport capacity is also limited in terms of fleet size. For instance, in the late 1980s, the State Water Transport Company operated a fleet of 37 boats representing a river cargo capacity of only 13,000 metric tonnes annually (UNCTAD 1992a:34).

Institutionally-determined entry barriers have sustained high fees which hamper Lao–Thai transit trade:[15] border trade with Thailand and transit trade through Thailand are solely dependent on ferry services at the authorized border crossings; and to date these remain monopolized.[16] The southern Lao provinces are at an additional disadvantage in cross-border trade with Thailand because of low transport capacity.[17] In 1993, the government opened additional ferry-serviced border crossings to facilitate transborder trade flows.

An Australian aid-financed bridge, which opened near Vientiane in 1994 connecting the Lao road network with Thailand, is expected to improve the transport situation. It will speed up border traffic by replacing the ferry service and link up the low-income countries of the eastern wing of South-east Asia (Vietnam, Cambodia and the Lao PDR itself) to the high-growth performance countries (Thailand, Malaysia and Singapore) on the western wing. The main west–east overland route, connecting the Lao PDR with the port outlets in Vietnam, which has recently been rehabilitated, should also facilitate trade with and through Vietnam. Current major road rehabilitation and construction projects, funded by 44 per cent of the ODA commitments for 1991, should improve domestic and international trade flows when completed.

Transport costs are increased by a lack of import cargo, implying a low back-loading factor. Thus, truck load capacity might well come to be better utilized if the Lao PDR were a transit country.

4   PROSPECTS FOR TRADE DIVERSIFICATION

This section reviews trade flows in selected commodities and services with a view to identifying the diversification potential of the Lao PDR. The suggestions are tentative: they have not been examined for financial and economic viability, nor have they been screened for social or ecological implications. The potential of products and areas of economic activity is discussed solely for the purpose of initiating a debate on the policy environment in which private and state-owned enterprises can realize these potentialities.

4.1 Natural-resource-based Production and Trade

Hydropower

The Lao PDR probably has the largest hydropower potential, estimated at 18,000 Mw., in South-east Asia, but at present only one per cent has been developed. Currently, two plants, Nam Ngum and Xeset, are in operation (the latter since 1993): about three-quarters of electricity from each of the two plants is exported to Thailand (Khammone 1992:1). The value of electricity charges comprises 70 per cent of Lao's recorded export to Thailand.[18] Electricity is Lao's second-largest export item and accounts for approximately 19 per cent of the total export earnings.

Hydropower is an obvious choice for further export development. The Lao PDR has commissioned a number of feasibility studies on medium- and large-scale hydropower plants along the Mekong river, and three new hydropower-generating schemes are in the pipeline (see Lam 1994).

The bulk of the electricity to be generated would be exported to Thailand; in the longer run, options may develop for the Lao PDR to export electricity through an expanded ASEAN grid to other South-east Asian countries. In the short run, the government will need to carefully monitor its commitments: there is a danger of financial overcommitment given the government's equity participation in schemes that are very large in comparison with the economy's size. Although the risk is spread considering the financial arrangements under the build-and-operate (BOT) modality, economic vulnerability remains a problem as long as Thailand retains its monopsonistic position, determining demand development as well as revenue flows.

Last but not least, the issue of environmental impact is unresolved. Given the one-party political context of the Lao PDR, the lack of NGOs with a political agenda, or strong civil society, the development of hydropower schemes proceeds in the absence of a critical environmentalist lobby in the country. This sharply contrasts with the strong opposition against hydropower schemes, for example, in neighbouring Thailand. Apart from political reasons, the less vocal environmentally-inspired opposition in the Lao PDR is also because of the low population density in areas where schemes are to be implemented so that the extent of relocation required is limited.[19]

Timber

Timber is a major export item from the Lao PDR; the recorded exports of wood, wood products, bamboo and other forest products amounted to approximately US$103 million for 1992. Two destinations, Taiwan Province of China, and

Thailand, accounted for 75 per cent of the total export value of wood and wood products. The Lao PDR is unable to meet the strong demand from Thailand (created by a ban on logging in force in Thailand since 1988), and because of its own ban on the export of unprocessed wood. The sector is tightly regulated, at least in the Vientiane area, through a quota system, in an attempt to upgrade wood exports into processed wood products.[20]

A vast improvement in the management of forestry resources is necessary if the forestry sector is to move towards a sustainable level of production. Regulation and control of the forest resource, for example, in the form of severe penalties on illicit logging or policing of shifting cultivation, are unlikely to be effective unless they are coupled with positive incentives to improve forest-resource management.[21] Land leases or proprietorship guidelines and legislation for individuals or communities to usufructuary rights to benefit from rehabilitated forests are an example of such incentives. Community forest development projects, undertaken on a pilot basis in the northern region, indicate that small plots can generate wood for local construction in a sustainable way, if tree nurseries and extension services are provided. However, reducing the pressure on forest lands will first and foremost require an improvement of the productivity of the agricultural lands currently under cultivation.

Mining

Anthracite and gypsum mining – until recently exclusively for CMEA markets – is continuing on a medium scale. Projects with a focus on further mineral exploration and exploitation have been licensed since October 1988; additional surveying and prospecting is currently undertaken by various foreign companies. Foreign investment opportunities in the minerals sector are considered good. Considerable deposits of both precious and semi-precious stones (in particular sapphire, aquamarine and amethyst) as well as fossil fuels (coal, oil and natural gas) are also being exploited.[22]

The current mining and exploration activities may require environmental impact studies, such as on mine tailings. Tourism development may also be jeopardized by particular forms of mining that destroy landscapes. The trade-offs between mining development and other types of economic activities also remain to be examined, especially with respect to their impact on local labour markets. The development of labour-intensive mining might face a shortage of workers, if other types of labour-intensive manufacturing are developing simultaneously, given the country's small labour force.

Fauna and flora-based trade

Traditionally, exotic reptiles and game have been used in local upmarket cuisine and for medicinal purposes; for these needs, hunting and trapping occur on a small scale. The greater commercialization since the opening-up of the Lao economy in 1988 appears to have intensified hunting of these species. They are increasingly marketed in urban areas of the Lao PDR, Thailand and China, so cross-border trade in wildlife resources is beginning to threaten certain species. Trade in endangered species continues despite the 1991 *Decree on the Protection of Endangered Species*. Tentative estimates of the returns to sales of rare and endangered mammals, birds and reptiles, based on extrapolating from incidental surveys of daily turnover of market vendors, suggest a lucrative and sizeable market.[23]

Introducing the farming of exotic reptiles in order to benefit from an expanding market, while respecting environmental exigencies, is a possibility which warrants discussion and feasibility studies as it seems to have great potential in the Lao context.

Rare and precious herbs, flora and spices (for example, cardamom) are other valuable forest resources which could be exported. With a view to diversifying income sources within the rural economy, the market potential of these and other forest-based commodities could be explored.

4.2 Agricultural Commodities

Conventional agricultural and livestock products

Perennial crops, in particular coffee and tea, seasonal crops such as rice, and livestock, for example, cattle, contribute to the formal and informal export flows of the Lao PDR. The recorded exports of these products for 1992 amounted to $3.2 million; 91 per cent of this is composed of coffee and tea, more than half of which was sold to Russia.

Cotton and silk production will need to be developed with a view to exploiting forward linkages into the nascent textiles, garments and accessories industries.

The rice production level of the Lao PDR is minuscule, if compared with output figures for neighbouring countries, for example, Vietnam and Thailand. Lao rice production remains vulnerable to climatic conditions since most of it is rain fed or dependent on river-based irrigation. In the longer term, as the irrigation network expands, the international rice market may be worth exploring. However, the transport constraint might call for joint marketing arrangements with exporters from Vietnam or Thailand.

In terms of developing a new range of agricultural export commodities, diversification schemes could examine the feasibility of promoting 'ecological produce'. A combination of factors[24] has conserved an agricultural setting in the Lao PDR with extremely low or nil inputs of chemical fertilizer and pesticides. The Lao PDR could attempt to exploit this 'advantage of isolation' by emphasizing and marketing organically-grown agricultural produce. An examination of the marketing requirements of such produce, including grading, labelling and quality control, and of the potential market size for them in the subregion, notably, the metropolitan areas of Thailand, Japan, the Republic of Korea, Taiwan Province of China, Hong Kong and Singapore could be an important step towards public and private investment decisions in this area.

Non-conventional crops: opium[25]
The Lao PDR is considered a major producer of opium in South-east Asia. The production of, and trade in, opium and opium products is a matter of great sensitivity for the Lao government, for the governments of donor countries as well as for the international organizations working in this field.[26]

Opium is cultivated in all central and northern Lao provinces: the yields are reportedly highest in Xieng Khouang and Houaphan provinces. About 130–140 tonnes of opium were reportedly produced in the highlands in 1992. It is estimated that per household production may average 1 to 2 kg. per year earning them between $80 and $160 (National Commission for Drug Control and Supervision 1992:5, 11). Even though this is only an approximate figure, it is evident that opium provides an important additional 'windfall' income to households with extremely limited alternative opportunities.

An undisclosed share of total production is sold legally in international markets under the country's quota for pharmaceutical processing.[27] In addition, approximately 65 tonnes of opium were estimated to have been exported to Thailand illegally at a price of approximately $80,000 per tonne. For 1992, the Lao government estimated an approximate sales value of $5 to 6 million generated from opium smuggling: trafficking is concentrated in the border area between Thailand, the Lao PDR and Myanmar, but some refining appears to be taking place within north-western Lao PDR, with collusion of groups in Myanmar and Thailand (National Commission for Drug Control 1992:7 and UNDCP 1992:5ff.).

The mountainous northern provinces of the Lao PDR are, in terms of agro-ecological characteristics, exceptionally suitable for the growing of opium. Moreover, the crop's characteristics, such as ease of storage, high value-to-weight ratio, and hence the low transport costs make it suitable for the highlands. The illegal nature of this cultivation coincides with the inaccessibility of much of the region. Alternative crops are unlikely to yield comparable returns to their growers in view of extension and marketing/transport constraints. Consequently, substitution programmes are likely to depend on external technical and financial assistance for a long time.[28]

In view of Lao's comparative advantage in the production of opium – and consistent with its international obligations – an enlargement of the Lao quota in the legal global market for medicinal purposes could be explored in conjunction with the present drug-control programmes, which have hitherto exclusively focused on crop substitution. Clearly, any increase of such legal quota would have to be conditional on an improved monitoring and policing of production by the relevant authorities in the Lao PDR and internationally.

4.3 Manufactures

Textiles and garments appear to be a major area for trade expansion and diversification. Based on the country's rich traditions of silk and cotton weaving, households, NGOs and small-scale manufacturers have, over the past few years, resuscitated the production of fabrics, garments and textile-based accessories. On a larger scale, some state-owned garment factories in the Vientiane area have entered into joint ventures with Thai manufacturers, producing for the Thai market. The Thai interest is focused on the low wages as well as realizing market access privileges emanating from the rules of origin.

In the medium term, skills training, technology transfer and backward linkages to inputs such as cotton and silk fibres cultivated in the Lao PDR will be required if the industry is to evolve into a source of medium value added per unit of exported garment as well as generate sizeable employment. The scope for expanding sericulture is considerable and pre-feasibility studies for the sector are under way. At present sericulture is undertaken on a very small scale but the low-grade cocoons cultivated produce low-quality silk that does not meet the standards for export markets.[29]

4.4 Services

Tourism development
In 1990, some 6,500 tourists visited the Lao PDR, as well as a further 6,500 'day trippers' (including foreign nationals crossing the border for business purposes). Most international tourists tour the Lao PDR on a leg of a visit to neighbouring countries (Thailand, Cambodia and Vietnam in particular). Public revenue from tourism was estimated to have increased by about 59 per cent between 1990 and 1992 (Boun Oum Chan Chon 1992).

Tourism assets in the Lao PDR include: (i) the country's cultural image and heritage; (ii) abundance of natural resources, including an unpolluted environment and rich wildlife; and (iii) unique historical and ancient sites of architectural and/or religious interest (Boun Oum Chan Chon 1992). The National Plan for the Development of Tourism, formulated in 1990, and the creation of the General Tourism Authority and a National Tourism Company have been the main instruments for realizing the potential of these assets. The formation of national nature and wildlife parks is perceived as a significant step in this direction.

5   CONSTRAINTS ON TRADE DIVERSIFICATION

The constraints on expanding and diversifying trade in the Lao PDR are fivefold:

1. the high degree of micro-variation within an extreme topography, encompassing a small formal economy, combined with a variety of informal partly-monetized, isolated economic systems;
2. the economic and political predominance and buoyancy of some of the neighbouring countries which strongly influence the scope and direction of agricultural intensification and manufacturing diversification;
3. severe environmental constraints resulting from a fragile ecology resulting in complex trade-offs across regions and provinces as well as over the short versus the long term;
4. the transport-related obstacles, which will remain nearly unsurmountable because of the extreme topography, and landlocked nature, of the country; and
5. the limited administrative capability of the central government, reflecting not only the relatively small revenue base in the formal economy, but also the history and practice of self-rule and autonomy which the isolated regions and provinces have experienced.

Environmental trade-offs are at the core of the diversification choices, given the exceptional potential which natural-resource-based trade, such as hydropower, minerals, and forest resources, offers. The linkages between trade and environment have been observed to be negative in many developing countries: increased economic activity causing severe environmental degradation. For the Lao PDR, the questions regarding the environment are particularly poignant because environmental degradation, to date, is more limited than in many other developing countries, including its neighbours, Thailand and Vietnam.

It could be argued that international trade, which enhances the present and future value of these resources, could be made to contribute to their preservation, in particular timber, for which international prices are steadily increasing (see UNCTAD 1992b). To realize maximum economic rent from the resources in the medium to long term, and to move resource use towards sustainable levels would, however, require firm policies and measures.

The predominance of the Thai economy in the subregion may frustrate the development of an independent Lao trade policy, both in terms of the role of the Thai currency as the medium of transaction, and in terms of the comparative advantage of the Thai manufacturing sector. Apart from the head start which Thailand has *vis-à-vis* the Lao PDR, the lifting of the investment, trade and aid embargo against Vietnam by the United States will alter the subregional balance. In attracting foreign direct investment as well as official development assistance, the Lao PDR will also have to compete with this larger and increasingly powerful economy.

The expansion of Lao's formal economy, as part of a diversification process, will be hampered by the country's small population and limited number of skilled personnel: the government is already under a strain as many qualified officials leave the ministries to join the private sector, which is short of managerial expertise. In addition, numerous projected large-scale infrastructural schemes, for example, road and hydropower projects, require a labour force (skilled and unskilled) probably exceeding capacity of the Lao labour market.

Among the structural constraints on the development of tourism are inadequate hotel facilities and the difficulty of transport to the Lao PDR, as well as within the country. Other issues inhibiting the expansion of tourism are institutional: visas are exclusively granted by the Ministry of Foreign Affairs in the capital, Vientiane;[30] tourist travel inside the Lao PDR is regulated through travel permits, which are required for visiting other provinces, and through regulations stipulating the minimum time a tourist must stay in designated hotels. Policy changes are under consideration to relax these controls on tourism, for example, decentralization of the visa-issuing authority to Laotian missions abroad as well as at specific points at the border.

The issues of sensitive and illicit trade (opium, endangered species, unprocessed wood) need to be addressed more coherently by policy makers, but this will almost certainly involve the commitment of additional financial and human resources. The liberalization of the Lao economic regime, by reducing direct involvement in productive activities, may free resources for other forms of regulation. Nevertheless, this will need to be complemented by an expansion of central administrative capability.

6   CONCLUSIONS

Prima facie, the statistical evidence, though inconsistent, appears to indicate that the Lao PDR's international trade, compared to other LDCs, is reasonably diversified. Earnings are derived from trade/transit services, hydroelectric power, a wide range of natural-resource-based products and, to a limited extent, agricultural products and manufactured goods. However, a closer examination reveals that:

1. within these product ranges, most of the net balances are negative with imports of trade services, manufactures and agricultural products exceeding export values within the same subgroup of products – the main exceptions being wood products and electricity; and

2. manufactures 'exports' amount, in a considerable number of cases, to trading within firms owned by Thailand-based foreign companies.

Overcoming these features of limited geographical as well as product diversification poses a formidable challenge.

A realistic trade-diversification strategy may well prove to be one which focuses on maximizing the economic gains from the advantages which are inherent to the Lao economy and for which competition from abroad will remain limited. Hydroelectric power, trade- and transit-related services, and natural-resource-based products are likely to fall in that category. Conversely, the production of manufactures, such as garments, have poor prospects in the short run; their present importance and growth rates may be due to quotas, and/ or voluntary restrictions, for major exporting countries in the subregion, rather than to an inherent comparative advantage of the country's manufacturing potential. The changes in the international trade environment in the garment subsector, to be brought on by the conclusion of the Uruguay Round in 1994, are unlikely to offer continued advantages of such a nature to the Lao PDR in the long run.

In contrast, the opportunities for the resource-based strategy appear encouraging, certainly in comparison to other LDCs. Most of the products offer considerable scope for expanding the value added through vertical diversification, especially processing. However, in some of the cases of resource-based production reviewed above (for example, un- or semi-processed wood, minerals, hydroelectricity or exotic flora and fauna) an active role of the government in these subsectors might be warranted to limit environmental damage. Hence, the alternative strategies of a resource-based, versus a diversification, approach would, in fact, need to be integrated to the benefit of the development process. Environmental concerns as well as the limitations imposed by the small size of the population and the socioeconomic makeup of the country need to be borne in mind.

NOTES

1. For an introduction to the history and political and economic structures of the Lao PDR, see Stuart-Fox (1986) and Taillard (1989). For a more recent overview, see Bountheung Mounlasy (1992).
2. Commercial logging combined with the intensification of shifting cultivation, for example, has been threatening the ecological balance; droughts in the late 1980s were attributed to the degradation of upland watersheds; and deforestation is estimated to proceed at a rate of one per cent per year.
3. The non-monetized sector and informal-sector petty manufacturing, in particularly commerce, would modify the respective shares of sectors and per-capita income if they were amenable to measurement.

4. Prior to 1975, France, the US and Thailand were the main countries for training; between 1975 and the late 1980s, a fair share of tertiary education and vocational training took place in Vietnam and the CMEA countries; and since the mid-1980s, the respective shares in training and higher education provided by Thailand and Japan have been increasing.

5. Originally called the New Economic Management System (NEMS), the NEM is of dual origin: *Perestroika* in the former Soviet Union coupled with a weakening of ties with the COMECON, and the increasing influence, on domestic policy, of the international lending agencies (Koehler 1990).

6. For a detailed history of the banking system, see Vilaihongse (1992).

7. For an account of the development in real interest rates, see Vilaihongse (1992:68, 77).

8. Of these, only one-third were members of the Chamber of Commerce. This may indicate that the others are operating only on a micro scale (Communication of the Lao Chamber of Commerce, March 1993).

9. In 1993, the minimum daily wage was 125 baht (or $5), and 1,000 kip (or $1.40) in Bangkok and Vientiane, respectively.

10. At least two privatization schemes failed because the foreign investment partner did not have sufficient capital or collateral to finance initial operations and the investment proper.

11. Assistance from the Russian Federation, China, Mongolia and Cuba amounted to only $1.5 million in 1991, a very steep decline from the annual average of $87 million during the first half of the 1980s.

12. For example, total aid amounted to $132 million in 1990, but increased sharply to $230 million the following year; the disbursement ratio was 70 per cent (1989), 114 per cent (1990) and 62 per cent (1991).

13. For example, the explosion in expatriate expert presence is putting great demands on government and other professionals as well as on institutional infrastructure in overstretching the capacity of government and nascent NGOs to handle the many activities resulting from aid inflows.

14. Proponents of the trade in services-based development strategy argue that developing the transport services would serve to attract finance for an international railway network linking, *inter alia*, Myanmar and Vietnam.

15. The 1987 transit agreement with Thailand was to reduce transit costs by 35 to 40 per cent, but Lao authorities confirmed a reduction of only 21 per cent. Despite accords reached in 1992, the Lao PDR may still be paying a premium on transit cargo (Entreprise de Transport Lao communication, Vientiane, March 1993).

16. Savanakheth/Mukdahan by a Thai firm; Thanalang-Nong Khai by the Laos River Transport Company (UNCTAD 1992a).

17. Capacity at the Pakse border crossing was limited to 6,000 to 7,000 metric tonnes p.a. in the late 1980s (UNCTAD, 1992a:33).

18. For Thailand, imports of Lao electricity constitute only 1 per cent of its total electricity supply. Southern Laos imports electricity from Thailand, since a trunk transmission line within the Lao PDR is missing (Ishida 1992:128).

19. Total estimated compensation for the Nam Theun II hydroelectric power project was $4.4 million. This estimate, however, does not include any provision for the loss of future income for the relocated households, other than a one-off compensation payment for 858 hectares of forest land estimated at $1,200 per hectare; nor does it place any financial value on the irreversibility of the environmental impact (for further details, see Snowy Mountain Engineering Co. 1990:6, and Tables 3, 4 and 5; and Tropical Forestry Action Plan 1990:15).

20. Exports of unprocessed logs appear to continue in areas not under direct government control, allegedly with Lao–Thai collusion: given the particular geographical conditions of the Lao PDR, cross-border illicit timber exports are almost impossible to monitor.

21. The Forest Management and Conservation Project, supported by an IDA-credit of $11.6 million in 1992, attempted to improve post-harvest management and the use of standardized grading and scaling systems for forest resources.

22. The first oil production-sharing contract was signed between Hunt Oil and the Lao government in 1989 followed by further contracts with British and French companies. Drilling has been undertaken; the contracts allow companies to pump oil for 20 years and the Lao government gets a 50 per cent share of the oil produced (*Asian Energy News* 1992).

23. At the That Luang Fresh Food Market, Vientiane, daily sales were observed to the tune of $440 per day (in July–October 1991), amounting to $160,000 annually, assuming constant turnover (Srikosamatra, Boun-oum and Varavudh 1992:10, 16–18).

24. These include relatively high soil fertility in Mekong valley lands, sufficient availability of natural plant- and animal-dung-based fertilizer, and a lack of transport facilities, as well as of cash and/or foreign exchange to import chemical agricultural inputs.

25. For an overview of this issue, see, for example, Delbrel et al. (1991).

26. According to the US State Department, opium cultivation covered 42,000 ha. in 1989 and decreased to approximately 26,000 ha. in 1992–93. Quoted in *Far Eastern Economic Review* (1994:23).

27. The Single Convention on Narcotic Drugs governs an international control system which 'provides for restricted cultivation of limited amounts of the opium poppy carefully calculated to correspond to the estimated annual medical requirements of each State'. This is because opiates have a recognized medical value and substitutes for certain applications have not yet been developed or approved (United Nations 1987:31). Australia, India and Turkey are the main providers of opium for the pharmaceutical industry.

28. The costs of integrated rural development projects in 12 districts, selected from six northern upland provinces, developed to improve food production and security, reduce the use of slash-and-burn techniques and to promote legal cash crop substitutes range from $0.5 to $3.0 million per district over a 4 to 6 year period; the annual recurring costs of the projects are estimated at $1.0 million.

29. With support of the Japanese government, some large-scale mulberry plantations are being developed on a trial basis in order to develop new varieties of silkworm. Communication of the FAO Country Representative, Vientiane, March 1993.

30. Applications are made through travel agencies, and tourists normally wait in Bangkok for about three to four days for their visas to be approved. (Communication of the general manager of a Thai–Lao joint venture hotel in Vientiane, March 1993).

REFERENCES

Accord général sur les tariffs douaniers et le commerce (1991), *Accord commercial entre le Royaume de Thailande et la République démocratique populaire Lao*, 29 November, L/6947, Bangkok.

Asian Development Bank (ADB) (1993a), *Asian Development Outlook*, Manila/Oxford: ADB.

Asian Development Bank (ADB) (1993b), *Key Economic Indicators of Developing Asian and Pacific Countries*, Manila/Oxford: ADB.

Asian Energy News (1992), vol. 2, no. 10, October, Asian Institute of Technology, Bangkok.

Banque du Commerce Extérieur du Lao RPD (BCEL) (1993), Communiqué no. 8, 13 January, Vientiane.

Bosaikham Vongdara (1992), 'Summary of the mineral potential of the Lao PDR', Forum on Investment Opportunities in the Lao PDR, mimeo, Vientiane.

Boun Oum Chan Chon (1992), 'Lao Country Report', Seminar on the promotion of sustainable tourism development in the Least Developed Countries of the ESCAP region, Pattaya, 26–30 October, Tourism Authority of the Lao PDR, mimeo, Vientiane.

Bountheung Mounlasy (1992), 'Recent Policy Changes and Prospects for Growth and Development: Laos' in *Vietnam, Laos and Cambodia in Transition: Reconstruction and Economic Development*, Tokyo: Sasakawa Peace Foundation, pp. 3–20.

Council of Ministers, Decree No. 47 on the state tax system, 26 June 1981. Amended by Decree No. 12 of 26 February 1991 (translated by Vientiane International Consultants).

Delbrel, G. (1991), *Geopolitique de la drogue*, Paris: Editions la Découverte.

ESCAP (1989), *1988 Economic and Social Survey of Asia and the Pacific*, New York: United Nations.

ESCAP (1992), *Mobilization of Financial Resources in ESCAP Least Developed Countries*, New York: United Nations.

Far Eastern Economic Review (FEER), Hongkong, various issues.

International Monetary Fund (IMF), *Direction of Trade Statistics Yearbook*, various years, Washington, DC: IMF.

Ishida, M. (1992), 'Issues for Reconstruction and Development: Energy Development', in *Vietnam, Laos and Cambodia in Transition: Reconstruction and Economic Development*, vol. 2, pp. 129–136, Tokyo: Sasakawa Peace Foundation.

Khammone Phonekeo (1992), 'Private power opportunities in the Lao PDR, Forum on Investment Opportunities in the Lao PDR', mimeo, Vientiane.

Koehler, G. (1990), 'Of Structures and Restructuring. The Case of the Lao PDR', Paper presented to the Canadian Learned Societies Conference, mimeo, Victoria, Canada.

Lam, N.V. (1994), *External Assistance and Lao PDR: Issues and Implications for Development Policy*, in Mya Than and J. Tan (1994), pp. 267–308.

Ministry of Agriculture and Forestry (1989), 'Development Strategies on Shifting Cultivation Stabilization and Environment protection', International Symposium on Forestry and the Environment, mimeo, Vientiane.

Ministry of Economy, Planning and Finance (1990), *National Statistical Centre, Basic Statistics 1975–90*, Vientiane: Government of the Lao PDR.

Ministry of Economy, Planning and Finance (1992), *Medium Term Policy Framework and PIP 1991–95*, Vientiane: Government of the Lao PDR.

Mugione, F. (1993), 'Transnational Corporations and Selected Services Industries in the Lao PDR', mimeo, ESCAP/TCMD Joint Unit on TNCs, Bangkok.

Mya Tha and J. Tan (eds) (1994), *Laos' Dilemmas and Options: The Challenges of Economic Transition in the 1990s*, Singapore: Institute of South-East Asian Studies.

National Commission for Drug Control and Supervision (1992), *Drug Control in 1991*, Vientiane: Government of the Lao PDR.

OECD (1993), *Geographical Distribution of Financial Flow of Developing Countries, 1988/91*, Paris: OECD.

Snowy Mountain Engineering Co. (1990), *Nam Theun II Hydroelectric Project, Preliminary Environmental Assessment*, mimeo, Vientiane.

Srikosamatra Sompoad, Siripholdej Boun-oum, Suteethorn Varavudh (1992), 'Wildlife Trade in Lao PDR and between Lao PDR and Thailand', *Natural History Bulletin of the Siam Society*, vol. 40, no. 1, pp. 1–47, Bangkok.

Stuart-Fox, M. (1986), *Laos, Politics, Economics and Society*, Boulder: Lynne Rienner Publishers.

Taillard, Ch. (1989), *Le Laos. Stratégies d'un état tampon*, Montpellier: Reclus.

Tourism Authority of the Lao PDR (1990), *National Plan for the Development of Tourism*, Vientiane.

Tropical Forestry Action Plan (1990), Vientiane: Government of the Lao PDR.

UNCTAD (1992a), 'Technical assistance needs of Bhutan, Lao Peoples Democratic Republic, Mongolia and Nepal in the area of transit transport. A historical perspective and future challenges', mimeo, Geneva, UNCTAD/RDP/LDC/50/Rev.1.

UNCTAD (1992b), *Commodity Yearbook 1992*, New York: United Nations.

UNCTAD (1993), *The Least Developed Countries 1992 Report*, New York: United Nations.

UNCTAD (1994), *The Least Developed Countries 1993–94 Report*, New York: United Nations.

UNDCP (1992), *UNDCP in the Lao PDR*, Vienna: United Nations.

UNDP (1993), *Lao PDR, Development Cooperation Report 1991*, Vientiane: United Nations.

UNESCO (1992), *Statistical Yearbook 1992*, Paris: United Nations.

UNICEF/ESCAP (1987/1988), *Asian and Pacific Atlas of Children in National Development*, Bangkok: United Nations.

UNICEF (1994), *The Progress of Nations*, New York: United Nations.

United Nations (1987), *Report on the International Conference on Drug Abuse and Illicit Trafficking*, Vienna: United Nations.

Verbiest, J.P. (1992), 'The Economies in Transition of Southeast Asia and China, New Frontiers, on the Pacific River', paper prepared for the Conference on Economic Development of the Republic of China and the Pacific River in the 1990s and Beyond, Asia and Pacific Council for Science and Technology, Manila.

Vilaihongse Sirisay (1992), 'Domestic Savings Mobilization: The Case of the Lao PDR' in *Mobilization of Financial Resources in ESCAP Least Developed Countries*, New York: United Nations.

World Bank (1993), *World Debt Tables 1993*, Washington, DC: World Bank.

8. Trade diversification in Mozambique: prospects and constraints

Khalil Rahman and Willem van der Geest

1 ECONOMIC STRUCTURE AND GROWTH PROFILE

1.1 Introduction: An Economy in Transition

With an estimated per-capita GDP of US$63 in 1992, Mozambique is one of the poorest countries in Sub-Saharan Africa (SSA). It inherited a distorted economic structure from the colonial period, when it was used primarily as a service economy to provide port and transport facilities to the neighbouring countries, in particular South Africa and the former Rhodesia. Agricultural export originated mainly from estate farming, while traditional peasant agriculture suffered neglect. The natural resources, including minerals and coal deposits, remained largely untapped. The manufacturing sector was dominated by high-cost enterprises which depended on imported machinery and raw materials. The lopsided structure of the Mozambican economy rendered it highly susceptible to external shocks.

External receipts accrued mainly from the export of agricultural and agricultural-based products, provision of transit facilities to the neighbouring countries and remittances of Mozambican wage labourers in South Africa. The lack of educational and training facilities for the local population led to a very low level of human resources development, compared to SSA standards. The Portuguese settlers dominated employment, skilled as well as semi-skilled, in the modern sector, including export and import trade.

Mozambique's economy has evolved through a number of stages since independence. The early years of transition (1975–77) were characterized by an economic vacuum caused by the abrupt departure of the settlers, particularly many skilled and semi-skilled workers. At the time of independence, when the government found itself saddled with a large number of abandoned enterprises as well as estates, it could count only about forty indigenous university graduates. The difficulty of economic management, inherent in this situation, was exacerbated by the destabilizing consequences of the civil war. The impact of the deteriorating situation in the southern African region was serious and the cost of implementation, by Mozambique, of United Nations sanctions against South Africa, proved to be very high. However, the recent changes in South Africa and the removal of sanctions are likely to improve the situation for Mozambique. The signing of the peace accord in October 1992 between the government and its principal adversary, RENAMO, and the planned national elections have also ushered in the possibility of a transition to political normalcy.

Despite mounting constraints, economic growth remained moderate during the 1978–81 period. Subsequently, however, the acute personnel, managerial and import constraints faced by public-sector enterprises, overcentralization of the administration, intensification of external aggression, and natural disasters, contributed to a substantial decline in output. The overall production declined by about 30 per cent by 1986, with exports falling by three-quarters, necessitating import compression by one-third. The industry and transport sectors suffered the sharpest decline. Agricultural output declined at the rate of about 6 per cent per annum.[1]

In 1987, the government launched structural adjustment measures under a three-year Economic Rehabilitation Programme (ERP). Notwithstanding the heavy social costs of adjustment, the ERP is credited with arresting economic deterioration and improving financial discipline and management practices. Mozambique embarked on a second phase of its adjustment programme, the Economic and Social Rehabilitation Programme (ESRP), 1990-92, with particular focus on the social dimensions of adjustment.

1.2 Evolution of Development Policies

It was not until the late 1970s that planned economic management began in Mozambique. The government's principal preoccupation in the immediate aftermath of independence was to establish political and economic control over the country with its very limited human and institutional capacities. In 1981, the government approved a ten-year plan with targets that proved overoptimistic. The plan emphasized large-scale development projects and the creation of huge state farms, but soon shifted to promoting small development projects using local raw materials, division of large farms to smaller and manageable units, and an increased role for private initiative. To cope with the deepening economic crisis of the early 1980s, the government began extensive consultations with the World Bank and the IMF in 1985 which culminated in the adoption of the Economic Rehabilitation Programme (ERP) in January 1987.

The ERP represented the conventional Bank–Fund approach of aggregate demand management coupled with liberalization. The most important achievement during the ERP was a GDP growth rate of about 5 per cent per annum during 1987–89, which is remarkable considering the war situation and the persistent decline in the preceding years. In addition, there were significant increases of external resource inflows, more determined attempts at augmenting macroeconomic efficiency and a revival of an orderly relationship with development partners.

The growth achieved during the ERP was largely due to the massive inflow of external resources, which accommodated the country's imports and provided incentive goods in urban markets. With exports stagnating at a very low level, external financial flows allowed Mozambique a widened current-account deficit which reached $873 million in 1990. At the same time the non-grant element, notwithstanding a decline, stood at about 40 per cent of the overall assistance in 1989. Mozambique has successfully participated in the Paris Club's debt-rescheduling process since 1984. In 1990, $707 million was rescheduled under the Toronto terms, bringing the total amount rescheduled to about $1.94 billion.[2]

The implementation of ERP measures, such as removal of consumer subsidies and raising of fees for basic services, led to considerable social costs, mainly for the poorer sections of the urban population. Malnutrition intensified in urban centres, enrolment rates for primary education dropped, and health facilities were unaffordable by the poor because of higher user fees.

The recognition of declining social conditions, and of the need for poverty alleviation, led the government to design the Economic and Social Rehabilitation Programme (ESRP), with particular emphasis on the involvement of the poor in the rehabilitation and growth process: its primary focus is the agricultural sector, particularly the family and private commercial subsectors. Its other objectives include improving domestic security, enhancing the incentive framework, support for light industry, and financial stabilization. The central policy instruments for implementing the ESRP include management of the government's fiscal balance; mobilization of concessional external resources; removing constraints on the expansion of domestic sources of credit to the non-government sector, and the management of exchange-rate policy.

The ESRP period, however, has been associated with a lower growth rate culminating in a fall in real GDP and lower export earnings in 1992. Adverse weather conditions (for example, drought and cyclones) have been important factors explaining economic performance. The social and food security situation in Mozambique also remained extraordinarily adverse throughout the ESRP period. Famine conditions and severe deprivation prevailed throughout the second half of the 1980s and early 1990s. A poverty assessment paper prepared for the Ministry of Finance estimates that the percentage of population in absolute poverty conditions in the early 1990s was between 25 and 45 per cent in urban areas, approximately 50 per cent in the sub- and peri-urban areas and 100 per cent in rural areas severely affected by war, and among refugees and displaced people.

In response the government developed a number of safety nets for the poor. In addition to the ESRP, the government is also pursuing the National Reconstruction Plan (NRP), which was presented to the Consultative Group Meeting in 1993. The NRP is regarded as an economic and social rehabilitation and development plan to be implemented in two phases. The immediate phase aims at rural resettlement and recovery of production and includes three salient elements:

1. the demobilization of soldiers and their integration into civilian society;
2. the organization of national parliamentary and presidential elections; and
3. the resettlement of refugees and displaced persons with a focus on agricultural recovery through the provision of basic inputs and other support services.

The NRP, in its second phase, would include larger integrated reconstruction and development programmes based on the geographical distribution of the population resulting from the resettlement of rural communities during the first phase of the implementation of the Plan.

2   TRADE PERFORMANCE

2.1   Performance of the Trade Sector

The most notable aspect of the recent trade performance of Mozambique is the contrast between the growth of exports and imports: while exports have gradually recovered from the sharp collapse during the early 1980s, imports have experienced an explosive growth resulting in sharply widening trade gaps.

The collapse of export earnings from $280 million in 1980 to $76 million five years later was mainly due to a drastic decline in the production of major items: levels of production of cashew, sugar cane and cotton in 1985 were merely one-third, one-sixth and one-tenth of the corresponding levels in 1981. Export of tea collapsed from $29 million in 1981 to $0.4 million in 1987 as output shrank from more than 90,000 tons to less than 2,000 tons during the same period. The export prices for some of the major agricultural items remained depressed throughout the early 1980s, and producers' prices suffered further because of domestic insecurity. Farmers had to sell their products cheaply to anyone who could transport them.

Arresting the decline in export value was made possible by an initial increase in the export volumes of cashew nuts and cotton in 1987, and has later been sustained by the growth of non-traditional items and miscellaneous exports, mostly chemical and metal products. Prawns remain the largest single source of export earnings accounting for about one-third of the overall export value.

Contributions of some of the important traditional export items including tea, copra and sisal continue to be marginal. Nevertheless, recent increases in export earnings, from $77 million in 1985 to $162 million in 1991, have been facilitated by the limited recovery of some important agricultural products. In addition, favourable export prices, in certain cases, and exchange-rate liberalization have contributed to the increase in export earnings.

Total value of imports in 1992 stood at $880 million, representing a doubling of the 1985 level. Import of all categories of products has been increasing steadily, but the largest increase has occurred in the consumer goods category, which accounts for more than 40 per cent of the overall import value. While food imports have increased by one-half since 1985, non-food imports registered fourfold growth during the same period. Import of primary materials accounts for nearly 30 per cent of total imports.

The direction of Mozambique's external trade does not reveal any major changes from the earlier pattern. About a third of Mozambique's total exports between 1989 and 1991 (increasing to approximately half in 1992–93) were to the OECD countries, principal among them being Spain, the US, the UK, Japan and Portugal (the share of the UK fell drastically between 1991 and 1993). The important partners in import trade include the US, France, Italy, Japan and Portugal (Table 8.1).

2.2   Unrecorded Cross-border Trade

The volume of unrecorded cross-border trade flows is believed to be quite significant. This includes smuggling of consumer items from South Africa, Swaziland, Zimbabwe and Malawi into Mozambique, and prawns and copper wires (for example, stolen from electricity cables) out of Mozambique. It is believed that the bulk of smuggled goods come from South Africa, implying that the share of South Africa in Mozambique's imports may be higher than official trade statistics would suggest. The basic incentive to undertake illegal cross-border trade is the scarcity of imported goods, reflected in local markets through substantial price differentials with neighbouring countries. In Mozambique, persons displaced by the war have taken up smuggling in the absence of alternative employment opportunities. Smuggling has thus become a major informal-sector activity and explains the existence of an informal rand market in the country.

To cope with the situation, the government has set up customs collection points in a number of areas along the frontier. Imports are allowed into the country upon payment of appropriate duties. The fear that clamping down on smuggling may cause a rise in delinquent activities as displaced traders seek other sources of survival is the key reason for not attempting to eliminate informal cross-border trade altogether.

Table 8.1 Direction of recorded trade, 1985–1993

	1985	1989	1990	1991	1992	1993
	(Exports as per cent of total exports)					
Industrial countries	47.6	39.9	33.6	34.1	48.2	55.8
of which						
Belgium-Luxembourg	0.1	0.4	0.3	0.2	0.4	0.5
France	1.6	1.4	2.9	1.2	1.8	1.4
Germany	2.7	1.8	1.8	1.0	2.2	1.4
Italy	0.2	0.4	1.0	1.0	1.1	1.8
Japan	10.6	3.7	3.9	5.0	5.1	8.3
Portugal	4.3	7.8	3.6	3.8	11.6	17.0
Spain	5.0	3.7	3.1	10.3	13.4	16.1
United Kingdom	6.6	3.7	4.4	1.0	1.4	0.9
United States	12.3	11.9	6.8	5.5	6.9	3.7
Developing countries	46.5	56.0	64.9	64.3	49.3	40.5
of which						
Africa	1.5	5.0	2.7	4.5	8.3	10.4
Côte d'Ivoire	..	..	..	0.2	0.7	0.9
Kenya	0.1	0.5	0.3	0.2	0.4	0.9
Malawi	0.2	0.5	0.3	0.2	0.4	0.9
South Africa	..	2.3	1.0	1.3	1.8	2.8
Zimbabwe	0.1	..	0.3	1.3	1.8	2.3
	(Imports as per cent of total imports)					
Industrial countries	64.4	57.7	56.8	59.3	62.0	52.4
of which						
Belgium-Luxembourg	1.5	0.9	1.5	1.9	2.2	2.1
France	11.0	6.0	3.9	5.5	10.3	4.0
Germany	2.9	4.5	5.7	4.1	3.3	3.5
Italy	8.1	10.9	8.4	7.8	3.1	7.1
Japan	3.2	5.6	4.7	5.0	3.2	6.3
Portugal	5.7	5.2	5.1	4.8	4.2	5.8
Spain	0.7	1.2	1.7	2.8	2.5	1.9
United Kingdom	3.8	4.8	5.6	4.3	3.7	4.8
United States	14.6	5.8	5.9	13.0	18.7	5.7
Developing countries	31.7	41.6	43.2	40.7	38.0	47.6
of which						
Africa	6.2	10.3	12.3	9.3	10.2	14.3
Côte d'Ivoire	..	0.1	3.1	2.3	2.5	3.6
Kenya	1.4	1.3	0.2	0.2	0.2	0.3
Malawi	0.9	1.7	1.7	2.0	2.2	3.1
South Africa	..	..	..	..	..	..
Zimbabwe	3.3	6.1	6.6	4.6	5.3	7.5

Sources: IMF, *Direction of Trade Statistics Yearbook*, 1991 and 1994.

2.3   Structure of Export Marketing

Diversification of exports will require further growth of the numbers of firms trading internationally. There are at present some 200 of these trading houses of varying sizes registered with the Ministry of Commerce. During the first quarter of 1991, only 20 of these accounted for more than 85 per cent of the overall export of the country. Prior to ERP, the government had extensive control over the export economy, particularly over agricultural items such as prawns, cotton, sugar, tea, coal and copra. Under ERP, there is a substantial private participation in export trade, in particular, the export of prawns and copra with market shares of 63 and 58 per cent, respectively, for the private sector.[3]

Although the public sector continues to handle a large share of agricultural-sector exports (for example, cashew nuts) and has a monopoly over some (for example, sugar), the private sector has significant weight as regards the export of all other major products. Notwithstanding these developments, the market structure for cashew nut exports has not changed since 1987, while the new private firms exporting prawns command only a small share of the market. It may not be easy to increase competitiveness of the export sector in the short run, given institutional, financial and human-resource constraints, the implications of which are examined below for the prospects of export expansion and diversification.

Six major organizations in Mozambique support enterprise development: the Chamber of Commerce, the Industrial Association of Mozambique (AIMO), the Association of Mozambican Private Enterprise (AEPRIMO), Agrarios, the Association of Hotels and Tourism, and the Association of Women Entrepreneurs and Executives. The Chamber of Commerce, created by the government, is the oldest enterprise association. The AIMO has both public- and private-sector enterprises as its members, while AEPRIMO represents mostly small companies. Agrario represents smallholders in agriculture. The recently-founded women's enterprise association constitutes an important step towards acknowledging their role in the economy.

Development of indigenous enterprises is at an early stage, reflecting both colonial and post-colonial legacies. Setting up companies in manufacturing as well as services sectors, including trade and commerce, involves obtaining a series of permissions from different ministries and government departments. Undertaking a feasibility study and proof of bank deposit are obligatory for all firms, irrespective of their sizes. The national parliament has responded to these procedural complications recently by enacting a bill providing for substantial simplification of the procedures. Other specific constraints include general shortage of qualified personnel, limited access to credit, and a virtual absence of underwriting facilities, public or private, for risk-bearing capital.

2.4 Human and Institutional Capacity in the Trade Sector

The severe lack of upper- and middle-level professionals in government institutions dealing with the external trade sector, including the Ministry of Commerce, the Customs Department, the Department for Promotion of Foreign Investment (GPIE), the Institute for Export Promotion (IPEX) and the Department for Import Programme Coordination (GCPI), imposes another serious constraint on the trade-diversification prospects of Mozambique. Less than 5 per cent of the officials of the Ministry of Commerce, are university graduates; and IPEX and other newly-created departments within existing institutions are under-staffed.[4] At the time of departure of the Portuguese, the Customs Department was left without a single Mozambican professional staff member. This paucity of technically-qualified personnel impedes the reaping of full benefits from external support measures like STABEX or GSP schemes, and is critically felt as the trade sector strives to expand its activities and network. The sparseness of the banking network reflects a similar constraint.

Measures taken by the government to ease the human-resources constraint include, the establishment of training programmes in all critical areas, and allowing private-sector enterprise associations to obtain training funds from bilateral and multilateral sources. It is also considering a further simplification of procedures in trade, investment and commerce as a supplement to these measures.

2.5 Tariff and Non-tariff Instruments

Tariff instruments
The trade policy instruments adopted by the Mozambican government include tariff as well as non-tariff controls. The tariff structure has been simplified in recent years: specific categories of items are exempted from import duties, either for reasons reflecting privileges of the final user, or because of priority in the use of the goods.[5] The last type of exemptions are granted on a case-to-case basis by the Ministry of Finance upon the recommendation of the Customs Department, leaving considerable discretionary powers at the administrative level.

Earnings from duties
The situation of customs earnings has greatly improved since 1987, when imports were first liberalized. The hard currency equivalent of effective earnings from duties more than doubled during the ERP from $34 million to $74 million between 1988 and 1991, and are expected to stabilize during the ESRP.

Non-tariff instruments

Imports of all types of goods and services require a licence, issued by the Ministry of Commerce on a case-by-case basis, specifying the place of embarkation and disembarkation of items and the amount and currency of payment. Priority is accorded to imports of raw materials, spare parts, food, medicine and petroleum. Imports in most cases are made on the basis of irrevocable and confirmed letters of credit. All exports are also subject to licensing.

2.6 Foreign Direct Investment (FDI)

The promotion of FDI is an important aspect of current external-sector policy. The government enacted a law on foreign investment in 1984 and promulgated a foreign direct investment ordinance in 1987, which provides the legal and policy framework for FDI. The incentive framework for FDI includes profit repatriation and taxation regimes.

The profit repatriation regime allows an investor to repatriate after-tax profits and dividends, as well as the original value of capital assets in the event of closure. In cases where profits are not generated in foreign currency (for example, import-substitution production), specific allocation of the foreign exchange for profit repatriation may be allowed on a case-by-case basis, subject to foreign-exchange availability. The taxation regime includes exemption of customs duties on capital goods which are not locally produced; a tax holiday ranging from 2 to 10 years on income and profits (the actual time frame is decided on a case-by-case basis); tax deductions on interest on loans; and tax deductions on training costs of Mozambicans. Income tax on expatriate personnel, however, is levied at source.

The Department for Promotion of Foreign Investment (GPIE), set up by the government in 1985, under the Planning Ministry for promoting and coordinating foreign investment, receives and evaluates investment proposals. Final authorization is given by the Planning Minister, or the Council of Ministers, depending on the size of the project. The approval time for an application is, on average, 90 days. Further simplification of procedures is being implemented with a view to shortening the approval time to 30 days. GPIE is also involved in promoting 'industrial free zones', which would offer investors exemptions from import and export duties, taxes on income, profit and sales.

FDI flows, which amounted to US$9 million in 1990, increased substantially to US$106 million in 1991. Business visits by foreign investors to Mozambique have also risen significantly. Areas in which interest has been shown by foreign collaborators cover a wide spectrum, including venture capital companies, insurance and tourism businesses, prospecting for gold and other minerals, fisheries and so on. Sources of FDI are primarily European: the main investors are UK companies (especially Lonrho) which accounted for about 36.5 per cent of the total value of FDI in 1991; followed by those from the United States (13.3 per cent), South Africa (10.8 per cent), Portugal (9.8 per cent) and the Netherlands (8.7 per cent).[6]

3 FOREIGN-EXCHANGE REGIME AND POLICY

3.1 Exchange-rate Adjustment

Up until the end of 1986, exchange rates were not considered an economic policy instrument under the government's planned economy approach with nominally fixed rates. Recognizing that a flexible exchange rate would be crucial to the strengthening of external accounts, providing economic incentives, and integrating the official and parallel exchange markets, the government started deregulating the foreign-exchange markets. In the first of a series of major and minor devaluations in January 1987, the mid-point rate of the meticais per US dollar was adjusted from Mt. 39 to Mt. 202. By mid-1993 when an open market policy was adopted, the value of the currency stood at Mt. 3,700 per US dollar.

On the whole, the devaluation of the meticais and the expansion of the secondary market resulted in a significant closing of the gap between the official/secondary rate and the parallel market rate.

3.2 The Administrative Control of Exchange

The extent of exchange-rate liberalization is limited by the fact that nearly three-quarters of the total foreign exchange available needs to be allocated to fixed objectives including tied-aid programmes, investment projects, debt service and export-retention schemes, leaving only about a quarter for allocation through the market. This administrative allocation involves the preparation of an annual foreign-exchange budget by the National Planning Commission in consultation with the relevant central and provincial government agencies. Within the limits established in the foreign-exchange budget, licensing of imports and exports is authorized by the Ministry of Commerce which also issues monthly advice on types and ceilings on importables. Finally, the Bank of Mozambique releases foreign-exchange funds in accordance with foreign-exchange availability. Transactions in foreign currency can be made through any bank operating in the country.

The government has also taken a number of steps towards liberalizing access to foreign-exchange allocations. These include the enlargement of the foreign-exchange retention scheme to cover the non-traditional exporters and the equalization of the rates of retention among exporters; full liberalization of imports up to US$500; creation of mechanisms for further liberalizing imports (consumer as well as capital goods and raw materials); and the establishment of a system of non-administrative allocation of foreign exchange (SNAAD). The SNAAD funds, which comprise non-tied grant resources channelled by the donors, was initially used for designated purposes, such as spare parts for construction and agricultural equipment. It has since then been expanded significantly to cover a larger number of items including industrial spare parts, certain raw materials, fertilizer, agrochemicals, and so on. The unwillingness of donors to channel resources to the secondary market, however, remains a major impediment to enlarging SNAAD.

While economic rationale favours a complete move to an open market for foreign currencies, the optimal path of transition to liberalization, in the context of Mozambique, does not simply require the withdrawal of all restrictions. Two specific issues deserve consideration: (i) increasing danger of overshooting of the exchange rate; and (ii) limited supply responses in a context of post-war reconstruction or production could necessitate a level of domestic demand compression beyond desirable or tolerable limits.

3.3 The Current-account Deficit

The large current-account deficit, financed by multilateral programme lending, combined with a commodity-based bilateral grant flow, has far-reaching implications for the volume and composition of imports. Two points warrant particular consideration: policy disincentives and the inherent tension between controlling the use of aid and liberalizing imports.

Policy disincentives
The extent of commoditization of grant aid imports has profound implications for public finance. The sale of food and other emergency relief materials through government channels secures immediate pubic revenue. However, this could discourage food production by depressing food prices. Such policy disincentives with regard to the rehabilitation of the agricultural sector need to be reviewed carefully. Any strategy to rehabilitate the agricultural sector will require the utmost determination, if, concurrently, it results in loss of public revenue.

Aid and import liberalization
For a variety of reasons, political as well as commercial, a considerable share of bilateral grants under projects are tied to particular uses. Trade liberalization, an integral part of the economic reform programme adopted by the government since 1987, needs to find a matching commitment from donor sources. This raises three specific problems:

- the rationalization of import supply is severely constrained, given prior commitments to donors;
- the substitutability of the sources of supply is limited: this may lead to inefficient use of scarce foreign exchange resources; and
- the availability of foreign exchange on the secondary market where the purpose can be decided by the final user is reduced, increasing the devaluation pressure on the meticais.

The above problems are likely to persist because of continued tying of aid, including import support funds. While the tying of the latter has decreased in the early 1990s the availability of such funds, on the other hand, has not increased during this period.

4   POLICY ISSUES FOR TRADE DIVERSIFICATION

4.1   Managing External and Internal Imbalances: Criteria and Scenarios

Medium-run scenarios of Mozambique's external sector can only be formulated once the criteria for their evaluation are clearly spelled out. The following criteria need to be taken into account:

- domestic-resource costs (DRCs) and comparative advantage;
- regional balance within Mozambique;
- intraregional market considerations within the Preferential Trade Area (PTA) and with South Africa;
- human-resource availability;
- financial-resource availability;
- availability of technology;
- market structure constraints; and
- environmental sustainability and renewability of resources.

This extensive set of criteria reflects the extraordinary situation in Mozambique in the early 1990s. In a well-developed market economy, with good information and competitive product and factor markets, a single economic measure, such as the DRCs, may encapsulate all the relevant information. In the present context of Mozambique the above set of criteria needs to be considered explicitly; and developed in much greater detail than is feasible within the constraints of this diagnostic study, for the purpose of formulating a comprehensive trade-diversification strategy.

Domestic-resource costs (DRCs)
The most commonly-used economic criterion for deciding whether or not a particular economic activity (for example, specific industry) is efficient is the

concept of DRCs. The DRC compares the domestic cost of production (labour, capital and inputs) to the foreign-exchange value of the value added, that is, output minus the costs of capital and non-traded inputs. The measure indicates whether foreign exchange can be earned through exports of the products generated by that activity.

The DRC is only an indicative measure, as it has many weaknesses. First, any valuation of labour and capital in terms of foreign exchange will be difficult, particularly in view of fluctuating margins between the official and the parallel market rates. Moreover, the DRC measures costs at a single point in time, and incorrect estimates for low capacity utilization or unusual input prices may be very difficult to remedy. Finally, the measure draws on the partial equilibrium framework, assuming that expanding production will be possible without exhausting supply on input markets or driving up price and wage levels because of scarcity. Hence, DRC estimates must be looked at with considerable caution.

Regional balance

The northern, central and southern regions each have substantial transport and transit potential through their seaport and onward transport facilities (railways). Nacala in the north links Malawi's southern region to the sea, Beira in the central part of Mozambique links Zimbabwe to a sea outlet, and Maputo in the south links Swaziland and the northern part of South Africa to the sea. The three coastal areas could become 'growth centres' if they combine transit trade facilities with export-processing zones (EPZs).

Intraregional market

Intraregional market considerations centre on the potential demand for goods and services within the southern African region. The PTA agreement could be used as an instrument of regional trade diversification. At present, trade with the neighbouring countries has increased following the peace accord of October 1992. Trade with South Africa, which has also been expanding in recent years, may further intensify in the aftermaths of political transition in that country. To consolidate gains from these trends, an active process of seeking trade expansion within the region will be required.

Human-resource availability

Human-resource constraints, in particular skilled personnel, limit the options for trade diversification considerably. Resettlements to rural towns and villages of the refugees and displaced population, once the national security situation has improved, continue as a major priority. A considerable share of the forced migrants may, however, continue to seek employment opportunities in the major urban areas, thereby creating a relative scarcity of labour in the rural areas and high unemployment in the cities. The possibility of an increase in the number of Mozambicans attracted to work in South Africa may also affect the availability of human resources. These likely trends indicate that urban-based semi-industrial production may have to be an integral part of the trade-diversification strategy.

Financial-resource availability
Even in a peace context, the lack of investible resources will limit the feasible rate of growth severely: only some 3 per cent of GDP is available for private domestic investment. Notwithstanding the immense investment opportunities, the likelihood of Mozambique attracting massive foreign investment in the short run seems low, considering, *inter alia*, competitive bidding for such funds by other countries in the region, in particular South Africa.

Availability of technology
The technological constraints are particularly severe because of the significant deindustrialization since the 1980s. The implications of this process of erosion of the technological base need to be comprehensively assessed.

Market-structure constraints
The slow rate of change in the market structure, in particular of export marketing, seems to indicate that programmes to encourage small and medium-sized enterprises to venture on to international markets have so far not achieved much success. Although entry barriers have been reduced, significant impediments to growth in the export-marketing sector remain, primarily reflecting the fragility of the emerging private sector and the legacy of widespread state control of the economy and trade in the past.

Environmental sustainability and renewability of resources
It should be considered to what extent *ad valorem* charges should be levied to ensure sustainability in natural-resource exploitation (for example, timber). This could take the form of requiring exporters to replenish depleted stock. In the case of non-renewable resources, such as minerals, coal and other energy items, there should be a careful evaluation of intertemporal choices. In the case of mineral-based products, there is the need for enhancing vertical integration to generate higher value added.

5   PROSPECTS FOR DIVERSIFICATION

5.1   The Semi-industrial Sector

As indicated in a World Bank (1990a) industrial-sector study, a number of enterprises in Mozambique reveal DRC ratios less than unity, implying that production is economically efficient as it generates foreign-exchange gains. Items produced with reasonable efficiency include truck tyres, cardboard, electric cable, bicycles, water pumps, paints, certain metal products, shoes, cartons and laundry soap. Other studies have identified various semi-industrial goods as having export potential within the PTA. Table 8.2 presents major potential markets for non-traditional export products.[7]

Textile goods and garments, especially those using local source textiles, may not be an unambiguously efficient line of production in terms of the DRC criterion. In the EU markets, the absence of quota and quantitative restrictions will be important in determining the cost effectiveness and scope for export expansion, although following the conclusion of the Uruguay Round, competition from non-ACP countries may intensify as preferential tariff margins diminish.

Table 8.2 Potential non-traditional export products

Products	Main markets
Agricultural horticulture	
Fresh fruits	Western Europe
Vegetables	Western Europe
Cut flowers	Germany, United States, France, UK and the Netherlands
Minerals	
Precious and semi-precious stones (11 specific items)	United States, Japan, UK, France and the Netherlands
Handicrafts and jewellery	Portugal, South Africa and former centrally-planned economies
Granite and marble	Italy and Middle East
Semi-industrial goods	
Tyres and tubes	PTA
Textile goods (e.g. cotton yarn)	Western Europe
Garments (e.g. fabrics, workmen's clothes)	Western Europe
Wall clocks	PTA
Water meters	PTA
Dry cell batteries	PTA
Glassware	PTA
Radio sets	PTA
Ballpoint pens	PTA
Razor blades	PTA
Builders' hardware	PTA
Wagons and rolling stock	PTA
Plastic footballs and mini basketballs	PTA

Source: Constructed on the basis of information contained in Commonwealth Secretariat (1989).

5.2   The Agricultural Sector

For agricultural products, the picture is only slightly less ambiguous: products such as cashew nuts exported through the Caju de Mozambique are undoubtedly profitable to export with a DRC ratio of 0.57. However, sugar is not, because on the basis of current capacity utilization levels and technology, the DRC ratio does exceed unity.

In particular, two main areas of economic diversification will need to go hand in hand with trade diversification. As a priority, a great deal of import substitution for agricultural products will be necessary, entailing a focus on the rehabilitation of rural production and trade. Rehabilitation of the agricultural sector, including rural economic and social infrastructure, will require continued external assistance.

Constraints to the rehabilitation of the Mozambican agricultural sector relate to agricultural policy and planning as well as to the state of rural inputs, production and marketing infrastructure. Data on physical, socioeconomic and other indicators are extremely unreliable as they are based on pre-independence surveys. Agricultural planning for rehabilitation, and hence estimates of its potential, may be misguided if such data are accepted uncritically.

The absence of draught power and the paucity of fertilizer in smallholder agriculture is compounded by the lack of appropriate seed varieties. Even in the context of improved security, any mechanism to ensure incentive pricing is likely to be frustrated by the absence of a basic marketing organization. The reintegration of the many *deslocados*, who live as squatters around Maputo and major provincial towns, will require considerable financial resources and, among other things, a well-defined land-use legislation, to be successful. Weaknesses in policy making and planning, and in basic rural infrastructure, as well as the enormous social problems associated with resettlement, will delay regeneration of agricultural and export production.

However, in the medium term, there is a considerable scope for vertical diversification of agricultural production into agribusiness, including food processing, cashew nut packaging, cotton ginning and baling, and tea drying and packaging.

5.3   Services and Energy

Concurrent with agrarian and industrial rehabilitation, special efforts should be made to revitalize the transmission of electricity from Mozambique to its neighbours on a long-term basis for investment in other sectors. Electricity has a high-earning potential, both through import savings as well as through export earnings from Zimbabwe, Zambia, Malawi and South Africa. The absence of customs duties, if continued, could guarantee the commercial viability of such transmission, but electricity charges would need to be set at levels which facilitate exports. Repairs pertaining to activities in the services sector and the rehabilitation of transmission facilities should be undertaken rapidly. The Cahora Bassa project, whose rehabilitation is expected to begin in mid-1994, could steadily supply South Africa with some 1,800 MW of electricity and leave about 180 MW for Mozambique. Another Mozambican electricity system linking Zimbabwe could serve as the least-cost way of meeting the latter's anticipated power shortage from the mid-1990s. Further, the second phase of the Cahora Bassa scheme, involving a 1,648 MW power station, could produce exceptionally low-cost electricity.

The potential for revenues from transit services to neighbouring countries is significant. The ports at Beira, Nacala and Maputo are potentially the most strategic facilities for Zimbabwe, Zambia, Zaire and Malawi; moreover, South Africa has been using the Maputo port. Internal insecurity and sabotage of the transport system had led to diversion, or considerable reduction, of traffic by the transit partners. A number of projects have been initiated, and, in certain cases, significant progress has been made to rehabilitate the ports and railway lines, particularly upgrading the Beira port, which alone can handle half the regional traffic, and the reconstruction of the Beira railway corridor linking Zimbabwe, Malawi and Zambia. The road network was seriously damaged during the civil war and needs urgent rehabilitation, which may cost as much as $24 billion. Some major repair work began in 1994 (for example, roads linking Maputo with South Africa and Swaziland), and the government has begun to receive some external funding for road rehabilitation.

6   CONCLUSIONS

In view of the tremendous trade imbalance, there is a pressing need for Mozambique to formulate a strategy with respect to the management of its external sector. As regards the level of imports of goods and services, further expansion of the current-account deficit or a compression of the demand for imports are among possible options. The first option will require a steady growth of external-resource inflows. However, it seems unlikely that the deficit could increase further without jeopardizing Mozambique's future income level since excessive external debt and the ensuing debt service obligations would increase uncertainty.

Stabilization or contraction of the current-account deficit will require a rapid growth of exports (at a rate some 8 times exceeding that of imports). Exports of goods and services in the medium run could probably increase to their 1973 level of $300 million. Even if disbursements from bilateral and multilateral sources remain at the same level, the rate of growth of imports would need to remain below 5 per cent per annum (in dollar terms), a level that would compress the value of capital goods and raw materials imported by Mozambique.

The share of raw materials and equipment in total imports has, since inception of the ERP in 1987, been limited, given the pressing need for imports of basic consumer items. The only option for reducing the share of imports of basic necessities and increasing the share of critical equipment import is sustainable import substitution,[8] which has profound implications for the focus, nature and the extent of trade diversification that can be undertaken.

Within the exportable cash crop sector (cashew nuts, tea, cotton) a restoration of levels of production to those obtained in the mid-1970s could be realized within the medium term. This in itself would necessitate a substantial diversification of exports, both geographically as well as in terms of products. Nevertheless, it would be important to bear in mind the effects of possible shifts in world prices on export earnings for these items.

Trade diversification into semi-industrial exports is severely limited by the availability of convertible currency resources. The choice of technology, within the constraints of dynamic comparative advantage, will thus need to focus on labour-intensive technology with output oriented to the domestic and regional markets. The focus of industrial production is likely to be on medium-income-level household consumer items (for example, ready-made garments and textiles, travel bags, shoes, tyres, batteries, bicycles and TV sets).

A determined attempt should be made to induce FDI in the context of industrial free zones. In view of the skills constraints a joint management approach of FDI in these zones is desirable.

NOTES

1. See World Bank (1992:13) for detailed information on GDP performance during 1980–89.
2. The ERP programme involved a Structural Adjustment Facility (SAF) of the IMF of 42.7 million SDR (June 1987 to June 1990) and an extended SAF of 100.7 million SDR for June 1990 to May 1993 and a four-phase ERP from the World Bank (a 300 million SDR/IDA credit). See UNCTAD (1994:Table 36).
3. In the case of prawns, this excludes the share of one company which is a joint venture between the Mozambican government and a foreign private firm (Banco de Mozambique).
4. In 1991 the number of graduates of economics and management in 1991 stood at only 13 and 17, respectively. This brought the total number of graduates for the country in these fields to approximately 270. There was in 1991, for example, not a single Mozambican holding a PhD degree in economics and only about 15 with masters degrees in economics.
5. These include users for (i) defence and security and (ii) goods imported under diplomatic conventions. Case-by-case exemptions may be granted for (i) emergency items for free distribution, (ii) import of raw materials and equipment for projects to reallocate displaced population, (iii) equipment for railways and port rehabilitation projects and (iv) raw materials for producing export items with a minimum of 35 per cent value added.

6. Some double counting may occur due to joint ventures originating from investors of various countries.
7. See also World Bank (1990b) and Commonwealth Secretariat (1989).
8. Sustainable import substitution requires that the sectoral and technological choice adheres to the requirements of dynamic comparative advantage as well as international price constraints.

REFERENCES

Commonwealth Secretariat (1989), *Report on Export Development Programme for Mozambique*, London: Commonwealth Secretariat.

International Monetary Fund (IMF), *Direction of Trade Statistics Yearbook*, various years, Washington, DC: IMF.

UNCTAD (1993), Handbook of International Trade and Development Statistics, New York: United Nations.

UNCTAD (1994), *The Least Developed Countries 1993–1994 Report*, New York: United Nations.

World Bank (1988), *Agricultural Sector Survey*, World Bank Report no. 7904–Moz, Washington, DC: World Bank.

World Bank, (1990a), *Mozambique: Industrial Sector Study*, Washington, DC: World Bank.

World Bank (1990b), *Mozambique: Restoring Rural Production and Trade*, Report no. 8370–Moz, Washington, DC: World Bank.

World Bank (1992), *Strategy and Programme for Managing the Transition to National Reconstruction*, prepared for the Meeting of the Consultative Group for Mozambique, Paris: World Bank.

9. Trade diversification in Niger: prospects and constraints

Lev Komlev

---

1   INTRODUCTION: THE MACROECONOMIC SITUATION

Niger, the largest landlocked country in West Africa, has been on the United Nations' and Lomé Convention lists of LDCs since these were established. Its socioeconomic situation since the early 1980s has been one of continuous decline. Trends in economic indicators have been among the worst in the LDCs. For example, over the 1980–92 period, Niger's annual growth rates of GDP and per-capita real GDP were negative –1.5 and –4.6 per cent, respectively, compared with 2.1 and –0.5 per cent for all LDCs; and the annual average growth rate of investment was –4.6 per cent, far below the LDC average of 0.5 per cent (UNCTAD 1994; and Government of Niger 1994). To stop this decline, and promote development, the country will need, *inter alia*, to diversify its economy and external trade.

This need is particularly pressing because of two main reasons:

1. more than 70 per cent of its export earnings are from the uranium market, which is in a deep recession; and
2. the economic policy of Niger's southern neighbour, Nigeria, with whom Niger has a flourishing informal cross-border trade, has negatively affected Niger's economy and external trade over the years.

The question that arises is: to what extent is economic and trade diversification feasible? This chapter analyses:

1. the possibilities and constraints for diversification of trade;
2. the country's experience of economic and trade diversification;
3. the existing potential for exports in the near future; and
4. preconditions for revitalization and diversification of trade.

2   DIVERSIFICATION: POSSIBILITIES AND CONSTRAINTS

2.1   General Constraints on Development

There are several constraints on Niger's development. The domestic market is narrow: for example, in 1994, per-capita GDP was less than $200 of which more than 80 per cent was produced in the informal sector. The human-resource constraint is severe and the prospects for relieving it are not bright.[1] The quality of the productive sector is low and the prospects for improvement in the near future are limited given the negative growth rates of GDP and investment, and the declining share of the modern sector in the formal economy. The supply of energy for domestic consumption has yet to be developed; per-capita energy consumption is one of the lowest in the world,[2] and industrial development remains very low. The share of manufacturing in GDP was 6.5 per cent in 1990 of which 1.3 per cent was in the modern sector and 5.2 per cent in the informal sector (see Table 9.1).

Table 9.1 Share of informal sector in GDP, 1980–1989 (percentages)

Year	1	2	3	4	5	6	7	8	9	10	11
	\multicolumn{11}{c}{Sector of activity*}
1980	100.0	1.7	69.7	..	16.0	81.6	48.7	67.2	92.2	..	72.4
1981	100.0	3.7	79.4	..	30.1	75.6	43.8	62.4	85.7	..	75.4
1982	100.0	4.1	80.7	..	32.0	80.8	41.7	63.8	84.1	..	77.9
1983	100.0	3.9	78.1	..	33.9	83.3	53.6	67.2	83.3	..	78.4
1984	100.0	4.2	82.6	..	42.5	83.4	52.0	73.4	87.1	..	77.5
1985	100.0	4.2	81.6	..	56.6	84.0	47.6	75.3	78.8	..	78.1
1986	100.0	6.2	81.4	..	47.0	82.9	43.1	78.0	78.0	..	79.0
1987	100.0	6.7	83.2	..	47.8	85.0	43.9	79.9	76.0	..	78.6
1988	100.0	8.1	86.7	..	63.0	84.9	46.8	84.4	78.0	..	81.0
1989	100.0	9.5	85.8	..	63.8	86.8	50.0	87.7	80.0	..	81.7

Notes: * Definition of sectors is as follows:
1   Agriculture and cattle breeding.
2   Mining.
3   Manufacturing.
4   Electricity and water.
5   Construction.
6   Commerce, hotels and restaurants.
7   Transport and communication.
8   Bank and real estate activities.
9   Social services.
10   Bank servicing.
11   Total as percentage of all market activity.

Source: Gouvernement du Niger (1991a).

High production costs, an adverse investment climate and the absence of an external trade strategy militate against diversification. Production costs in the industrial sector are very high compared with those of neighbouring Nigeria.[3] The investment environment is hostile to private investors because of a lack of access to financial resources, excessive administrative formalities, and the absence of valid commercial and labour legislation, among others.

The country is open to external trade, partly through its informal-sector trade, especially, with Nigeria. Niger's economy is directly affected by the economic policies in neighbouring countries, and the country's membership of the franc zone limits its economic policy options. For example, this denies it the use exchange-rate adjustment as an instrument of trade policy because its currency was on a fixed parity with the French franc until its devaluation in early 1994 (see Chapter 4, on Benin).

Moreover, since the second half of the 1980s, the economy has suffered continual setbacks, mainly because of a downturn in the price of its main export, uranium, but also because of the continual depreciation of Nigeria's currency, the naira, increasing smuggling and custom fraud, as well as poor economic management. The deterioration in the country's terms of trade amounted to losses of about 10 per cent of real GDP between 1987 and 1992.

2.2 Diversification of Tradables

It is possible for Niger to reach self-sufficiency in selected cereals, and to achieve the export potential of other agricultural products. Active measures against desertification might stop the erosion of arable land. The application of green revolution methods, coupled with appropriate policies, could allow intensification and diversification of agriculture. However, the constraints are severe: climatic drawbacks[4] are complicated by the traditional organizational framework of the rural sector, shortages of agricultural credit and poor agricultural marketing structures.

The potential for cash crops (for example, cotton, groundnuts, sugar-cane) is limited by a shortage of arable land and the primacy of ensuring food security. The possibilities for diversifying exports of both food and cash crops will be limited by the competition from neighbouring countries producing the same products at lower costs.

As a savannah country, Niger has a comparative advantage in stock-rearing over tropical forest countries of the subregion, such as Côte d'Ivoire, Ghana and Nigeria. However, droughts have repeatedly decimated livestock, either through death, or because of the removal, of livestock to neighbouring countries.[5] The risk of drought makes the diversification of livestock imperative: ovines, caprines and camelines which are more adaptable and are easier to restock after drought should probably be favoured. Diversification in the livestock sector was severely constrained by Nigeria's policies of adjustment, and by increased export competition after the devaluation of the naira *vis-à-vis* the CFA franc. The 1994 change of parity between the naira and CFA franc may, however, have changed the situation in favour of Niger.

Niger's mineral wealth is not fully explored: investment needed for prospecting and exploration has not been easy to find because of the saturation in the major mineral markets. However, existing knowledge of Niger's mineral wealth shows that besides the reasonably assured uranium resources, estimated at 173,710 tons,[6] there are 650 million tons of proven iron ore resources (at Say), 200 million ton deposits of calcium phosphates (at Tapoa), and some commercially exploitable resources of cassiterite, a tin-bearing ore (in the Aïr region). There are also indications of gold deposits (Tillaberi region) and petroleum deposits (along the border with Chad) (*Africa South of the Sahara* 1993:639). However, the high estimated exploitation costs and the unknown quality of minerals hardly attract foreign investors. Horizontal and vertical diversification of the mineral sector and exports do not therefore appear likely in the short to medium term.

The short- to medium-term prospects for vertical diversification in the agricultural sector are modest. Bearing in mind the present level of economic development of the country, vertical diversification may be limited to processing of dry vegetables and fruits, of meat and milk products, and of skins.

2.3 Problems of Market Diversification

Given the limited horizontal and vertical diversification possibilities of tradables, and the pattern of consumption of its trade partners, the scope for market diversification appears severely restricted. For example, uranium, the main export commodity of Niger, can only be exported to countries with a nuclear industry. Hence, uranium exports are centred on the industrialized countries, notably France. On the other hand, the country's main livestock and agricultural products are consumed mostly in countries of the subregion, especially in Nigeria. Nevertheless, some new markets could be developed for out-of-season agricultural products, hides and skins, jewellery and cottage-industry goods.

Niger may benefit from some of the facilities provided under the Lomé IV Convention in support of economic diversification to the ACP countries and particularly to the least-developed countries.[7] As an LDC, Niger receives favourable treatment under all generalized system of preferences (GSP) schemes which could, in principle, provide a stimulus to its trade diversification. However, Niger's problem in market access does not appear to be product coverage or a lack of exporters' knowledge in utilizing different GSPs, but rather one of limited availability of tradables, their production costs and quality.

Niger could attempt to utilize its comparative advantage *vis-à-vis* other developing countries by diversifying its market within the region for exports, such as cattle, cotton, cowpeas and other vegetables. Diversification of trade between Niger and other countries of the subregion in the area of mining and manufacturing exports seems unlikely: other countries of the subregion feature similar production patterns in manufacturing, but at lower production costs. Niger needs subregional programmes of specialization more than other countries, otherwise its capacity to benefit from facilities such as the Lomé Convention will remain hypothetical.[8]

2.4 Transit-transport Problems

The scope for diversification is further limited by the country's landlocked status, which increases its import bill by at least 30 per cent. Access to seaports is ensured by three transit-transport corridors:

1. through Benin, connecting Cotonou with Niamey (1,060 km.);
2. through Togo, connecting Lomé with Niamey through Burkina Faso (1,241 km.); and
3. through Nigeria, connecting Lagos with eastern Niger (1,525 km.).

In the early 1990s, two-thirds of transit volume went through the Benin corridor (252,000 tons) whereas 89,000 tons or 24 per cent went through Togo and 37,000 tons or 10 per cent through the Nigerian corridor. A study by the World Bank on the transit-transport problems of Niger shows that harbours, carriageways and the railway infrastructure of these corridors are in a good state, and their capacities are in excess of the actual volume of the country's transit requirements, even for a long-term period (Banque Mondiale 1990:58). The functioning of all three corridors protects Niger from possible political and technical hazards in any of the transit countries, and reinforces its bargaining power in negotiations with any single transit country. Moreover, the Ghanaian and Ivorian corridors can be used for limited quantities of Niger's transit goods without additional investment from Niger. A switching of Niger's transit among the existing corridors, with a focus on economic efficiency and security, could be beneficial.

This overview shows that real possibilities for diversification in Niger are limited by numerous constraints: geographical, structural and policy related. The first two cannot be alleviated in the short-to-medium term, but the last could be overcome by sound economic policies.

3 ECONOMIC- AND TRADE-DIVERSIFICATION EXPERIENCE

3.1 Attempts to Diversify Production and Trade

After independence in 1960, a number of measures were taken to diversify the country's economy and foreign trade. These resulted in the creation and development of the uranium sector. Initiated by France, production from Niger's large uranium deposits shot up rapidly in response to increased world demand after the 1974 and 1979 energy crises. Starting from scratch in 1970, the share of uranium output in GDP increased by 1975 to 6 per cent, accounting for 60 per cent of the country's exports.[9] High GDP growth rates fuelled by uranium production, rapidly increased gross domestic investment to 37 per cent of GDP in 1980. As a result, industrial production based on agricultural and natural resources (flour milling, meat production, tannery, spinning, weaving, printing and cement works) as well as industries based on mixed resources (beer, beverages, soaps, perfume and detergent, metal works) developed in the 1960s and 1970s, expanded rapidly. At the same time, new product lines (batteries, painting, joiners' work) were created with many of these continuing to expand until the mid-1980s.

However, the financial results of the industrial enterprises – and thus the financial returns on the use of uranium export earnings – were mediocre, mainly because of unsound investment decisions, flawed pricing and marketing policies, excessive state interference, lack of financial discipline and shortage of qualified staff. The losses and/or low returns from these investments were initially cushioned by increasing uranium export earnings and by the monopolization of a large part of these earnings by the state for financing state-owned enterprises which supplied essential goods and services at low prices.

In the early 1980s, uranium export earnings dropped sharply with the slump in world market prices. At the same time agricultural production declined, due to recurrent droughts and the failure of the state-managed farms sector to improve performance. Until 1983, the government continued to borrow commercially to finance its development programme, but the situation continued to deteriorate. By 1983, external debt, of which three-quarters was public or publicly guaranteed, stood at 54 per cent of the country's GDP (Graybeal and Picard 1991:286). Unable to meet repayments, the government went to the Paris and London Clubs, and obtained an agreement on rescheduling its debts within the context of a rigorous IMF-stabilization programme launched in 1983. Niger also entered into an agreement with the World Bank for structural adjustment lending in 1986. The policy orientation previously agreed with the World Bank was included in the 1987–91 development plan (Gouvernement de Niger 1987). As part of the stabilization measures, subsidized industrial production of a number of goods was stopped within the context of an imposed austerity budget; procurement of supplies and equipment was sharply reduced; credit was restricted; and foreign borrowing cut.

During the first phase of the structural adjustment programme (1986–89), production in some sectors recovered: beverages, soap, skins, woven cotton fabric and meat. However, by 1989 the production of groundnut oil, skins and batteries was discontinued. The effect of the structural adjustment measures, for example, reducing the size of the parastatal sector through privatization, while failing to provide incentives to the private sector, increased the share of the informal sector in manufacturing value added which rose from 82 per cent in 1985 to 86 per cent of GDP in 1989 (see Table 9.1). Dismantling of tariffs (1987)[10] and external trade liberalization (1990),[11] as well as the de facto openness of the country's frontier with Nigeria,[12] significantly reduced the scope for Niger's industrial production.

The expansion and diversification of tradables projected in the development plan appear to have been unsuccessful. Moreover, during 1991–93, the economy continued to deteriorate. The uranium and manufacturing sectors contracted considerably with significant negative balances at the enterprise level. The fiscal position continued to degenerate and domestic and external payment arrears accumulated.

In parallel, the country experienced a long period of political transition, leading to the installation of a democratic government in April 1993. To arrest economic deterioration, the new government adopted an internal adjustment programme in 1993 under which public-sector salaries were reduced by about 13 per cent on average, and measures were taken to limit smuggling and fraud. The devaluation of the CFA franc in January 1994 should also help to improve the competitiveness of the country's exports.

3.2 Trends in Recorded and Informal External Trade

The changing economic situation in Niger was reflected in the country's external trade. Between 1960 and 1970, the country's export configuration remained broadly the same. In 1973, however, uranium became the major export commodity, and accounted for about two-thirds of all export earnings within two years. Its share of exports peaked at 87 per cent in 1979, but it has since declined to 68 per cent in 1990. The share of exports of livestock and agricultural products fluctuated because of drought and the volatile share of uranium revenues in total export revenues.

The pattern of the country's imports has not changed substantially since the 1970s. An increasing share of capital goods in Niger's imports in the early 1970s could be partly explained by uranium exploitation as well as by expanding manufacturing activity. Capital goods imports were maintained at a relatively high level during the 1970s but they declined during the 1980s. The early 1990s were characterized by an increased share of food and private vehicle imports, and a decrease in capital goods and petroleum-product imports. These changes are attributed to the crisis in the uranium sector, episodes of drought, political and social disorders and the decline of overall economic activity.

During the 1980s and the early 1990s, there was a decline in the volume and value of recorded exports and imports. By the end of 1991, the export of manufactured goods from Niger was virtually nil; uranium remained almost the sole official export. Import compression, which led to a decline in the share of capital goods, reduced the opportunities for horizontal and vertical diversification of the productive sectors in the early 1990s. Some opportunities for diversification may, nevertheless, be associated with the devaluation of the CFA franc, which, together with other structural adjustment measures, may enable Niger to regain its competitiveness.

3.3 Trends in Direction of Trade

Niger's external trade has been, and continues to be, characterized by the dominance of France as a major trading partner. However, some geographical diversification has taken place in the post-independence period.

During the 1980s, France, which had lost its importance as an export destination since Niger's independence, regained its position, absorbing more than 80 per cent of exports in 1991–92. The share of the industrial countries in Niger's exports averaged just over 90 per cent between 1989 and 1992, largely due to France but also to newcomers among destination countries such as the US. Over the same period, Nigeria's share in Niger's exports declined drastically, most probably because of a shift in export flows from the formal to the informal sector. Côte d'Ivoire emerged as the country's main export destination in Africa taking just under 50 per cent of Niger's total African exports during 1991–93 (Table 9.2).

Available data on recorded trade flows show that over the past three decades, Niger's imports have become relatively diversified: recorded imports from Nigeria, for example, decreased from 7 per cent in 1985 to about one per cent in 1990–93, although this is also most likely to be the result of the shift from formal to informal trading channels. Imports from developing countries fluctuated between 20 and 30 per cent during 1985–93, due to the increasing substitution of Asian developing countries for European countries as sources of capital and manufactured goods (Table 9.2).

France continues to be the main source of capital goods for Niger, but other industrialized countries have taken supplies of agricultural and manufacturing equipment, notably track-laying tractors and tractors for trailers (Japan); steam power units and grain-working machinery (Germany); milking machines, welding and brazing machines, electrical equipment and industrial food-processing machinery (United Kingdom).

Table 9.2   Direction of recorded trade, 1985–1993

	1985	1989	1990	1991	1992	1993
	(Exports as per cent of total exports)					
Industrial countries	79.1	96.5	93.0	90.9	89.2	63.4
of which						
Belgium-Luxembourg	0.1	..	..	..	..	..
France	65.6	73.9	66.2	84.1	80.5	54.2
Germany	0.1	..	..	..	..	0.4
Italy	1.2	0.7	1.1	0.9	0.5	0.4
Portugal	..	7.3	0.4	0.4	0.5	0.4
Spain	5.8	9.8	7.7	..	..	..
United Kingdom	0.1	0.7	0.7	0.4	1.1	2.1
United States	0.1	0.7	15.4	2.2	1.6	2.5
Developing countries	20.6	3.1	6.4	8.3	9.7	35.7
of which						
Africa	20.5	1.8	4.7	7.6	8.5	7.5
Burkina Faso	0.5	..	0.4	0.4	0.5	0.4
Côte d'Ivoire	1.7	0.7	0.7	3.0	3.8	3.7
Nigeria	13.7	0.7	2.9	1.7	2.7	2.1
Togo	0.2	0.3	0.4	0.4	0.5	0.4
	(Imports as per cent of total imports)					
Industrial countries	60.2	57.7	56.9	53.5	50.9	43.7
of which						
Belgium-Luxembourg	1.4	2.0	2.2	1.7	1.7	2.8
France	27.7	30.1	28.1	23.6	21.6	22.1
Germany	5.5	4.6	3.6	5.7	4.2	3.8
Italy	2.6	3.7	3.8	3.5	2.7	2.6
Portugal	..	..	0.2	..	..	..
Spain	0.5	0.7	0.5	0.7	0.4	0.8
United Kingdom	2.0	2.9	5.0	5.5	10.5	1.8
United States	11.4	2.4	3.4	3.0	2.9	3.4
Developing countries	32.8	22.3	20.5	20.8	25.2	29.4
of which						
Africa	18.2	14.9	13.0	11.6	10.8	12.1
Burkina Faso	0.3	0.2	0.2	0.2	0.2	0.4
Côte d'Ivoire	7.2	7.8	9.6	8.4	7.8	8.7
Nigeria	6.7	4.6	1.0	0.7	0.6	0.8
Togo	0.8	0.7	1.0	1.0	1.0	1.2

Sources: IMF, *Direction of Trade Statistics Yearbook*, various issues.

4 TENTATIVE EVALUATION OF EXPORT POTENTIAL

Considering the constraints on diversification and the recent developments in the country's economy and external trade, it is difficult to imagine that Niger could achieve, before the end of the century, new industrial-diversification projects, except for small-scale agroindustrial development. The goods most likely to be traded are uranium, livestock and agricultural products, as well as manufactured and handicraft output (see, for example, ITC 1989a, 1989b and 1991b).

4.1 Uranium

Niger is one of the world's main producers of uranium. The sector is operated by the Société des Mines de l'Aïr (Somair) and the Compagnie Minière d'Akouta (Cominak). Both enterprises were created by the French government, with participation of French private interests in Somair, and Japanese and Spanish interests in Cominak. These companies have the necessary production technology and a developed market network, but relatively high operational costs in comparison with other producers, at a time of a fall in uranium prices,[13] led to a deterioration of their financial situation. Without premium prices on sales to its principal consumer, France (20–30 per cent above prevailing world prices), the companies would not be able to sustain their activities. To improve their financial situation, these companies need to reduce their operational costs.[14] Unless the devaluation of the CFA franc enables them to improve their competitiveness, they face a risk of cessation. The value of uranium exports continued to fall from $200 million in 1991 to $160 million in 1993; a further drop is projected for 1994. This decline will only be partially offset by the increase in other exports. The problems in the uranium sector increase the urgency of expanding and diversifying the production of other tradables.

4.2 Animal Products

Live animals
Traditionally, Niger exports live animals to Nigeria (85 per cent) and to Algeria, Côte d'Ivoire, Libya, Benin and Togo. During the 1980s, official exports of live animals were first suspended, then restrained and subjected to licences and quotas in order to build up the numbers of livestock decimated after the drought years (ITC 1989a:28ff.). Informal exports of live animals (estimated to account for 90–93 per cent of total exports) also declined during this period. Total export potential of live animals is about $30–40 million a year. After the drought years, the government recommended horizontal diversification of livestock in favour of camelines and small ruminants which are more resistant and

more reproductive (Gouvernement de Niger 1987:76ff). This change in the livestock pattern could eventually lead to a diversification of Niger's livestock exports. Geographical diversification may be possible for informal-sector exports, but official exports are likely to be focused on countries with convertible currencies.

Meat

In spite of its potential, the export of meat is limited in practice by inadequate processing and cold-storage capacity.[15] As in the case of live animals, the $2.9 million revenue from meat exports recorded for 1989 reflects only official trade, while total trade turnover may have been as high as $53 million, according to Sydonia, based on observations at frontier markets implying a share of the unofficial sector of 95 per cent (ITC 1989a:30). The main market for meat is Nigeria, but further market research in Côte d'Ivoire, Benin and Togo may be justified. In the early 1990s these countries were importing EC chilled meat at the price of 450 CFA francs per kilo, which includes subsidies of 250 CFA francs per kilo. After devaluation, official exports of Niger's meat to those countries may become competitive even without a decrease or abolition of these subsidies (*Africa International* 1994:14).[16]

Hides and skins

The export of hides and skins is increasingly left to the informal sector. When the Société Nigerienne des Cuirs et des Peaux (SNCP) was privatized, the new owners encountered financial and organizational problems causing a deterioration of equipment, decreasing quality and declining production. Consequently, equipment must be upgraded and SNCP's hides and skins trade network reestablished. This is important as there is a demand for both raw materials and finished goods in France, Italy, the Netherlands and Ghana. The potential positive effect of devaluation needs to be supported by measures in the areas of quality control and marketing.

4.3   Vegetables and Fruits

The export volume of onions increased fourfold between 1975 and 1989. Further growth of this market will depend on factors such as conservation technology, export credits, commercial procedures, packaging conditioning techniques for export markets and freight costs. Copro-Niger and Sonara are the main companies in the sector. Potentially important markets exist in Côte d'Ivoire, Benin, Togo and central African countries.[17]

In spite of drought and weevil attacks during the 1980s, cowpea production has increased. The high quality of the product facilitated exports to Nigeria. The devaluation of the Nigerian naira hindered recorded exports and increased the share of informal exports to about 90 per cent. However, the devaluation of the CFA franc may reverse the situation. Other important markets include Benin and Togo.

Niger could produce and export off-season vegetables, such as the green bean 'bobby', cultivated between October and April. Potential markets include France, Germany and Belgium in Europe, Benin, Togo and the Côte d'Ivoire in West Africa, and Congo, Gabon and the Central African Republic in Central Africa. Between 1984 and 1987, the Société JIC Niger produced some 150 to 200 tons of beans annually (ITC 1989a:3). However, JIC could not resolve problems of air transport,[18] customs and administrative formalities and had to close down. Competent and determined investors would be needed to resuscitate production and exports. Agreement with air and land transport companies should be sought, and preferential treatment should be given by importing countries in transit tariffs, customs and administrative formalities.[19]

There are also ample comparative advantages in the cultivation of potatoes and garlic for exports to neighbouring countries. There were a number of attempts to export citrus fruits, but the saturation of markets in the region does not provide opportunities for exports in the short term.

4.4 Cotton

The domestic official market for cotton in Niger is disappearing. Finding markets abroad beyond the unofficial ones in Nigeria remains problematic as demand for short-fibre cotton is limited. The Société Nouvelle Nigerienne des Textiles (Sonitextil), a company under the control of the international group Scheffer, with minority participation of the Niger government, is the major producer of cloth in Niger. Its products cover domestic demand, and export volumes have been growing since 1982. Exports to the West Africa subregion include coloured threads, natural, bleached and printed materials. In 1989, the company was exporting 20 per cent of its production with roughly equal shares going to Côte d'Ivoire, Senegal, Togo, Benin and Liberia. However, protectionist measures in Côte d'Ivoire (an import ban) and Senegal (increasing value-added tax from 7 to 30 per cent) threatened its traditional regional markets. In addition, Niger's trade liberalization stimulated official and unofficial imports of textile products from Nigeria, Mali and the Côte d'Ivoire. As a result, the turnover of the company halved.[20] In 1991, the company was preparing to curtail its spinning-mill and cloth-mill production in Niger. Demand for textile products exists in Gabon and Togo, but administrative problems continue to block negotiations. Some improvement could be achieved through import-protection measures, energy and market-access subsidies, as well as through waiving of export taxes. Another important issue is information on transport costs and market conditions of African countries outside ECOWAS. The markets of East Africa, for example, may provide opportunities for exports, given the direct air connection between Niamey and Addis Ababa.[21] Another possibility is diversifying styles to include, for example, African designs for European consumers.

4.5 Perfumery, Soap and Cosmetics

The markets in Niger and other countries of the subregion provide opportunities for perfumery and soap products adapted to the conditions and tastes of the indigenous population. However, the Société des Produits Chimiques au Niger (SPCN) controlled by Unilever, decreased its production and virtually stopped its exports, mainly because of fraud. In order to reduce production costs and stay competitive in the domestic market, the company also compromised on the quality of its products. As in the case of Sonitextil, the continuation of productive activity of the SPCN may require some government incentives. The realignment of the currency could have a positive impact in this particular case.

4.6 Handicraft Products

Among handicraft products, the most sophisticated include dressed leather goods (such as bags, cases, wallets and belts) and jewellery. While the low quality of leather and tanning, and of melting and hallmarking of gold and silver, does not jeopardize their marketing in tourist markets it does limit their export potential. The export of small articles made of mahogany or ebony is possible, but constrained by the competition of similar articles from Mali, Burkina Faso, the Côte d'Ivoire and Senegal. Similarly, competition from these countries, together with high transport costs, limits the export of larger-size articles made of mahogany or ebony. Opportunities for the export of carpet could also be exploited, although Niger could face stiff competition from some Asian countries, particularly in the European markets.

The development of handicraft products for export is hindered by weak commercial motivation and the lack of an organized commercial or marketing network. Increasing the export potential of handicraft products would therefore require a resolution of these problems as well as a significant improvement in the quality of articles, and augmenting the range of artisanal skills.

4.7 International Tourism

International tourism could be an important source of foreign-exchange earnings, enhanced by the depreciation of the real exchange rate. Niger has considerable opportunities in this area, but currently tourism is hampered by the limited number of hotels with facilities for international tourists and problems of transportation (including the shortage of motor vehicles) to attractive tourist zones, such as Agadez, Zinder, Arlit, Tahoua and Maradi.

The development of international tourism would require significant foreign investment in hotels and ancillary tourist facilities which may be difficult to attract in Niger's present circumstances.

To sum up, the export-diversification potential of Niger does appear restricted in comparison with other LDCs, such as Uganda or Bangladesh. Even in those products where the country enjoys some comparative advantages there are significant constraints to increasing production for export markets. In addition, in creating the conditions conducive for attracting foreign investment in these sectors, infrastructure and technology would have to be updated. Other constraints relate to administrative and institutional difficulties, lack of information on requirements in different export markets, and high transportation costs. The escalation in informal cross-border trade covering products such as cowpeas, live animals, meat, hides and skins may also have to be tackled if the government is to benefit from increased foreign exchange or revenue that would accrue from its diversification efforts.

5   CONDITIONS FOR REVITALIZATION AND DIVERSIFICATION OF TRADE

In order to revitalize production and exports, and encourage further diversification of tradables, there is the need for changes in policies relating to investment, trade promotion, the agricultural, livestock and uranium sectors, and the influx of goods via informal cross-border trade. In addition, transit policies have to be streamlined, and export-diversification efforts need to look at options for improving the geographical spread of destinations. An ITC (1989a) study explored the viability of selective marketing in various African and international markets (Table 9.3).

Investment in Niger declined steadily during the 1980s: the share of investment in GDP declined from 36 per cent in 1980 to less than 6 per cent in 1993 (ITC 1989a:38). The proposals for establishing a favourable investment climate for private investors presented in the Plan de Développement Economique et Social 1987–91, and especially the recommendations of the Private Sector Round Table (June 1988), merit attention. The Round Table recommended, *inter alia*, a new investment code, reduction of administrative formalities, a commercial code and new labour legislation, and rehabilitation of the credit sector.

Some progress has been made on improving conditions for attracting foreign investment: a new investment code, published in the *Journal Officiel du Niger* in December 1989, is in line with the mid-term and long-term development objectives of the country, as well as with the recommendations of the Round Table. It grants privileges to:

• the agricultural sector and agro-based industries;

Table 9.3 Potential export markets for Niger's products

Products	Markets
Uranium	France, other EC countries, Japan.
Onions	Côte d'Ivoire, Benin, Senegal, Congo, Gabon, Cameroon.
Live animals	Nigeria, Togo, Algeria, Mali, Libya, Côte d'Ivoire.
Meat (chilled and dry)	Côte d'Ivoire, Benin, Togo, Gabon, Cameroon, Nigeria, Algeria, Saudi Arabia.
Hides and skins	Ghana, Italy, France, Spain, Holland, Algeria, Nigeria, Togo, Benin, Côte d'Ivoire, Senegal.
Leather goods	Côte d'Ivoire, Senegal, but mostly EC, United States and Canada.
Fruits and vegetables (off-season)	EC, Scandinavian countries, Togo, Nigeria.
Bobby beans	EC, mostly France and Belgium, Netherlands.
Cowpeas	Nigeria, Mali, Senegal, other African countries.
Woven cotton fabrics	West African countries, Liberia, Ghana, Sierra Leone, Guinea.
Textiles, dresses	West African countries, Côte d'Ivoire, United States, Canada.
Handicraft products	EC, United States, Canada, Switzerland.
Soap and cosmetics	ECOWAS, East Africa.
International tourism	Tourists from DMECs.

Source: ITC (1989a:50).

- the use and transformation of local raw materials;
- the production of exports;
- small and micro-enterprises;
- the imports of necessary equipment; and
- the organization of vocational training.

The code does not restrict conditions for genuine competition and, generally, is more attractive to investors than similar codes of other countries of the subregion (PNUD 1991). However, other measures, such as tariff dismantlement (1987) and external trade liberalization (1990), eliminating protection from imports of competitive goods might complicate the situation and discourage private investors.

To improve the investment climate, the new investment code needs to be complemented by a commercial code and new labour legislation. External commercial legislation is based currently on a large number of different, and sometimes contradictory, texts. The commercial code should mainly cover external trade; it should also be compatible with international agreements and be based on a liberal economic doctrine, but as far as possible contain measures to promote the production of tradables by local firms. Niger's labour legislation was adopted almost 30 years ago and is out of date. For any entrepreneur, labour legislation is critical to investment decisions. Rehabilitation of the banking sector should be continued, in particular through the strengthening of the newly-created SONIBANK, and support given for the reactivation of the Fonds d'Intervention en Faveur des Petites et Moyens Entreprises du Niger (FIPMEN).

Second, special programmes, with short- and long-term components for tradable livestock and agricultural products, as well as for manufacturing, will have to be designed. Short-term programmes should be oriented to create the minimal conditions to stop the regression in the tradable sectors. Rehabilitation programmes should support enterprises that:

1. produce tradables, and/or increase the value added of natural resources;
2. are able to find partners in export markets; and
3. make low demands on capital, energy and water consumption.

Long-term programmes should be oriented towards:

1. setting up a large and diversified productive base by increasing the value added from domestic natural resources;
2. upgrading the competitiveness of enterprises by reducing their operational costs and by enlarging and diversifying the markets for them;
3. developing human resources through education and vocational training; and
4. integrating the informal into the formal sector.

Third, a vital condition for revitalization and diversification of trade is the adoption of external trade-promotion policies, including:

1. identification of domestic opportunities for exports;
2. strengthening infrastructural facilities (electrification, handling facilities at airports, cold storage chains, and so on);
3. simplification of export procedures, especially for perishable products;
4. reduction of export tariffs and taxes;
5. establishing commercial attachés abroad;
6. facilitating financing for export operations (for example, trade and pre-shipment finance); and
7. establishing a system of insurance for export credits.

Entrepreneurs should be requested to:

1. reorganize and coordinate foreign trade activities through the formation of collective interest groups;
2. adhere to quality standards; and

3. familiarize themselves with international market practices, in particular through specialized training.

The Chamber of Commerce (CCAIAN), and especially the Centre Nigérien du Commerce Extérieur (CNCE), should:

1. explore the possibilities of access to new markets for Niger's products at different stages of processing/manufacturing (review customs requirements, import restrictions, quality restrictions, prices charged by competitors, and so on);
2. strengthen export enterprises, including their reorganization and rehabilitation;
3. provide information to exporters on the standard and style of products suitable for export; and
4. provide institutional support for external trade development and diversification.

The implementation of these recommendations will take time given the lack of training centres in the country. At present, Niger has four vocational training centres, but only one of them, the Centre National pour le Perfectionnement à la Gestion (CNPG) could readily start adequate trade-promotion training.

Fourth, although diversification of transit-transport corridors may not be justified, redistributing Niger's transit among existing corridors, bearing in mind economic efficiency and security, could benefit trade. Diversification of transport companies operating in transit-transport corridors, as well as diversification of sea transportation by using tramp vessels and non-conference vessels, would decrease transport costs; further decreases in cost are possible through eliminating customs bottlenecks.

Fifth, any measure to increase and diversify production and exports will have only a slim chance of succeeding without resolving two problems. The first is to reduce the risk of a further sharp fall of export earnings from uranium, and to maintain earnings, at least at the present level. The second problem is to restrain the influx of goods from abroad (mainly from Nigeria through informal cross-border trade channels) at prices which undermine the production of almost all tradables in Niger.

It is difficult to resolve the uranium problem internally, but exploitation efforts could be concentrated on deposits with low operational costs in order to maximize returns.

The second problem, influx of imports, may have been partly resolved through the devaluation of the CFA franc which reduces production costs and increases the costs of imported products. Thus it will be less advantageous for Niger to 'buy Nigerian' or South-east Asian goods re-exported from Nigeria. However, neither the devaluation of the CFA franc, nor the factual revaluation of the Nigerian naira[22] may decisively improve the situation since the inflow of imported goods results, to a considerable extent, from the interest of some entrepreneurs to obtain CFA francs. This incentive could be radically reduced following the limitation of currency exchange to BCEAO units only. The devaluation makes it necessary to adjust external tariffs; and some temporary non-tariff measures to stimulate the recovery of manufacturing tradables are probably necessary as well. The government should also continue to strengthen its customs' services by using skilled staff and modern equipment, and by increasing their commitment to effective and honest work.

6　CONCLUSION

The constraints to trade diversification in Niger are onerous, and the potential to realize its objectives in the short term is limited.

The decline of uranium export earnings, and in agricultural and livestock production, and the failure to improve performance of the state-managed sector, have exposed the fragility of Niger's economy since the mid-1980s. Faced with the economic crisis, the government adopted rigorous stabilization and structural adjustment measures which were aided by the January 1994 devaluation of the CFA franc. The adjustment policies would, however, need to be supported by other measures before any revitalization of production and further diversification of tradables can be achieved. These would require commitment and support at the national and international levels, in particular with reference to the issues discussed in Section 5 above.

NOTES

1.　In 1990, Niger's illiteracy rate was more than 87 per cent (91 per cent for women and 81 for men). School enrolment ratios were very low: 19 per cent for combined primary and secondary education; and 0.8 per cent for tertiary education. Only 2 per cent of young women and men received secondary education. Existing centres of vocational training do not measure up to the pressing needs of economic development; and education is primarily oriented to preparation for administrative service and does not train for technical production skills.
2.　39 kg. in 1992 (UNDP 1995, p. 177).
3.　For example, salary, electricity and fuel costs at an industrial unit in Maradi (Niger) were respectively, 3, 3 and 5 times higher than those of a unit of the same profile and category in Kano (Nigeria) (see ONUDI 1991).
4.　The climate of Niger is arid and two-thirds of the country is desert; moreover, the desert is expanding. Only 12 per cent of the country's territory is cultivable, of which 5 per cent is currently under cultivation.
5.　The size of the cattle herd declined by two-thirds between 1972 and 1975, and by one-half in 1984 and 1985. It takes several years to rebuild cattle herds.
6.　Equivalent to more than 10 per cent of reasonably assured uranium resources of all developed and developing market-economy countries, with costs ranging up to US$80 per kgU or US$30.77 per 1b U3 O8.
7.　See Lomé Convention, Articles 52 and 53 regarding the promotion of agricultural production, Article 93 regarding industrialization, Articles 135 and 136 covering diversification of trade and Article 214 for the use of Sysmin in *The Courier* (1990).

8. It is very unlikely that the Programme de Coopération Industrielle 1988–1992 of CEAO, as well as the Additional Protocol on less industrially developed member states of ECOWAS would generate practical results for Niger.
9. In 1990 the share of the uranium sector in GDP fell slightly to 5 per cent but its share in total exports was more than 68 per cent.
10. Import duty on some product lines was reduced by about 40 per cent, while other product lines were exempted from duty.
11. Licensing and quantitative restrictions for all imports, except petroleum were eliminated (see Decree No. 90–146 of 10 July 1990 on liberalization of merchandise imports).
12. The customs service has only 800 poorly-equipped officers to monitor a 1,500 km. border.
13. Reasons for the fall in uranium prices include relatively low prices and a surplus in the petroleum market, the accidents at Three Mile Island in 1978, the Chernobyl catastrophe in 1986 and the existence of large stocks of uranium in uranium-importing countries.
14. By way of comparison: in 1989 the maximum operational costs in Niger were about US$31 per pound of U3 08 and its free-on-board Cotonou price was US$35 per pound. The average price paid by US buyers for imported uranium in 1988 was US$19 per pound. US spot prices in 1989 were US$9 per pound (according to NUEXCO, the uranium dealer) Gouvernement de Niger (1991a:109; UNCTAD 1991:276; and data provided by the Central Bank).
15. Three new modern slaughterhouses (in Zinder, Maradi and Tahoua) have not radically changed the situation (see ITC 1989a:30).
16. According to the Ministère d'Agriculture et d'Elevage du Niger, the country can export chilled meat to Côte d'Ivoire, Benin and Togo at a price of 1,000 CFA francs per kilo (communication with Darre Issoufou, the Secretary-General of the Ministry). Copro-Niger, a mixed company controlled by the state, also sees the possibility to export dry beef meat to the Côte d'Ivoire (communication with Massana Nababa, the Chef de Service Approvisionnement of the Company). Also see PNUD (1991).
17. According to the Ministère de la Promotion Economique de Niger (now Ministère de l'Industrie et de l'Artisanat), a project on production and exports of dehydrated onions is under examination (Communication with Brigitta Dia, then Director, Department of Industry and Private Investments Promotion).
18. Air freight is very expensive – about US$0.7–1.0 per kg. – and unreliable. The risk of heavy financial losses is high.
19. Customs and administrative formalities are time consuming and highly expensive, comprising up to 70–75 per cent of the market price achieved in Côte d'Ivoire.
20. Sonitextil's turnover dropped from US$33.5 million (1985) to US$13.9 million (1990) while the company's exports dropped from US$3.4 million to US$0.4 million.
21. Communication with Mr Faignee, Financial Director of Sonitextil.
22. Shortly after the devaluation of the CFA franc, Nigeria fixed the rate of its naira at 22 to the dollar and abolished the parallel rate of the currency which was about 46 nairas to the dollar. The devaluation of the CFA franc together with the revaluation of the naira resulted in an approximate 75 per cent decrease of the former against the latter (see *Africa Research Bulletin* 1994 and Gaud, M. 1994:15).

REFERENCES

Africa International (1994), 'Dévaluation – premier bilan. Niger: Grèves à répétition', no. 274, July/August, p. 14.
Africa Research Bulletin (1994), vol. 31, no. 1, 16 January–15 February, p. 11569.
Africa South of the Sahara 1994 (1993), 23rd edn, London: Europa Publications Ltd.
Amselle, J.-L. and E. Grégoire with D. Bagayogo (1988), *Politiques nationales et réseaux marchands transnationaux – les cas du Mali et du Niger-Nord*, Paris: Club du Sahel (OCDE), Ministère de la coopération, and 23rd edn, Ouagadougou: CILSS.

Banque Mondiale (1990), *Corridors de transport en Afrique sahelienne. Le cas Niger*, Rapport No.8814–NIR, Washington: Banque Mondiale.

Charlick, R.B. (1991), *Niger. Personal Rule and Survival in the Sahel*, London: Westview Press, Inc.

Gaud, M. (1994), 'De la réévaluation à la dévaluation' (1994), *Afrique contemporaine*, no. 169, 1st quarter, pp. 15 ff.

Gouvernement de Niger (1987), *Plan de Développement Economique et Social du Niger 1987–1991*, Texte Integral, Ordonnance No. 87-015, 30 April, Niamey: Ministère du Plan.

Gouvernement de Niger (1991a), *Annuaire Statistique*, 'Series longues', Niamey: Ministère du Plan.

Gouvernement du Niger (1991b), *Direction de l'Industrie*, Base de données, various years, Niamey: Ministère de la Promotion Economique.

Gouvernement du Niger, Ministère du Plan/Direction de l'Analyse Economique et de la Prévision (DAEP) (1991c), 'Information', mimeo, Niamey.

Government of Niger (1994), *Niger: Statement of Economic and Social Policy*, Niamey: Ministère du Plan.

Graybeal, L.N. and L.A. Picard (1991), 'Internal Capacity and Overload in Guinea and Niger', *Journal of Modern African Studies*, vol. 29, no. 2.

IMF, *Direction of Trade Statistics Yearbook*, various issues, Washington DC: IMF.

IMF (1994), *IMF Survey*, from the Executive Board, 21 March, p. 91, Washington, DC: IMF.

International Trade Centre (ITC) (1989a), 'Niger: Etude des potentiels d'exportation', Project No. 87/008, ITC/DTC/89/999, mimeo, Geneva.

International Trade Centre (ITC) (1989b), 'République du Niger. Promotion du Commerce Extérieur', Project No. NER/87/008, ITC/DTC/89/1102.22, Geneva: ITC.

International Trade Centre (ITC) (1991a), 'Niger: Rapport de mission d'analyse prospective (1991)', ITC/DTC/91/1402, mimeo, Geneva: ITC.

International Trade Centre (ITC) (1991b), 'Revue du secteur industriel au Niger', Project DP/NER/90/025, 19 April, Geneva: ITC.

'Les effets de la dévaluation sur le secteur manufacturier au Niger' (1994), paper presented by the delegation of Niger at the UNDP/UNIDO workshop on impact of the CFA franc devaluation on the manufacturing sector of countries in the Economic and Monetary Union of West Africa, Bamako (Mali), 13–15 June 1994, pp. 102–6.

'Lomé IV Convention' (1990), in *The Courier*, Africa–Caribbean–Pacific–European Community, no. 120, March–April.

OECD (1990), *Uranium. Resources, Production and Demand*, Paris: OECD.

Organisation des Nations Unies pour le developpement industriel (ONUDI) (1991), *Rapport de visite d'usines du Directeur de l'ONUDI*, Niamey: ONUDI.

Programme des Nations Unies pour le developpement (PNUD) (1991), *Revue de Secteur Industriel au Niger*, Project DP/Ner/90/025, Niamey: PNUD.

The Courier (1994), no. 143, January–February.

UNCTAD (1990), *Niger 1990. Country Presentation*, Second United Nations Conference on the Least Developed Countries, Geneva: United Nations.

UNCTAD (1991), *Commodity Yearbook 1991*, New York: United Nations.

UNCTAD (1994), *The Least Developed Countries 1993–1994 Report*, United Nations publications, Sales No. E.94.II.D.4, New York: United Nations.

UNDP (1995), *Human Development Report 1995*, New York: United Nations.

UNICEF (1990), *Ajustement structurel et satisfaction des besoins essentiels. Une étude de cas à partir de l'expérience du Niger (1982-1989)*, New York: United Nations.

World Bank, Database, Niger.

10. Trade diversification in Uganda: prospects and constraints

Willem van der Geest[1]

1 ECONOMIC STRUCTURE AND GROWTH PROSPECTS

The main phases of Uganda's recent political and economic history revolve around the economically disastrous sequence of events which unfolded after the military coup by Idi Amin against the Obote regime in 1971. The Amin regime operated through fear and there was no guarantee of security of life and property. The subsequent bitter battle for control eventually engaged Tanzania's army and, at the time, it seemed to have reached a conclusion with the restoration of the Obote II regime from 1980 onwards, after a disputed election. As became clear in the period 1983–85, the instability and civil and military strife was, however, by no means resolved. When the Obote II regime fell in July 1985 the country faced complete economic ruin. A temporary military government held power until January 1986, after which Yoweri Museveni assumed the Presidency.[2]

The structural economic changes during and after the period of instability and civil war are well documented and will be restated only briefly here. The growth of GDP halted throughout 1971–86, and the per-capita GDP in 1986 stood at only 57.5 per cent of its 1970 value. Other economic features of the period were a sharp decline of the manufacturing sector and a reversal of the agricultural sector into the subsistence non-monetized mode. Agricultural production declined at 0.7 per cent, resulting in a fall in its share of GDP during the 1970s. Table 10.1 below summarizes the key macroeconomic indicators during the rehabilitation period from 1986 onwards, which was characterized by the reverse of the decline of per-capita GDP.

1.1 Rehabilitation and Growth Prospects

The strategic issues which the Uganda government will need to address during the Rehabilitation and Development Plan relate to:

Table 10.1 Key macroeconomic indicators, 1986–1991 (average annual percentage change)

Growth of GDP	5.9
Per-capita GDP growth	3.4
Gross domestic investment (% of GDP)	13.0[a]
Current-account deficit (average % of GDP)	−10.8
Export of goods NFS[b]	−15.8
Import of goods NFS[b]	16.5
Inflation	97.0[c]
Exchange-rate depreciation	65.7[d]

Notes:
a. 1986–90.
b. In US$ value terms.
c. Average inflation 1987–88 to 1991–92.
d. Official devaluations May 87 to July 91.

Sources: MPEP/MFEP, *Background to the Budget* (various issues).

1. perceiving rehabilitation as a process of assessing and creating opportunities, rather than as returning to its previous productive and export profile for which it no longer has a dynamic comparative advantage due to changes in international commodity and capital markets;
2. the appropriate sequence of economic rehabilitation and structural adjustment measures. Does liberalization of the trade regime (removing import restrictions, lowering tariffs and so on) impair or promote the rehabilitation effort? Should reform of domestic marketing structures be undertaken before, at the same time or only after external-sector liberalization has proceeded?

2 MACROECONOMIC MANAGEMENT ISSUES: PUBLIC AND TRADE DEFICITS

2.1 Macroeconomic Policy Framework and Objectives

The formulation of a consistent and coherent macroeconomic strategy for the medium term received a high priority from the Museveni government and was actively supported by donors including the United Nations Development Programme (UNDP) and the World Bank. Uganda's macroeconomic database has recently been extensively revised. On the basis of the 1989 Household Budget Survey the time series for the growth of gross domestic product (GDP) were revised upwards – reflecting an improved recording of service-sector activities, in particular rural transport and marketing.[3]

The strategic components of the macroeconomic statement (MFEP 1992c) focus on:

1. increased resource mobilization through positive real interest rates;
2. prudent fiscal and monetary policies and liberalization of the trade and payments regime in order to stimulate and attract private investment;
3. increasing and diversifying exports to ease the foreign-exchange constraint and augment import capacity to obtain capital, investment and intermediate goods;
4. promotion of exports through an appropriate exchange rate, the scrapping of marketing board monopolies and the rationalization of export procedures.[4]

Trade development and export diversification are seen as a central macroeconomic objective, to be realized through export promotion, efficiency-oriented reform of agricultural policy and foreign investment promotion, including the introduction of a foreign investment code, the establishment of the Uganda Investment Authority and the rehabilitation of the Departed Asian Properties Custodian Board.[5]

It was emphasized that the style of government needed was one which enabled initiatives, rather than one of direct control. In particular, the *kibanda* informal foreign-exchange markets were to be legalized. Institutional and structural reform were to be complementary to the macroeconomic strategy, including improving the efficiency of the civil service through retrenchment and the privatization of a significant number of parastatals under the Public Enterprise Reform and Divestiture project (PERD). These measures were expected to have positive effects on both the public finance and the external trade deficits. (See MFEP 1992b.)

Uganda's accumulation of external debt (in particular debt on concessional terms)[6] reflects the problem of insufficient domestic-resource mobilization in both public and private sectors, resulting in limited domestic private investment and a continued imbalance between public revenue and expenditure. Significant budget deficits have accompanied the rehabilitation process, because attempts to improve revenue collection, to date, have had limited success.[7]

2.2 The Macroeconomic Environment for Trade Diversification

Public deficits and exchange-rate adjustments
The present external imbalance, with current-account deficits ranging between $195 million to $263 million per annum during 1988 to 1991, is primarily the result of public deficits: the private sector's incomes and expenditures are close to balancing. Hence any reduction of the trade deficit will require a reduction in the public expenditure level, improved revenue collection, improved export earnings, higher net private transfers and/or import compression.

Exchange-rate policy

The liberalization of the export produce markets, which has been virtually completed for coffee and is in progress for cotton and other crops, was sequenced to follow the liberalization of the foreign-exchange market. Foreign-exchange liberalization had started and progressed rapidly, partly in response to budget pressures. The practical implication of this sequencing of liberalization was twofold:

1. exporters could retain their earnings in full and could freely buy foreign exchange for input supply and other purposes; and
2. the incentives for capital flight were reduced and attracting foreign investment became easier.

In retrospect it appears that this ordering of adjustment policy measures – focusing on the foreign-exchange market early in the structural adjustment process – has facilitated a new inflow of private foreign investment as well as a certain degree of diversification away from coffee during the years from 1989 to 1993. Nevertheless, sequencing the process of liberalization in this fashion was never an explicit decision, but rather a response to the pressures of the informal financial markets. With the benefit of hindsight, it appears that the rapid foreign-exchange market liberalization seems to have shortened the period of damaging hyperinflation and its associated uncertainties: a parallel market premium of 885 Ugandan shillings in 1991 had disappeared by 1993.

3 EXTERNAL-SECTOR PERFORMANCE DURING REHABILITATION

3.1 Conditions Pre- and Post Civil War

A certain degree of diversification which had characterized Uganda's export structure in the early 1970s was entirely lost during the civil war. In 1970, coffee constituted some 58 per cent of the export earnings of commodities followed by cotton (20 per cent), copper (9 per cent), tea (5 per cent) and animal feedstuff, hides and skins and other products accounting for the remaining 8 per cent. Only coffee exports, though in sharply reduced volumes, were maintained throughout the period of instability. Hence, coffee accounted for nearly all of the export earnings in the early rehabilitation years from 1986 to 1990. Against this background, the twin objectives of the macroeconomic strategy – improving the balance of payments and reducing the public finance deficit in a growth context – are closely associated with the drive for export expansion and diversification. Such diversification will need to be complemented by capturing the opportunities for efficient import substitution.

3.2 Export Performance

The crisis of Uganda's exports is reflected in both a decline of its earnings as well as an unprecedented concentration and dependence on coffee. Export revenues in US dollar terms have been declining since the mid-1980s, while imports increased by roughly 50 per cent; the resulting increasing trade deficit of about $250 million to $350 million from 1987 to 1992 was one of the triggering factors for export promotion (MFEP 1993b).

Uganda had virtually become a monocrop exporter by the end of the 1980s with coffee comprising almost 97 per cent of total export earnings. Measured in current prices, the 1988–89 export revenue had plummeted to 79 per cent of its 1980 value, partly because the world coffee prices dropped dramatically and partly because export sales in the international cotton, tea and copper markets had collapsed. The changed concentration of exports can be observed from Table 10.2. In 1967 the three main commodities accounted for 85.5 per cent of the total export earnings, but two of these (cotton and copper) earned nearly one-third of the total. Throughout the 1980s, the contribution of coffee was

Table 10.2 Long-term structural change of Uganda's commodity exports, 1967–1991

	Value ($ millions)				Percentages	
	1967	1970	1980	1991	1967	1991
All commodities	180.98	243.61	349.76	184.26	100.0	100.0
Traditional items						
Coffee	96.88	142.03	340.73	117.38	53.5	63.7
Cotton	42.45	49.17	4.19	11.73	23.5	6.4
Copper	15.31	20.57	1.00	–	8.5	–
Tea and mate	9.74	13.24	0.32	6.78	5.4	3.7
Tobacco (unmfd)	0.10	1.05	–	4.53	–	2.5
Non-traditional items						
Animal feed	6.41	6.72	0.00	–	3.5	–
Hides and skins	3.54	3.74	2.04	4.33	2.0	2.4
Oilseeds, nuts, kernels	1.36	1.00	0.10	10.64	0.8	5.8
Crude vegetable materials	0.85	0.31	–	5.77	0.0	3.1
Non-ferrous base metal ore	0.82	1.10	–	–	0.5	–
Crude animal matter	0.38	0.43	–	0.35	–	0.2
Remainder	3.15	4.26	0.57	22.75	1.7	12.3*

Notes: * Other non-traditional export items recorded for 1991 were (percentage of total export value in brackets): gold (5.2%), fish and fish products (2.9%), cereals (2.4%), electric current (0.5%) and timber (0.2%).

Sources: UNCTAD (1993b) and Ministry of Finance and Economic Planning (1993c).

about 97 per cent of total recorded earnings of commodity exports. Hides and skins, animal feedstuff and oilseeds, which had made sizeable contributions to export earnings before the war, had completely lost their importance by 1980.

In terms of recorded trade flows, trade with the Preferential Trade Agreement (PTA) area has begun expanding since 1990. However, in view of the professed intention of the countries in the PTA region to create a common market, it is unlikely that this will expand the revenue base for trade taxation. For the industrialized countries, the United States and the UK have lost their importance as major export markets: France, Spain, and Germany have emerged as the main destinations for Uganda's exports in 1990–93 (Table 10.3).

Unrecorded border trade
'Non-traditional' exports, as reported in Table 10.2, are likely to be underestimated, because recorded external trade does not fully capture the ongoing informal cross-border trade flows. Hence, while the traditional export crops (coffee, cotton, tea and tobacco) have remained the main source of export revenue, the export sector is probably more diversified than the official trade data reflect. Uganda's informal cross-border trade covers a variety of basic foods and household consumer goods. Food crops sold in the informal sector or bartered to neighbouring countries throughout the years of civil war include bananas and other fruits, vegetables, cereals (rice, wheat, maize), and cassava, edible oils and seeds, and fish.

Rehabilitation and export diversification
Reflecting the importance of restoring the external balance, the government formulated an Export Diversification Plan (henceforth EDP) up to the year 2002. The strategy includes a review of policy changes required, an identification of the institutional and promotional constraints, and is complemented by specific sectoral programmes. The main new programmes outlined in the EDP include:

1. strengthening of the Export Credit Guarantee Scheme which has been in operation since 1991 under the aegis of the Bank of Uganda (supported by the World Bank);
2. strengthening the Uganda Bureau of Standards; and
3. establishing an Export Development and Promotion Council.

This council would coordinate the various institutions involved in export development and promotion, in particular the Export Policy Analysis and Development Unit (EPADU), whose export development duties are being transferred to the Export Promotion Council (EPC). The services to be provided to exporters by the EPC and other bodies include:

1. export market research and analysis;
2. dissemination of export market information;

Table 10.3 Direction of recorded trade, 1985–1993

	1985	1989	1990	1991	1992	1993
	(Exports as per cent of total exports)					
Industrial countries	88.3	90.7	89.9	89.4	84.1	85.2
of which						
Belgium-Luxembourg	1.5	3.3	3.3	2.3	2.3	3.0
France	7.0	12.0	13.2	14.4	12.0	12.7
Germany	8.0	8.7	6.1	9.8	9.7	9.7
Italy	6.6	6.2	8.8	6.9	5.1	6.7
Portugal	0.9	1.8	3.3	3.4	4.6	6.7
Spain	9.9	9.8	5.5	9.8	11.4	12.7
United Kingdom	15.1	11.3	10.5	6.3	8.6	7.5
United States	28.3	14.5	7.7	10.9	6.9	7.5
Developing countries	10.9	4.8	10.1	10.6	15.9	14.8
of which						
Africa	1.2	1.6	4.8	2.0	1.3	2.5
Kenya	..	0.4	..	0.6	0.6	1.5
Rwanda	..	0.7	1.6	..	0.6	0.7
Tunisia	..	..	2.8	1.1	..	..
Zimbabwe	..	..	..	..	..	..
	(Imports as per cent of total imports)					
Industrial countries	54.5	59.9	49.8	64.5	60.7	58.8
of which						
Belgium-Luxembourg	3.5	2.2	1.7	3.2	3.3	2.9
France	1.7	2.4	2.2	4.0	3.6	4.2
Germany	6.5	11.5	8.3	7.9	7.6	8.4
Italy	6.3	5.0	8.8	6.9	3.8	3.7
Portugal	0.1	1.1	..	..	..	..
Spain	0.6	3.3	0.2	4.2	3.6	1.3
United Kingdom	19.7	15.4	13.3	17.3	14.2	13.2
United States	1.8	5.4	5.0	3.7	4.6	6.0
Developing countries	44.1	39.5	50.2	35.5	39.3	41.2
of which						
Africa	33.5	21.2	38.3	14.0	16.9	19.3
Kenya	..	20.4	36.2	12.6	15.3	17.6
Rwanda	..	0.3	0.2	..	..	..
Tunisia	..	..	0.7	0.5	..	..
Zimbabwe	..	0.4	1.0	0.5	1.4	1.3

Sources: IMF, *Direction of Trade Statistics Yearbook*, various issues.

3. promotion of foreign investment;
4. coordination of donor-funded export development;
5. preliminary appraisal of investment proposals;
6. policy analysis regarding the scope for reducing domestic costs, capturing opportunities for quality premia, the use of fiscal instruments for export incentives and appropriate exchange-rate management; and
7. underwriting of export finance.

3.3 Import Performance

Import composition
The shares of both industrial and developing countries in total recorded imports have remained largely the same during 1985–93, but the share of Africa has declined sharply in the rehabilitation period: in particular, Kenya's share declined from more than a third in 1990 to an average of 15 per cent in 1991–93 (Table 10.3).

The import data from three estimates differ considerably: the value of imports for 1991 on cash basis was $149.8 million, on recorded entry it stood at US$411.1 million and for the balance-of-payments purposes it stood at $488.3 million (preliminary estimate).[8]

Import-duty structure
The average nominal rate of tariff duties was 28 to 29 per cent of total recorded import c.i.f. value. The structure of the customs duties ranges from zero to 80 per cent on an *ad valorem* basis on non-petroleum goods. Recent harmonization of tariffs has reduced the nominal tariff from much higher levels; a recent study found that more than three-quarters of the total import revenue come from the goods subject to lower bands, in particularly the 10 to 30 per cent band (UIA 1993:23). The nominal rates of duties increase with the degree of manufacturing and processing. Further sales taxes are levied on the basis of the sum of the c.i.f. import value plus the dutiable amount – in effect causing a cascading tax structure. Further reduction in the levels of duty and simplification of its structure has been announced in the Budget speech of 1993–94.

Effective protection
The average nominal protection rate for selected industrial goods is 18.8 per cent;[9] and the average effective protection rate for production for domestic markets and for exports is 62.1 and –14.5 per cent, respectively[10] (UIA 1993).

As observed by the UIA (1993:3), the protection offered domestic producers through the negative list system and duty exemptions on inputs limits economic growth and employment by restricting the ability of potential industries to expand.

Efficient import substitution

The Export Diversification Plan points to the need to study to what extent cost-effective import-replacing production may be feasible. In particular, products which use mainly local materials as their intermediate inputs would qualify, including: (i) foods and beverages; (ii) salt; (iii) sugar; (iv) cigarettes; (v) textile fabrics and ready made garments; (vi) cement; (vii) lime; (viii) footwear; (ix) stationery supply; (x) soaps and detergents; and (xi) ethanol packaging materials.

In 1990, imports of these items amounted to approximately US$55 million, some 9 per cent of the total import value. Uganda's soap manufacturers import tallow and coconut oil; the former could be obtained from the domestic meat-processing industry and production of palm oil is deemed technically feasible. Cotton textile mills in Uganda produce at only 16 per cent of installed capacity and supply only one-sixth of the local demand. Nevertheless, any expansion and rehabilitation will need to be selective, taking into account the present state of the textile mills, the costs of their rehabilitation and the projected development of international prices.

To assess the feasibility of efficient import substitution will require an improved recording of import inflows. The improved database could be used to compute nominal and effective rates of protection for a wider range of products, as well as domestic-resource cost indicators. Comparing the economic cost of domestic production with the costs of imported substitutes would offer considerable guidance for the selection of import-substituting projects. Privatization through the PERD project is likely to attract foreign firms into the domestic import-substituting production, with possible eventual export expansion into the PTA region.

4   PROSPECTS FOR TRADE DIVERSIFICATION

Export-diversification prospects of Uganda will depend on, *inter alia*:

1. the volume and price development in global commodity and manufactures markets;
2. global trade regimes;
3. upgrading output quality and reliability of supplies; and
4. maintaining the real effective exchange rates.

Moreover, the ability to consolidate informal trade flows and to enhance subregional ties will also be crucial to achieving geographical as well as product diversification.

4.1 Projections of Export Growth

EDP presents a preliminary projection of traditional and non-traditional export sectors; it forecasts a very considerable increase in export volumes based on certain assumptions, for example, establishment of an export-processing zone; the negotiation of a cobalt extraction contract. The target increase of total export value (in US dollars) is 25 per cent per annum for a four-year period, from 1992–93 to 1996–97. Export value growth during the subsequent years up to 2002 is expected to be slower at 13.5 per cent per annum.

The projections are undoubtedly 'optimistic'; for the traditional agricultural exports of coffee, cotton, tea, for example, the projections assume rising or steady prices.

This section will review the prospects for Uganda's:

1. traditional exports, in particular coffee and cotton;
2. non-traditional exports, for example, horticultural development;
3. the services subsector, in particular tourism; and
4. the FDI commitments made since the middle of 1991.

4.2 Traditional Exports

Agricultural diversification

Since traditional exports of Uganda were primarily agricultural, diversification of the agricultural sector will be one key condition to improving export performance.[11] The short-term agricultural strategy focuses on regaining the market shares for Uganda's traditional exports, in particular of cotton and tea, as well as expanding coffee exports. The problems which perennial crop exporters face are manifold, but relate in particular to world market prices. The projected long-term price trend of tea indicates only a weak increase of prices, while for cotton a slow recovery towards the second half of the 1990s is expected to be followed by a subsequent decline (see below).

Agricultural diversification and intensification will be a precondition for export expansion. Crops such as cotton (beans and maize for PTA countries); and horticultural products, including, spices (especially, vanilla, cardamom, dried ginger and dried chilli), banana, cashew nuts and fresh cut flowers, have a potential for exports.

Export market identification and the consequent product development have remained problematic, and market information has not yet been available systematically. Although some individual traders have made efforts to sell fish, chillies, ginger and so on to foreign buyers, export promotion is still in an infant stage, and international marketing expertise is lacking.

The nature of international and domestic cost constraints to exports are discussed below for the perennial crop coffee and the seasonal crop cotton, and for horticultural products in general. The description of the constraints for the expansion of these commodities applies equally to other agricultural crops and products.

Coffee export development

Robusta coffee has been Uganda's main export product throughout the past thirty years, with arabica accounting for only 6 per cent of the output. Yields of the robusta crop stand at approximately 75 to 80 per cent of the level which should be expected for the prevalent low-input smallholder cultivation practices, in view of Uganda's favourable soil, rainfall and agro-ecological conditions. The relatively low yields and falling quality of robusta may be explained by the ageing of the trees, a lack of new planting materials, competition from food crops leading to intercropping (often with banana) and poor field practices.

Uganda's performance in the depressed world coffee market has been better than that of most other Sub-Saharan African coffee-producing countries:[12] it has regained some of its lost share of world coffee production, increasing it from 2.19 per cent in 1979–81 to 2.66 per cent by 1991.

The positive supply responses of coffee in Uganda have been muted by drought as well as by the downward trend in international coffee prices. Another problem of the subsector in the post-liberalization phase relates to coffee processing: cartelization seemed to persist. Even with a very considerable excess capacity and low utilization, in some cases less than 20 per cent, charges for coffee processing did not adjust downwards. Overall, the liberalization of coffee markets has had some positive effects, in particular the price gains for farmers, through the emergence of private traders, who are reported to compete effectively with the unions which were appointed buyers for the Coffee Marketing Board (CMB).[13]

Cotton export development

The short-term export action plan developed in the joint Government/World Bank agricultural sector review focuses on cotton because it is perceived that

1. its profitability will remain acceptable;
2. farmers' production responses will be rapid given enhanced security in the cotton-growing regions; and
3. the main sectoral policy changes – increasing competition through revoking monopsonistic marketing – can follow the successful example of the coffee subsector.

Cotton output peaked in the early seventies when some 86.9 thousand metric tons of lint were produced. In sharp contrast, purchases by the Lint Marketing Board, which has the right to purchase all cotton for export, in 1990, stood at a mere 5.9 thousand tons. The government's new policy stance is to liberalize the ginning and marketing of cotton. The agricultural-sector review recommends a decentralized system with competitive prices and open access to the markets for cotton at the farm gate and cotton lint produced by the ginneries.

The short-term strategy for cotton may be understood primarily as rehabilitating a crop which was very successful in the years prior to Uganda's civil unrest. However, the analysis provided by the agricultural-sector review does not unequivocally support the choice of cotton as a prime candidate for rehabilitation and export development, because of, *inter alia*: unfavourable international price trend; low earnings from cotton, estimated at only US$0.42 per person day,[14] assuming low-input low-output techniques; and high production costs which are above those of competing countries, such as neighbouring Tanzania. Indeed, total production costs exceed the average export price – in other words, the parastatal Lint Marketing Board continues to incur a financial loss while exporting.

Exchange-rate adjustment through further devaluation would tend to increase the foreign cost components of cotton production, even though it could potentially reduce the domestic labour costs.[15] Reducing the producer prices directly would inevitably entail even further reduction of the farmer's earnings. Hence, macroeconomic adjustment by itself will not be able to deal with the low earnings and high processing costs; additional microeconomic measures may prove necessary.

4.3 Non-traditional Exports (NTEs)[16]

Uganda's NTEs amounted to $30.8 million in 1990–91, which was less than one-fifth of the total export value, and include for example: timber, minerals and agricultural produce such as maize and sesame seed. The underrecording of agricultural NTEs is believed to be considerable, but no reliable estimates are available. The prevalence of informal cross-border trade indicates that small-scale and informal business can be an important source of export development, especially for trade within the PTA region.

Horticulture

Horticulture has been identified by the government of Uganda as one of the agricultural subsectors with considerable export-diversification potential. Production data for fruit and vegetables are subject to considerable margins: it is estimated for 1991 by the Kawanda Research Station staff that tomatoes, cabbages and onions are the main vegetables cultivated (amounting to nearly 200,000 tons) and that the production of pineapples, mangoes, citrus fruits, avocados, papayas and passion fruits amounts to approximately 190,000 tons. Although fruits are grown all over the country, the south-west (Mpigi, Masaka, Mukono, Luwero and Mubende districts) and Kapchorwa district on the eastern border were reported to support more than 500 hectares of fruit cultivation in 1988. The value of horticultural exports for the three-year period 1988–90, as estimated by the EPADU on the basis of customs data, amounted to $2.5 million with bananas, pineapples and ginger alone accounting for more than 80 per cent of this value.

From an institutional point of view, the Uganda Horticultural Farmers' Association (UHFA) and the Horticultural Exporters' Association of Uganda (HEAU) represent the subsector at the official level and attempt to deal with the problems of the availability and quality of farm inputs, processing, packaging and air freighting as well as obtaining appropriate technical assistance. The constraints on expanding horticultural exports are reviewed below.

4.4 Trade in Services

Tourism

Tourism development in Uganda will provide both an opportunity to, and a test of, Uganda's ability to cast off its image of civil insecurity. Up to 1972, the basis of Ugandan tourism was the great abundance of wildlife species in well-organized parks and game reserves. In 1971, some 85,000 tourists generated foreign-exchange earnings of $18.9 million, making tourism the third-largest foreign-exchange earner, after coffee and cotton. Uganda's civil unrest had seriously damaged tourist facilities and destroyed tourism. It inflicted grave damage on wildlife, with herds of elephants reduced from an estimated 32,000 to 2,000 by 1980, and other species, including the white rhino, hunted to extinction.

The main assets of Uganda's tourist industry are its wildlife and game reserves which combine features of the West African tropical rain forests with the East African savannah vegetation.[17] The overriding concern in the planning of Uganda's tourism resources is to maintain a balance between achieving economic and conservation objectives. The 'special interest tourism' which Uganda could attract would include camping and walking safaris, mountaineering, bird watching, hunting safaris, gorilla tourism, sailing, fishing, and so on.

Since 1986, visitors arriving to Uganda have increased steadily, reflecting primarily the increased presence of multilateral and bilateral donors. The most recent estimate puts arrivals in 1986 at 32,840, which increased to an estimated 90,000 by 1991.[18] However, only approximately one out of every five persons arriving in Uganda was a holiday tourist.

Present positive developments in the field of tourism services include:

1. increasing the number of airlines routing to and through the international airport of Entebbe;
2. upgrading of the airport through an investment programme of the Civil Aviation Authority;

3. renewed commitment to protection of animals and the ecological system;
4. upgrading of hotel and lodging facilities in the national parks as a component of the UNDP/WTO Tourism Rehabilitation and Development Planning Project (second phase); and
5. increasing supply of tourist services through travel agents and tour operators.

4.5 Foreign Direct Investment (FDI)

Perhaps the most encouraging response to Uganda's rehabilitation process has been the interest from both foreign and non-resident Ugandan investors. It was estimated that total investment from 622 projects licensed by the UIA by December 1993 could be in the range of $435 million to $501 million over the medium term.[19] The UIA estimates that the actual flow of investment (including investment drawn from domestic sources) stood at approximately $50 million to $60 million for 1992 and was higher for 1993. The estimate assumes that the average disbursement cycle of a project is three years and that only one out of every three projects does actually result in investment (see UIA 1993 and 1994).[20]

The market orientation of the approved projects tends to be towards import-competing production for the domestic market. Only one out of nine approved projects may be considered as export oriented.

There can be little doubt that the key determinant of both 'new' as well as 'returning' foreign investment into Uganda is the expectation of a continuation of the recently-established political stability and the security of property rights. This will be contingent upon a peaceful transition to democratic rule following the Constitutional Assembly elections held in March 1994. However, the nature of the constraints on FDI is not merely confined to the political development and stability in the country.

5   CONSTRAINTS TO TRADE DIVERSIFICATION

To discuss the constraints to trade diversification may, in the case of Uganda, amount to discussing the constraints to its economic development in general – reflecting the fact that the problems of Uganda primarily relate to reorganizing and restarting productive activities. Nevertheless, a number of constraints concern more specifically trade policy as well as trade promotion, for example those which limit the supply of inputs to trade (such as trade services, transport, including transit through neighbouring countries) and those which relate to the specific nature of international marketing (market access, quality control and certification, standards, labelling and packaging, and so on).

The general constraints to Uganda's economic development, such as the weaknesses of the feeder-road systems, communication infrastructure, and so on, inevitably hamper the development of an export-oriented subsector. For example, while the constraints to expanding horticultural exports are manifold, they include quality and price variables regarding: (i) production at the farm level; (ii) transport, trade and processing, as well as (iii) access to the international markets for the highly-perishable commodities.

Table 10.4 lists the various types of constraints – and hence potential areas for donor support – for developing horticulture.

Table 10.4 Constraints on Uganda's horticultural development

Physical/production	
Farm inputs	Poor-quality farm seeds; no seed certification; limited availability and high prices of fertilizers and pesticides; low-quality planting material used;
Factor inputs	Limited casual labour used, reflecting cash and credit constraint; lack of appropriate farmer's training;
Institutional	
Extension	Integrated pest-management approach not implemented, with resulting high incidence of pests and diseases; no in-service training of extension workers; dynamic extension approach lacking;
Research	Inadequate funding; inadequate dissemination and feedback to farmers; insufficient experimental work; insufficient attention for post-harvest handling; few researchers with relevant experience;
Organizational	Horticultural training virtually absent; fragmented government support and weak coordination between export-promoting bodies;
Infrastructural	
Transport	Absence of feeder roads and so on in many areas; high airfreight costs; no cold chain exists; limited processing capacity;
Trade and market	Quality of fruits and vegetables inadequate for the international market; saturation of the domestic markets during peak supply periods;
Financial	Limited formal credit availability; gender bias against women; limited trade credit availability;
Other	Lack of a comprehensive overall plan for horticultural development.

Source: Netherlands Ministry of Foreign Affairs (1992).

5.1 Financial Aspects

Weaknesses in the present development finance system are, perhaps, the greatest obstacle to the expansion of exports. The present state of the development finance institutions (Development Finance Corporation of Uganda, Uganda Development Bank, East African Development Bank) is all but encouraging. These institutions face the problem of 'bad debts' attributable to mainly imprudent banking practices, but also to unanticipated large devaluations which have reduced the feasibility of import-dependent projects. At present no clear solution has been formulated: debt rescheduling (supported by foreign credits) generates further foreign indebtedness.

The Bank of Uganda operates an export-financing facility (for example, export crop finance) for 'serious' exporters, that is, those with clear expression of interest from foreign buyers. The facility provides US dollar denominated loans for a period of 90 to 180 days (in exceptional cases up to a year). Interest rates are linked to the international US dollar rate of interest, which was 9 per cent at end of 1992. The facility was designed as a revolving fund with an initial capital grant of $2 million. The size of the facility is perceived to be vastly insufficient, even though other banks such as the Ugandan Commercial Bank have started to operate similar export finance windows.

5.2 Obstacles to FDI

The main obstacles to foreign investment are the weakness of infrastructure as well as ingrained inefficiencies in the regulatory framework. The perceived or actual lack of transparency and uniformity in regulatory measures include, for example, the present system of high import duties, coupled with a high incidence of exemptions granted on a case-by-case basis. These are perceived to jeopardize a level playing field between new entrants and well-established entrepreneurs. The position of parastatals, which have been allowed to function without proper financial, auditing and budget control, within the commercial sector, reinforces the perception of unequal market access and operating conditions. Finally, land tenure for foreign nationals is not secure, restricting investment interests in large-scale commercial farming.

According to investors interviewed, the constraints on implementing planned projects related to the access to, and availability of, land, especially for greenfield investment, scarce and expensive warehousing facilities, and difficulties of securing medium- and long-term investment finance (see UIA 1994). Another survey of foreign investors' perceptions carried out in 1993 confirmed the above points and added:

1. the erratic nature of government policies and regulations;
2. the slow privatization and divestiture policy;

3. administrative delays; and
4. low labour productivity in comparison to Kenya or India (The Services Group 1993).

5.3 Demographic and Labour Market Constraints

One of the binding constraints to trade diversification will be the limited availability of trained and experienced personnel. The main cause is the weakness of educational policies, but pressure is heightened by the impact of acquired immune deficiency syndrome (AIDS). The high incidence of AIDS in Uganda is likely to lead to major social, economic and demographic changes (see Barnett and Blaikie 1992). The economic cost could be significant, in particular through its effects on the labour markets,[21] and may have important implications for agriculture, which is labour intensive.

5.4 Human-resource Development

Removing the human-resource constraint will depend to a considerable extent on improved education.[22] The problem areas of Uganda's educational system include continued illiteracy, high dropout rates at almost all levels, shortage of qualified teachers, and a widening gap between educational preparation and actual employment opportunities (see Uganda National Commission for UNESCO 1992). In 1992, for example, out of 940 faculty posts in Makerere University, only 68 per cent were filled; and of 64 posts for commerce and economics faculties, 67 per cent were filled. The limited availability of business and related skills in the country remains a constraint in accessing international markets.

5.5 Infrastructure

The key infrastructural constraints of Uganda are manifold and are known to include:

1. poor, sparse and costly internal road transport network;
2. poor railway facilities and the lack of containerization of its traffic;
3. the lack of a nation-wide cold-storage chain;
4. the lack of organized access to airfreight capacity and airport services;
5. poor and costly telecommunication facilities;
6. insufficient wholesale market facilities; and
7. erratic utility supply, especially water and electricity.

A network of macadamized roads connects Tororo near the Kenyan border to Jinja and Kampala and the west of the country bordering Zaire as well as the southern border with Tanzania. However, roads in the other parts of the country are not paved. The railway system is characterized by extremely low density (5 km./100km.[2]) (UNCTAD 1993c:39). However, Uganda's railway fleet has been upgraded in the recent past, and it is estimated that as much as 50 per cent of total traffic is moved by rail, though road transport is expected to increase as a result of road rehabilitation (World Bank 1990:31, 54).

Uganda's low share of exports in GDP is attributable, in part, to its position as a landlocked country. As in other landlocked countries, the costs and risks of transit tend to reduce volume and value of exports, while inflating import costs. In 1986, for example, Uganda was spending an equivalent of 41 per cent of the total value of exports for transport payments (UNCTAD 1992c Table 12).[23]

Transit-cost disadvantages tend to deter exports and hamper the development of new export goods; moreover, foreign investors are observed to be more reluctant to invest in landlocked countries.

5.6   Transit Administration

Transit trade has remained cumbersome, unreliable and costly. Diversifying risks and lowering costs of transit trade would require exploring or rehabilitating additional rail connections, for example, the Kampala–Kasese line within Uganda or the Musoma–Tanga line which would serve cargo transport across Lake Victoria. However, feasibility studies appear to indicate a low financial return as well as environmental damage (World Bank 1990). Nevertheless, upgrading the transport and transit networks is a prerequisite to accommodating intensified trade flows, both to overseas destinations, as well as to neighbouring countries.

6   CONCLUSIONS

The rehabilitation of the Ugandan economy has been characterized by bold and innovative macroeconomic reform and management. There are signs that these are beginning to yield results for the export sector. They include the slowing down of inflation and the steadying of the exchange rate, the easy availability of foreign exchange and, most importantly, the net inflow of new and returning investment. With respect to the export sector, some limited diversification has materialized in recent years and numerous pipeline activities give some grounds for export optimism; some diversification is taking place in the face of falling coffee export receipts.

The major constraint to reducing the persistent anti-export bias in taxes and tariff policies is the dependence of the recurrent revenue budget on customs duties. This problem is not likely to be 'solved' through further public expenditure reduction – it will require domestic-resource mobilization through tax reform and improved collection systems. Specialized technical assistance in this area may prove useful. International measures to assist in dealing with the public deficit will inevitably include debt rescheduling to reduce interest payments.

The incentives for exports, which were steadily eroded during the war and civil unrest, are being improved through microeconomic reforms such as scrapping public monopsonies and extensive implicit subsidies. Areas which will require further improvement relate primarily to the arena of commercial policy. Lowering import tariffs, while reducing exemptions, will help to create a level playing field between importers and domestic producers/exporters as well as between new and established firms. Such tariff changes could be designed to be budget revenue neutral in the initial years, pending improved revenue collection from non-trade taxes. Specific support for exports by the government would include export market information services as well as streamlining the cumbersome duty-drawback system. General support would focus on the extensive infrastructural improvements as identified in the export-diversification plan.

NOTES

1. The author would like to express his gratitude to R.H. Kajuka, Minister of Trade and Industry, B. Suruma, then Deputy Governor of the Bank of Uganda, Tedla Teshome, UNDP Resident Representative, Wilson Kwamya, UNDP Programme Officer, Margaret Temywa, Senior Commercial Officer and B.D. Jayal, Senior Adviser on Trade Policy, Ministry of Trade and Industry. Comments by Chandra Patel and Gabriele Köhler, LDC Division, UNCTAD and Mark Henstridge, Centre for the Study of African Economies, University of Oxford, on earlier drafts were helpful.
2. This government includes representation of former political parties as well as of the National Resistance Movement (NRM) led by Museveni. A constitutional committee defining the powers and functioning of the parliament reported in autumn 1993 and has laid down the principles for elections scheduled for 1994.
3. The GDP growth for the post-war years was revised upwards by 0.3 to 0.9 per cent per annum; over the ten-year period 1981–90 the upward revision amounted to some 15 per cent. The principal reason for the revision was the prevalence of the 'black markets' for goods as well as foreign exchange, reflecting administered 'official' prices. Sales at the official prices implied income transfers from the government to the consumer; these were not previously incorporated in the estimates of domestic production.
4. The Structural Adjustment Credit I (SAC I) which consisted of two tranches, approved in December 1991 and March 1993, had similar macroeconomic policy objectives: (i) easing trade restrictions; (ii) promoting investment; (iii) resolving departed Asians' property claims; (iv) improving revenue collection; (v) focus public expenditure on social priorities; and (vi) adopting civil service reform.
5. Restoring property rights to departed Asians has been a slow and contentious process, plagued by many legal difficulties. A recent announcement of the government has stated that all Asian property claims must be filed by October 1993 or title is forfeited. This may facilitate the process of privatization which to date has been hampered by the fact that the titles to public assets proved contestable.

6. The debt service flows for Uganda, as of September 1993, for the fiscal year 1993–94 on account of maturities payable by the government are calculated as US$110.5 million, consisting of interest of $33.7 million and principal of $76.8 million; this may prove to be as much as the total annual export earnings in the same year. Of the total payments, $64.2 million is owed to multilateral organizations.

7. The introduction of the custom's database system ASYCUDA is expected to improve collection of revenues from import duties. With the setting up of the Uganda Revenue Authority (URA) in 1991 to improve collection of taxes, total revenue in fiscal year 1992–93 reached 8.1 per cent of GDP, but this is lower than for any country in Sub-Saharan Africa for which comparable data are available (see World Bank 1992c).

8. The Bank of Uganda describes imports on a cash basis only and excludes imports financed through external loans and grants or private foreign exchange. The Bank also estimates aggregate imports in order to prepare the balance of trade. The Customs and Excise Department compiles another import estimate based on the recorded entry of goods. The total import value as per the Customs and Excise Department is considerably below the balance-of-payments estimate. Nevertheless, the estimate of import on cash basis will include some goods unrecorded by customs, in particular the so called 'suitcase' trade from Dubai.

9. Defined as the percentage with which Uganda's domestic price exceeds the international price for the same good. This is the unweighted average of 34 industrial items of which 10 had a nominal protection rate of zero. These results are tentative, because of the complexity of the system of tariffs and exemptions and the continuous changes in the system.

10. Defined as the percentage of increase of value added due to taxes and subsidies. (Unweighted average for 23 industrial production processes.)

11. Uganda's Agricultural Sector Memorandum carefully considers agricultural potential and constraints and distinguishes between a short-term export-oriented strategy and a medium-term strategy which includes actions on a broad range of production and institutional issues (World Bank 1992a).

12. Total world coffee production in 1991 stood at 101,159 thousand bags (of 60 kg.); this was an increase of 19.2 per cent over the 1979–81 average world production. In the same year, Africa's production stood at 19,463 thousand bags which was virtually identical to the 1979–81 level. This implied a reduction of its market share from 22.95 per cent in 1979–81 to 19.24 per cent by 1991 (World Bank 1992b).

13. For example, in 1991 the Mabaka Union attempted to force smallholders to accept a price of USh 170 per kg. of coffee, while private traders were in the market for USh 210 per kg. Farmers refused to sell to the Union and did not yield to any coercion.

14. The gross margin is defined as the value of output per hectare of cotton, using average yields and hand hoe technology, minus the value of material inputs. The gross margin is divided by the number of person days needed for the cultivation; it therefore includes an implicit allowance for land rents.

15. More than 90 per cent of the on-farm costs of growing cotton using traditional technology are local (for example, hired and family labour and transport services and so on); for the off-farm costs, some 50 to 60 per cent of them are local.

16. The distinction of traditional and non-traditional exports refers to the historical pattern of exports, rather than the type of good or the process through which it is produced.

17. For example, the Queen Elizabeth National Park, gazetted in 1952, combines lake, swamp, grassland, wooded savannah and forest. It is the home to elephants (estimated at 550, down from 3,000 in the early 1970s), wild game (for example, tree hyraxes, ant-bears, black buffaloes, waterbuck, Ugandan kob, topi, bushbuck, sitatunga and reedbuck) and the hippopotamus (some 4,000 in the Kazinga Channel alone), varied bird colonies and lake fish.

18. Ministry of Tourism, Wildlife and Antiquities (1992).

19. This should be regarded as a preliminary and very optimistic estimate. Moreover, it should be noted that the fixed capital formation component of the project approved will be approximately one-quarter of the investment outlay.

20. Personal communication of the mission with officials of the Uganda Investment Authority (UIA), December 1992.
21. Barnett and Blaikie (1992) note the sequence of loss of income-earning opportunities, the diversion of productive labour time to care for the sick, diversion of cash to medical expenses and at a later stage funeral expenses, withdrawal of children from school and additional orphans to care for within the household. See also UNCTAD (1994).
22. Recent educational statistics indicate that the number of primary schools increased over the 1985–91 period from seven to eight thousand and the enrolment expanded by some 400,000 pupils during this period. Recurrent expenditure by the Education Ministry has, in recent years, been the second largest after defence.
23. Only Malawi and Chad were worse off in terms of this ratio of transport payments to export value.

REFERENCES

Barnett, T. and P. Blaikie (1992), *AIDS in Africa*, London: Belhaven.
Bigsten, A. and S. Kayizzi-Mugerwa (1992), 'Adaptation and Distress in the Urban Economy: A Study of Kampala Households', *World Development*, vol. 20, no. 10, pp. 1423–41.
Directorate of Civil Aviation (1990), *AIR Uganda*, Fal3–3, Kampala: Civil Aviation Authority.
Edroma, E. (1992), 'Tourism Industry: Communication, Information and Education', *Uganda Travel and Tourism*, vol. 2, no. 2, Kampala.
EPADU (1991), *Export Strategy, Government Policy and Non-traditional Exports – Analysis and Recommendations for Action*, Kampala: Export Promotion and Development Unit.
Evans, A. (1992), 'A Review of the Rural Labour Market in Uganda', mimeo, School of Oriental and Asian Studies, University of Sussex.
General Agreement on Tariffs and Trade (GATT) (1993), *Multilateral Trade Negotiations The Uruguay Round: Communications from the Republic of Uganda*, MTN.GNG/MA/W/23 and MTN.GNS/W/193, Geneva: GATT.
Henstridge, M. (1993a), 'Stabilization and Structural Adjustment Policy in Uganda: 1987–1990', in W. van der Geest (ed.) (1993), *Negotiating Structural Adjustment in Africa*, pp. 47–68, London: James Currey Ltd.
Henstridge, M. (1993b), 'The Appraisal of the SACII for Uganda', mimeo, Centre for African Studies, University of Oxford for the Directorate General for International Cooperation/Ministry of Foreign Affairs, The Hague.
International Monetary Fund (IMF) (1994), *IMF Survey*, 24 January, Washington, DC: IMF.
International Monetary Fund (IMF), *Direction of Trade Statistics Yearbook*, various years, Washington, DC: IMF.
Ministry of Commerce, Cooperatives and Marketing (MCCM) (1991), *Exporters and Importers Guide*, Kampala: MCCM.
Ministry of Commerce, Industry and Cooperation (MCIC) (1992), *Background Information Paper on Export Diversification Plan 1992/93–1996/97–2002*, Kampala: MCIC.

Ministry of Finance and Economic Planning (MFEP) (1991a), 'Gross Domestic Product Uganda 1981–1990', Statistics Department, *Statistical Bulletin*, no. GDP/3, Entebbe: Statistics Department.

Ministry of Finance and Economic Planning (MFEP) (1991b), 'Index of Industrial Production', Statistics Department, *Statistical Bulletin*, no. IP/14, Entebbe: Statistics Department.

Ministry of Finance and Economic Planning (MFEP) (1991c), *External Trade Statistics of Uganda, Exports 1990*, Statistics Department, Entebbe: Statistics Department.

Ministry of Finance and Economic Planning (MFEP) (1992a), *Background to the Budget 1992–1993, Economic Performance 1991–92 and Prospects for 1992–93*, Kampala: MFEP.

Ministry of Finance and Economic Planning (MFEP) (1992b), *Rehabilitation and Development Plan 1991/92–1994/95*, Vols. I and II, Kampala: MFEP.

Ministry of Finance and Economic Planning (MFEP) (1992c), *The Way Forward I, Macroeconomic Strategy 1990–1995 and The Way Forward II, Medium Term Sectoral Strategy 1990–1995*, Kampala: MFEP.

Ministry of Finance and Economic Planning (MFEP) (1992d), 'Consumer Price Index Kampala', Statistics Department, *Statistical Bulletin*, no. CPI/2, Entebbe: Statistics Department.

Ministry of Finance and Economic Planning (MFEP) (1992e), *Key Economic Indicators*, 11th Issue, October, Statistics Department, Entebbe: Statistics Department.

Ministry of Finance and Economic Planning (MFEP) (1992f), *Final Results of the 1991 Population and Housing Census (pre-release)*, Statistics Department, Entebbe: Statistics Department.

Ministry of Finance and Economic Planning (MFEP) (1993a), *Background to the Budget 1993–1994, Economic Performance 1992–1993 and Prospects for 1993–1994*, Kampala: MFEP.

Ministry of Finance and Economic Planning (MFEP) (1993b), 'Imports and Exports, Uganda 1981–1992', *Statistical Bulletin*, No. Ext–1, Entebbe. Statistics Department.

Ministry of Finance and Economic Planning (MFEP) (1993c), *Key Economic Indicators*, 12th issue, October, Statistics Department, Entebbe: Statistics Department.

Ministry of Planning and Economic Development (MPED) (1985), *Background to the Budget*, Kampala: MFEP.

Ministry of Planning and Economic Development (MPED) (1989), *Background to the Budget*, Kampala: MFEP.

Ministry of Planning and Economic Development (MPED) (1990), *Background to the Budget*, Kampala: MFEP.

Ministry of Tourism, Wildlife and Antiquities (1992), *Uganda Travel and Tourism*, vol. 2, no. 2, Kampala: MTWA.

Netherlands Ministry of Foreign Affairs/Directorate General for International Cooperation (1992), *Horticultural Sector Support Mission*, The Hague: DGIC.

The New Vision, Kampala, various issues.

The Services Group (1993), 'Uganda Foreign Investment Survey for Export Development', draft report, Arlington, Virginia.

Tourism Consultancy Services (1992), *Tourist and Road Map of Uganda*, Kampala: TCS.

Uganda Investment Authority (UIA) (1992), 'Status Report on Progress with Investment Projects', mimeo, Kampala: UIA.

Uganda Investment Authority (UIA) (1993), 'Study of the Effectiveness of Policies, Facilities and Incentives for Investment Promotion (summary of the final report)', mimeo, Kampala: UIA.

Uganda Investment Authority (UIA) (1994), 'Investment Status Report July 1991–December 1993', mimeo, Kampala: UIA.

Uganda National Commission for UNESCO (1992), 'The Development of Education – Uganda 1990–1992', a report of the 43rd Session of the International Conference on Education, Geneva, 14–19 September, mimeo, Kampala/Geneva: UNESCO.

UNDP (1991), *Development Cooperation Uganda 1990 Report*, Kampala: UNDP.

UNCTAD (1992a), *Diversification of Trade in the Least Developed Countries*, UNCTAD /LDC/2, Geneva: United Nations.

UNCTAD (1992b), *The Least Developed Countries 1991 Report*, New York: United Nations.

UNCTAD (1992c), *Transit Systems for Land-locked Developing Countries: Current Situation and Proposals for Future Action*, Meeting of Governmental Experts from Developing Countries and Representatives of Donor Countries and Financial and Development Institutions, TD/B/LDC/AC.1/2, New York: United Nations.

UNCTAD (1993a), *The Least Developed Countries 1992 Report*, New York: United Nations.

UNCTAD (1993b), *Handbook of International Trade and Development Statistics 1992*, New York: United Nations.

UNCTAD (1994), *The Least Developed Countries 1993–1994 Report*, New York: United Nations.

World Bank (1990), *The Great Lakes Corridor Study*, Africa Technical Department/ PTA Transport and Communications Division, Washington, DC: World Bank.

World Bank (1991a), *Report and Recommendation of the President of the International Development Association to the Executive Directors*, Report no. P–5670–UG, Washington, DC: World Bank.

World Bank (1991b), *Uganda Transport Sector Memorandum: Sustainable Development and Maintenance Priorities for the 1990s*, Report no. 9364–UG, vols I and II, Washington, DC: World Bank.

World Bank (1992a), *Uganda Agricultural Sector Memorandum*, Report no. 10715– UG, Washington, DC: World Bank.

World Bank (1992b), *Market Outlook for Major Primary Commodities*, vols I and II, Report no. 814/92, International Trade Division, Washington, DC: World Bank.

World Bank (1992c), *1992 World Development Report*, Washington, DC: World Bank.

11. The Uruguay Round, trade diversification and the LDCs[1]

Samuel Gayi[2]

---

1 BACKGROUND

The Uruguay Round (UR) of multilateral trade negotiations, which was success-fully concluded with the signing of the Final Act in April 1994, is by all reckoning a historic event. It was the longest trade negotiation ever to be undertaken, having been inaugurated in 1986, and it recorded the highest number of developing-country participants, who, to some extent, influenced its agenda.[3] Moreover, unlike the previous seven GATT rounds of negotiations, it had a broader agenda covering new areas such as services, intellectual property rights (IPRs) and investment measures, while setting out for the first time a programme for agricultural trade liberalization and the full integration of the trade in textiles and clothing within the GATT framework of rules.

Long before the UR was concluded, it was hailed by experts as a momentous event that would usher in a new phase in international economic and trade relations: a multilateral trading system capable of generating enormous welfare benefits for all countries – developed, developing and the least developed – which include the unprecedented growth of world trade and long-term effic-iency gains. Despite the benefits suggested by some studies, it has also been noted that these will not be evenly distributed among countries. Indeed, the Ministers at the Marrakesh Ministerial Meeting acknowledged possible welfare losses for some poor African countries.

This chapter reviews the effects of the UR on LDCs;[4] in particular it exam-ines the consequences the UR may have for the trade-diversification potential of LDCs. It also discusses the policy options available to LDCs in their attempts to maximize net benefits from the UR: how can LDCs cope with the difficulties that may arise from the implementation of Uruguay Round agreements, and effectively utilize the opportunities? What support measures can the internat-ional community provide to facilitate the adjustment and structural changes required in LDCs to enable them to withstand increasing competition in, and take advantage of the opportunities offered by, the new multilateral trading environment?

A discussion of this nature requires two caveats. First, there is still a lack of clarity on some issues that prevent an unambiguous statement of specific effects.[5] Nevertheless, it is very likely that, whatever the anticipated long-term gains, the UR entails transitional costs for poor countries, including LDCs. Second, given the different trade patterns and configuration of LDC exports and imports, the wide range of issues covered by the UR and the sheer diversity of the LDC grouping, any conclusion reached from an a priori assessment of its overall impact should be treated with some caution.

1.1 Main Features of the Uruguay Round[6]

The key features of the Round include, first, the establishment of the World Trade Organization (WTO), to provide a common institutional framework for the conduct of trade relations among its members in respect of all the agreements and arrangements concluded under its auspices, including the entire results of the Uruguay Round. Second, tariffs on manufactures have been reduced on average by more than one-third. Third, with the gradual phasing out of the Multi-fibre Arrangement (MFA) and voluntary export restraints (VERs), non-tariff measures (NTMs) have been rolled back to a considerable extent. Fourth, an integrated dispute-settlement mechanism has been established, underpinned by more transparent and stronger rules, to apply to all multilateral trade agreements annexed to the agreement establishing the WTO. Fifth, the principle of differential and more-favourable treatment has been built into the various agreements in recognition of the special developmental, financial and trade needs of developing countries and the least developed among them.

Specific features of the UR include the following:

Special and differential treatment

Special and differential (S and D) treatment for LDCs has been incorporated into the various provisions of the multilateral trade agreements and in the 'Decision on Measures in Favour of LDCs' annexed to the Final Act. In the latter Decision it is agreed, for example, that:

> [I]f not already provided for in the instruments negotiated in the course of the Uruguay Round, notwithstanding their acceptance of these instruments the least developed countries, and for so long as they remain in that category, while complying with the general rules set out in the aforesaid instruments, will only be required to undertake commitments and concessions to the extent consistent with their individual development, financial and trade needs or their administrative and institutional capabilities. (para. 1)

The rules set out in the various agreements and instruments and the transitional provisions in the Uruguay Round should be applied in a flexible and supportive manner for the least developed countries. (para. 2 (iii))

[T]o keep under review the least developed countries and to continue to seek the adoption of positive measures which facilitate the expansion of their trading opportunities. (para. 3)

Agriculture

The UR aimed at achieving greater liberalization of international trade in agriculture, first by restricting the use of all direct and indirect subsidies to agriculture, second, by seeking reduction in export subsidies, and third, by reducing import barriers. Non-tariff measures (NTMs), including quantitative restrictions, are to be replaced with tariffs providing approximately the same level of protection. Tariffs resulting from this 'tariffication' process, together with other existing tariffs on agricultural products,[7] are to be reduced by unweighted average of 36 per cent over six years (1995–2000), by the developed market-economy countries (DMECs) and 24 per cent over 10 years (1995–2004), by developing countries (DCs). While LDCs are also required to tariffy NTMs and bind their tariffs, they are exempt from all reduction obligations applicable to other countries.

Textiles and clothing

The agreement in this sector is to progressively dismantle the quota system under the MFA and to fully integrate trade in textiles and clothing into GATT over a 10-year period starting from 1995. This is to be accompanied by increased growth rates in quotas and the gradual integration of products with recourse to a transitional safeguard for those products under restraint but not yet integrated into GATT.

TRIPs and TRIMs

The agreement on trade-related aspects of intellectual property rights (TRIPs) creates minimum common international standards for the protection of patents, copyrights, trade marks, industrial designs, geographical indications, integrated circuits and undisclosed information (trade secrets), and extends patent protection to 'processes' in addition to products. This increases current protection levels of intellectual property rights to fields of technology or areas not covered at present in LDCs. The agreement on trade-related investment measures (TRIMs) clarifies and strengthens existing GATT rules in respect of trade-distorting or trade-restrictive investment measures which are inconsistent with the GATT provisions on national treatment and on general elimination of quantitative restrictions.

Services

The General Agreement on Trade in Services (GATS) establishes a multilateral framework of principles and rules to govern global trade in commercial services. GATS has universal coverage and includes a comprehensive definition of trade in services covering four 'modes of supply' through: cross-border movement, movement of consumers, commercial presence and the presence of natural persons. It embodies commitments to general obligations by all WTO members which include, *inter alia*, the non-discriminatory application of the most-favoured-nation (MFN) principle, transparency of measures affecting trade in services and increasing participation of developing countries in trade in services. While the general obligations apply to all services, obligations relating to market access and national treatment apply only to those services included in the national schedule of commitments allowing members to apply specific conditions. It provides a framework for progressive liberalization of trade in services in future negotiations.

Multilateral trade rules

These rules have been strengthened and made more transparent, particularly in the areas of dispute settlement, anti-dumping, subsidies, balance-of-payments provisions, customs valuation, rules of origin, and so on.

World Trade Organization

The WTO is charged with strengthening the rule of law governing international trade, and ensuring its application through an effective dispute-settlement mechanism.

The main features of the UR and implications for DCs are summarized in Table 11.1.

2 POSSIBLE IMPLICATIONS

The available evidence (see, for example, GATT 1994a; Page and Davenport 1994; UNCTAD 1994a; Weston 1994, 1995; and World Bank 1995)[8] suggests that, in general, the global impact of the UR will be positive. The expected benefits include: a stable, secure and predictable trading system brought about by more transparent multilateral rules and disciplines and higher levels of tariff binding; higher global economic growth that will increase demand for DC and LDC commodity exports; and longer-term efficiency gains for DCs and LDCs due to competition engendered by increased liberalization.

The extent to which individual countries or different regions of the world share in these benefits will depend on their level of development defined by the pattern of, and participation in, international trade.

*Table 11.1 Summary of effects of some Uruguay Round agreements on
developing countries**

Main features of agreement	Implications for developing countries
1. Agriculture: decisions in three areas limit agricultural policies; (i) export subsidies reduced; (ii) domestic support restrained; (iii) border measures 'tariffied'.	Improved access for agricultural exporters, but: (i) concerns over uneven product coverage (sugar meats); (ii) agricultural net importers fear losses from higher prices.
2. Textiles and apparel: 10-year phase-out of MFA with elevated growth rates in quotas, sequential elimination of product coverage, but with temporary selective safeguards.	Potentially major gains to developing countries in area of prominent trade interest, but: (i) concern that adjustment in industrial countries concentrated in later years; (ii) concern over potential replacement by protective regime (anti-dumping); (iii) concerns of many countries that they will be un-competitive against other suppliers and will lose.
3. Tariffs and grey-area measures (VERs): tariffs to be cut by a comparable percentage to Kennedy and Tokyo rounds. VERs measures to be phased out (specifics of how not yet clear).	Tariff cuts will improve developing-country access, but: (i) will likely be small in areas of special developing country interest (textiles and apparel); (ii) tariffs already low (except apparel) in most developed countries; (iii) African countries concerned over erosion of margin of preferences under the Lomé Convention.
4. Services: broad principles agreed with sectoral exceptions and conditionality (MFN). Market access and national treatment embodied, with access commitments tabled.	Relatively few specific concessions tabled at this stage, which is more likely to prove the beginning of a process towards liberalization, rather than substantive liberalization in its own right.
5. Intellectual property: establishment of broad international minimum standards of protection in the three areas of patents, trademarks, copyright. Disputes to be settled under the integrated dispute-settlement body under the WTO.	Many developing countries had already moved close to the minimum standards, in part due to prior bilateral pressures. Key issues are in the pharmaceutical sector.
6. Dispute settlement: firm time limits over the stages of the dispute process, and the need for a consensus to reject a panel report strengthening the process.	Strengthened procedures in the interests of smaller countries bringing complaints against larger countries.
7. WTO: the world trade body established to give permanence to GATT. Two features are that: (i) countries acceding to WTO must accept all decisions in the Round as a package (unlike the Tokyo Round codes); (ii) acceding countries agree to be bound by an integrated dispute-settlement process covering the three areas of goods, services and investment.	Absence of menu choice in selecting which UR decisions to sign on to concerns some countries, as does the integrated dispute process. Some countries reportedly considered remaining as GATT Contracting Parties, rather than acceding to the WTO prior to the Marrakesh Ministerial Meeting.

Note: * Implications for LDCs are the same as for developing countries, but LDCs may fare worse than them in some cases, as discussed in the text.

Source: Hamilton and Whalley (1995:35–6).

In the developing world, a group of Asian countries, notably the newly industrializing economies (NIEs), have emerged as the 'growth pole' of the world and have rapidly altered their export baskets towards manufactures, as well as increased their participation in world trade. In contrast, the majority of DCs, in particular the LDCs, have seen their economic fortunes recede with increasing globalization and liberalization.

The share of LDC exports in world trade, which was about 0.7 per cent in 1975, has declined consistently since then. In 1992, only three LDCs, namely, Bangladesh, Botswana and Zambia, recorded exports above $1.0 billion (UNCTAD 1995d:5).

DC exports are biased towards primary commodities, mainly natural-resource-based and tropical agricultural products. These exports made up 70 per cent of total exports in 1992, with manufactures accounting for 30 per cent for LDCs. For DMECs, primary commodities accounted for 20 per cent of total exports, and manufactured goods for 80 per cent. The LDCs have lost substantial market shares in commodity trade over the past two decades: the value of LDCs' commodity exports in world-commodity trade decreased from 4.7 per cent (1970–72) to 1.4 per cent (1990–92) (UNCTAD 1995e:Table 3), *despite* the preferential treatment they enjoyed. Manufactured products, mainly garments, featured in the exports of a few LDCs: Bangladesh, Haiti, Lesotho and the Maldives (UNCTAD 1995d:5). Even for these countries, the share of manufactured products in total exports exaggerate the value added because of the high import content of such products.

Coupled with the above, LDCs are highly dependent on imports, not only of capital goods, but also of food. Net imports of major food items (cereals, edible oils and dairy products) were equivalent to 25 per cent of the total export earnings of LDCs in 1992; and the share of food items in the total imports of 27 LDCs is more than 20 per cent, higher than for any other group of countries (UNCTAD 1995d:5–6).

Evaluations of the impact of the UR within this context suggest that the new trading system it engenders entails transitional costs for LDCs, although the level and timing of such costs are in dispute. While much of the costs are estimated to be immediate, the benefits would accrue to the majority of LDCs in the long run, and, in part, depend on what policy adjustments are made by these countries in the short to medium run to improve their supply capabilities and efficiency of production in order to enhance their participation in world trade.

A number of studies suggest that the UR would result in substantial income gains for DMECs, in particular through a higher level of demand for textiles and agricultural products as restrictions are reduced (for example, Hamilton and Whalley 1995; Hoekman 1989; UNCTAD 1995d; Weston 1995). Among DCs, the East Asian economies are expected to be net beneficiaries, while income losses are forecast for Africa and South Asia, and the prognosis for Latin America is ambiguous.[9]

Overall, the anticipated costs of the UR centre around three areas. First, preference erosion, that is the diminution of trade-preference margins following the reductions in MFN tariffs. Second, there is the possibility of higher prices for food, and other critical imports, like pharmaceuticals and technology because of the agreements on agriculture and TRIPs. Third, costs are associated with compliance with notification requirements, policing the TRIPs agreement and increased participation in WTO activities.

Continuing the discussion, we first examine the likely implications of the UR for LDCs by discussing each of these issues. Second, we explore the effects the UR may have for the trade-diversification potential of LDCs.

2.1 Anticipated Effects of the Uruguay Round on LDCs

Preference erosion

One major concern for LDCs, especially African LDCs, is the erosion of the margin of preferences they enjoyed under the generalized system of preferences (GSP) or Lomé Convention, and its ramification for their competitiveness.[10]

Regarding tropical agricultural and natural-resource-based export items,[11] trade liberalization could entail some loss for LDCs in the short run. They are unlikely to benefit from the expected trade-creation effect, because of the low short-term supply elasticity of some of these products, for example, tropical beverages; and they may suffer from trade diversion due to erosion of their existing preferential margins. However, in the long run, it may be possible for LDCs with an agricultural potential to increase foreign-exchange earnings by expanding agricultural exports.

Textiles and garments are of substantial export interest to one-third of developing countries (GATT 1993). The domestic value added of these products is low because of a high import content, but they have provided the impetus to industrialization in some LDCs. The sector is particularly important to Bangladesh, Cambodia, the Lao PDR, Lesotho and Nepal, which face MFA and MFA-type restrictions in the Canadian and United States markets (and, in the case of Bangladesh, in the European Union (EU) market as well). Haiti also faces these restrictions in the United States market. To a minor extent, cotton yarn and fabrics feature in the export baskets of several African LDCs.

The phasing-out of the MFA and its associated tariff reductions, the provision for increased growth rates of MFA quotas and the improvement in the application of the flexibility provisions may expand, in the medium term, export opportunities for WTO-member LDCs – Bangladesh, Haiti, the Maldives and Lesotho. Consequently, current market shares of non-WTO LDC members – Cambodia, the Lao PDR and Nepal – may be threatened (UNCTAD 1995d:11). Intensified competition in export markets may lead to a loss of market share by some LDCs to more-developed DCs with stronger industrial bases, particularly in Asia (for example, China, India, Indonesia, Pakistan and Sri Lanka) but also in Latin America. It is projected, for example, that Africa's apparel output will increase by only 30 per cent, instead of 110 per cent, barring any change in the MFA, over the 10-year period (Hertel et al. 1995:22–3, cited in Weston 1995:10).

Competition may also increase among potential host countries for textiles and garment-related foreign investment and technology to the disadvantage of some LDCs which lack infrastructural and institutional preconditions critical for increasing FDI inflows.

On a trade-weighted basis, the overall loss of preference margins for all LDC products covered by preferences is about 8 percentage points for Canada, 3 points in the EU and Japan, and 2 points in the United States (UNCTAD 1995d:9).[12]

The extent of the loss of preference margins and its effects on the competitiveness of LDCs' exports depends on the rate of utilization of such preferences. If, as suggested by various UNCTAD studies, the rate of utilization of preferences was low (see Section 3.2 for the reasons), then the effects of preference erosion on LDC exports would seem to have been exaggerated. The possible preference erosion for some LDCs under the Lomé Convention on agricultural products such as sugar, cut flowers, vegetables and fruits, and beef, may also be limited as the liberalization attained for these products and others, of export interest to some LDCs, is restricted under the agricultural agreement.

In summary, the UR holds the prospect for increased participation of LDCs in global trade provided that they can overcome critical supply-side constraints to become competitive in international markets (see below). First, there may be the potential for increased exports from LDCs as a result of higher world demand. Second, the binding of MFN-tariff reductions, and to a lesser extent, the tariffication of NTMs by making NTMs more transparent, may enhance LDC market access.

Escalation in the prices of critical imports

For food items, studies have indicated that trade liberalization will inevitably result in higher world prices that will hurt food-deficit countries (for example, some LDCs), while food-surplus countries (for example, OECD countries) will gain. The possible negative impact of higher food prices for food-deficit countries was acknowledged by the Ministerial Decision at Marrakesh, but there was a dispute over the magnitude of price increases, and therefore losses to net food-importing countries.[13]

Countries with comparative advantage in agricultural production will gain in the long run from increased exports and better terms of trade. Cereals like wheat, rice and coarse grains for which protection and subsidies in the OECD countries were significant, are likely to cost more because of the possible effects of the three reduction commitments of the agricultural agreement on demand

and supply: the quantity of these products 'dumped' on the world market at subsidized prices will be reduced and DMECs' imports of these goods will increase (UNCTAD 1995d:12).

FAO estimates indicate 11 per cent (or $0.5 billion) of the projected increase of $4.5 billion in the food-import bill of Africa between 1987–89 and the year 2000 will be accounted for by the effects of the UR (Weston 1995:16).[14] Projections by UNCTAD show that if the UR agreement on agriculture is fully implemented, LDC overall trade deficits could worsen annually by between $300 and 600 million or by about 2.6 to 5.0 per cent of export earnings, amounting to $3 billion over a five-year period (UNCTAD 1995d:14). For the effect of the UR on the prices of selected commodities, see Table 11.2.

Table 11.2 Effect of the Uruguay Round implementation on world food prices by the year 2000 (percentage change)

Commodity[a]	FAO[b]	UNCTAD[c] (1)[d]	(2)[e]	OECD/WB[f]
Wheat	7.0	8.6	3.2	6.6
Rice	7.0	9.6	0.7	1.3
Maize	4.0	–	–	–
Millet/sorghum	4.0	–	–	–
Other grains	7.0	–	–	–
Coarse grains	–	9.0	2.9	3.3
Oil–seeds	–	7.7	3.8	–
Vegetable oils	–	5.9	2.5	4.6
Fats and oils	4.0	–	–	–
Beef	8.0	10.1	5.3	2.3
Pork	10.0	6.3	2.7	0.6[g]
Lamb	10.0	10.2	5.5	2.3
Poultry	8.0	9.3	4.9	0.6[g]
Dairy products	–	7.9	4.5	2.5
Milk	7.0	–	–	–
Sugar	–	11.3	4.5	3.0
Weighted average	6.6	8.6	3.8	3.3

Notes:
a. The three institutions adopted slightly different definitions for commodities, for example, FAO's 'other grains' includes 'coarse grains'.
b. FAO data taken from FAO document CCP:95/13, January 1995.
c. Revised figures from UNCTAD, 1995f, which are different from those in the original source, UNCTAD (1995e).
d. Assumes no price response in non-OECD countries to changes in world-market prices.
e. Assumes a price response in non-OECD countries.
f. OECD/World Bank's scenario allows for unemployment.
g. Other meats.

Source: UNCTAD (1995e, Add. 1, Table 11, p. 15).

Thus, the implication for LDCs of the UR agricultural agreement is the possibility of increases in their food-import bills which will impair their capacity to devote scarce resources to other areas of economic development. For example, during 1990–93, LDCs spent almost 40 per cent of their total export earnings on food imports (that is, about 4 per cent of GDP) (Table 11.3a and b).

Nevertheless, there are some uncertainties about the net effects of the agricultural agreement contained in the Final Act, especially as the effects will be partly dependent upon the pace of agricultural liberalization in the OECD countries.[15] There may be positive effects for LDCs if higher world food prices stimulate domestic production, and if enhanced market access to the OECD markets enables those LDCs with comparative advantage in agriculture to expand export earnings.

As food aid is exempt from export-subsidy cuts, there may be no short-term price increases for emergency food imports, although the long-term effect of this on the volume, and therefore price, of food aid is as yet uncertain, and depends, to a large extent, on policy responses in DMECs. If a fall in subsidies to commercial grain exporters induces a less than proportionate decline in total output, surplus food may continue to be directed to food-aid objectives to keep prices at, or near, pre-UR levels.

Table 11.3a LDCs' food imports as proportion of total exports, 1990–1993 (percentages)

Region	1990	1991	1992	1993	1990–93 (average)
Total LDCs	37.0	37.5	40.6	36.9	38.0
Africa	29.3	31.9	35.3	32.6	32.2
Asia	58.8	49.9	49.1	41.8	49.8
Oceania	64.1	62.1	53.4	56.2	58.4
America	136.7	128.2	313.3	376.1	191.1

Table 11.3b LDCs' food imports as proportion of GDP, 1990–1993 (percentages)

Region	1990	1991	1992	1993	1990–93 (average)
Total LDCs	3.8	3.6	3.8	3.3	3.6
Africa	4.6	4.8	5.3	4.7	4.8
Asia	2.8	2.2	2.3	2.1	2.3
Oceania	11.7	11.8	12.4	11.5	11.9
America	7.3	6.1	12.5	14.0	8.8

Sources: UNCTAD (1994d), *Handbook of International Trade and Development Statistics*, calculations based on data from FAO, *Production Year Book* (various issues).

The TRIPs agreement may lead to increased costs for importing countries of pharmaceuticals, agrochemicals, technology, and possibly for seeds in the short run. In the long run, high potential returns are possible on any transfer of technology attained in the process (UNCTAD 1994a), in particular if greater protection increases the willingness of intellectual property suppliers to supply LDC markets.

Other effects

These include costs relating to compliance with notification requirements, legislative changes and the corresponding reorganization of institutional infrastructure, and the opportunity costs associated with the deployment of scarce managerial and administrative skills to WTO assignments, and so on. These costs, and those relating to TRIPs and TRIMs, are not easily amenable to measurement, and hence are difficult to estimate.

2.2 The Uruguay Round and Trade Diversification

Apart from the specific effects, the UR may have some knock-on effects, not easily quantifiable, on the trade-diversification potential and development prospects of LDCs.

Trade-diversification programmes and policies have been implemented in LDCs to attain three separate but interconnected objectives: earnings stabilization, export-revenue expansion and raising value added. Stabilization of earnings and export-revenue expansion can be attained through horizontal diversification into commodities whose price fluctuations do not synchronize. Vertical diversification into higher value-added products, which entails processing domestic or imported inputs, may help a country increase value added as well as improve its trade earnings. A fourth objective of diversification may be to reduce a country's dependence on a limited number of export markets (geographical diversification). This section briefly discusses the effects that the UR may have on LDC capability to attain these objectives.

Despite the trade restrictions entailed in the MFA, it did guarantee NIEs' exports minimum quotas in DMECs' markets, and provided them with a catalyst for growth. Relocation of firms from NIEs to Bangladesh and some other LDCs, in order to 'jump' quota restrictions, provided a stimulus to the embryonic industrialization process of these countries. Quality upgrading within quantitative quota limits and diversion into non-quota markets have all contributed to product and geographical diversification (Trela 1995).

The gradual phasing out of the MFA will reduce and finally eliminate quota rents enjoyed by some LDCs, although tariff preferences where they exist may offer competitive advantage in the short run. The ten-year transitional period may, however, offer the opportunity to undertake strategic restructuring and development of the textile industry through upgrading of design and production technologies in order to face the post-MFA global competition.

Nevertheless, if phasing out the MFA does indeed lead to free trade in the textiles and garment sector (that is, if DMECs do not resort to anti-dumping and countervailing duties), it could be a tremendous boost to industrialization in the more-developed DCs (for example, NIEs and second-tier NIEs).[16] To the extent that tariff reductions in this sector in the long run translate into enhanced access to DMEs' market for LDCs, and provided, as suggested above, the necessary restructuring is undertaken, the textiles and garment sector in these countries could be rejuvenated to increase export earnings as well as augment value added.

At another level, tariff bindings contained in the UR, by setting maximum tariff levels, guarantee enhanced security in trading relationships which is conducive to long-term policy shifts such as those involved in trade-diversification programmes. The significant reduction in tariff escalation for many products in the major markets under the UR will provide a stimulus to LDC manufactured exports and enhance their diversification of production into higher value-added products (GATT 1994c:9).

As argued by some analysts, GSP schemes may have implicitly encouraged commodity concentration and dampened pressures for more effective export-promotion policies (Weston 1995:11). Thus, if they become less useful as instruments for managing trade due to possible preference erosion, pressure on LDC governments to engage actively in export promotion, including trade diversification, would intensify. Preference erosion could also expand and create new markets for LDC exports because a fall in MFN tariffs could erode advantages that DMECs grant each other, which would be to the advantage of LDC exporters (World Bank 1995:38). Moreover, if the UR does lead to the reform of GSP schemes, this may stimulate reforms that could facilitate the diversification of both products and markets, in particular if the reforms increase product coverage and enhance access to the markets of all preference-giving countries (see below).[17]

If the agreement on TRIPs guarantees confidence and security in LDC markets for suppliers of technology and other intellectual property, then the increased willingness to supply such markets should reduce current problems associated with transferring new technologies to LDCs. By improving the chances of technology transfer, TRIPs could facilitate vertical diversification and increase the value added of LDC exports. The potential advantages associated with this in the long run should more than offset the anticipated increased prices of technology in the short run.

By reducing distortions in world prices, the agricultural agreement may yet create opportunities for horizontal diversification. LDCs with comparative advantage in agriculture may find it profitable to export food items that were unprofitable to export under the previous price regime.

Overall, to what extent a country benefits from the UR will be determined by the degree of external orientation in its trade policy. A country with an outward-oriented trade regime, which is conducive to trade diversification, stands a better chance of utilizing the opportunities inherent in the UR.

Nevertheless, the adjustment of LDC economies in the post-UR world will be plagued with some uncertainties. Although the Agreements on Subsidies and Countervailing Measures (ASCMs) and TRIMs provide for flexibility through transitional periods in complying with the obligations in respect, for example, of granting subsidies (in the case of ASCMs) or other incentives (in the case of TRIMs) mandatorily contingent upon use of domestic over imported goods, it remains to be seen how this flexibility could be put into good effect within the allowed transitional period to have impact on domestic industrial capacity and trade diversification.

As yet, there are potential pitfalls, including the following, which create uncertainty and concern: contingency trade-protection measures, transitional safeguard mechanisms, unless scrupulously and sparingly used, could undermine the UR's potential benefits for LDCs.

These notwithstanding, the greatest obstacles to the LDCs' attempt to diversify trade and/or readjust to a new post-UR trade environment are their structural weaknesses. To the extent that LDCs are able to overcome their constraints in technology, social (human capital formation) and physical infrastructure, they should be in a position to promote trade diversification, and enhance their development prospects by attracting new FDI to the textiles and garment and other sectors (see below). However, this is only feasible in the long run when they may begin to reap systemic benefits from the UR. The possible effects of the UR on developing countries are summarized in Table 11.1.

3 MITIGATING POSSIBLE ADVERSE EFFECTS OF THE URUGUAY ROUND ON LDCs

To the extent that the risk of LDCs being marginalized in a liberalized global economy is real, uncertainty over their gains from the multilateral trading system has increased. The need for reorienting their economies to meet the new challenges by becoming more competitive in the production of tradable goods and services is paramount. While this has been acknowledged by LDC governments, supply-side factors have emerged as key impediments to LDCs' greater participation in international exchanges of goods and services on the one hand, and improving their access to foreign investments and technologies and know-how on the other.[18]

LDC economies are characterized by a variety of supply-side constraints or structural weaknesses which are a barrier to trade expansion and diversification (that is, the expansion of both traditional primary products and non-traditional products and efficient import-substitution production). These constraints include weak technological capacity, lack of entrepreneurial, managerial, marketing and technical skills including those for quality control, paucity of long-term finance, expensive trade credit and pre-shipment finance, and non-transparent legal and regulatory framework. Deficiencies in the physical infrastructure are also major constraints in many countries, especially because of restraints on public-expenditure programmes.

In an attempt to adjust to the increasingly competitive international environment, most LDCs have, over the past decade, implemented policies to liberalize their economies under the banner of structural adjustment programmes (SAPs) supported by conditional finance from the World Bank and the International Monetary Fund (IMF). These programmes have brought about some improvements in the macroeconomic environment, in particular macroeconomic stabilization in some LDCs, but policy measures to tackle supply-side constraints have remained limited, thereby retarding progress in this area.

The relative neglect of supply-side constraints is attributable to various factors: flaws in the design of reform programmes and continuing debate over the sequencing of different phases, lack of resources, both human and financial, the seemingly intractable nature of some of the constraints and lack of a consensus as to how they should be tackled. Analyses of countries undertaking adjustment have revealed that these issues are unlikely to be resolved in the foreseeable future, as problems of underinvestment in human-resources development, weak private-sector response, and debt overhang, among others, persist in these countries. To date, the limited trade expansion and diversification attained by LDCs despite these efforts (Kirkpatrick and Weiss, Chapter 2 in this book), underscore the fact that LDCs' ability to benefit from the multilateral trading system of the UR is predicated on their capability to produce traded goods and services competitively.

That there is a compelling case for external support measures to mitigate the possible adverse consequences on LDCs arising from the UR agreement is widely recognized. DMECs stand to gain more from trade integration with DCs than from more integration among DMECs. Potential gains will arise from a more efficient utilization of resources, increased investment and innovation, higher productivity as well as increased market size, competition and technology spillovers (World Bank 1995:3). However, external support measures need to be designed to correspond with domestic-policy responses. This is more so as the attainment of the trade-diversification objective requires a delicate interplay of macroeconomic management and microlevel enterprise support measures, and the elimination of legal, regulatory and structural impediments for which external assistance is required.

3.1 National (Domestic) Measures

The overall objective of domestic policy should be a complete overhaul of economic management to enhance LDC participation in international trade. This will necessitate policy and structural transformations to meet the new challenges.

Policy measures should be directed at reorienting the incentive framework in favour of the tradables sector, and at attaining improvements in the efficiency of production for domestic consumption (for example, food) and external markets in order to meet increased competition from abroad.[19] This calls for a flexible production system, underscored by flexible product and labour markets, which is in consonance with trade-diversification objectives.

As part of the overall economic restructuring being implemented under SAPs, trade-policy reforms bolstered by sectoral and microlevel reforms are in progress in most LDCs. These reforms, in particular those that create an enabling environment for private enterprise, must be concluded and/or deepened.

LDCs' ability to compete in a liberal trade environment depends on a skilled, educated and flexible labour force capable of adapting and integrating new technologies into the production process. Thus, human capital development has to be tackled more systematically through increased investment in education, in particular at the technical and/or vocational level, as the experience of NIEs has shown that investments in this type of training yield high returns. Regular on-the-job-training schemes can also help in updating skills of the workforce to enable them to cope with technological innovations. Training schemes oriented towards the provision of labour-intensive, long-distance services should enable LDCs to utilize their comparative advantage in the services sector which is one of the fastest-growing components of trade and FDI.[20]

To cope with the initial problem of high prices which may arise from the TRIPs agreement, LDCs must strengthen domestic administrative capacities to secure equivalent non-patented or off-patent products and procure technologies from competitive sources. More investment in research and development (R&D) by LDCs should help them in the long run to improve their technological capability and reduce the technological gap between them and the DMECs.

An efficient financial system that can provide long-term and risk finance, as well as trade and export credits, should be developed by implementing financial-sector reforms that encourage private-sector participation. Improved marketing channels in both domestic and export markets would enhance efficiency and facilitate increases in traditional as well as non-traditional exports. This should be accompanied by a more transparent legal and regulatory framework that is conducive to the development of efficient production structures.

The agricultural agreement gives some leeway to LDC governments to overcome some of their anticipated problems. Direct and indirect measures to encourage agriculture and rural development, including investment and input subsidies to low-income producers, are not outlawed. If properly targeted, such measures should be able to ease some of the initial difficulties of food-deficit LDCs, as well as to serve trade-diversification objectives. In the long run, sectoral policies should be strengthened to enhance food production by increasing the efficiency of agricultural production.

Generally, domestic policies should be designed and implemented in such a way as to ease supply-side constraints in order to facilitate the reallocation of resources by private agents into new lines of production (for example, horizontal and vertical diversification) to boost and stabilize foreign-exchange earnings.

3.2   International Support Measures

One instrument for improving market access for LDC export items could be the provision of additional trade preferences, for example, GSP. Other possible measures include supplementary financial and technical assistance from bilateral and multilateral sources to ameliorate supply-side constraints, improve the efficiency of domestic production, and provide market access and other trade- and investment-related support to enhance the supply capacity of tradable goods and services in LDCs.

The generalized system of preferences (GSP)

As evident from the discussion in Section 2, the implementation of the Final Act entails the risk of erosion of tariff margins under existing GSP schemes. Nevertheless, new opportunities are likely to emerge for improving GSP coverage due to the tariffication of agricultural products under the Final Act (see, for example, Davenport 1994).

As pointed out by various UNCTAD studies,[21] the utilization of, and benefits derived from, GSP schemes by LDCs have been limited for a variety of reasons. Primarily, this is due to weak supply capabilities and limited product coverage in the schemes of those countries that are the main markets of LDCs, relatively restrictive rules of origin, as well as procedural and other complexities associated with the system, including frequent changes of the eligibility criteria of individual schemes. Inadequate institutional and managerial capacities in many LDCs also limit their ability to benefit from schemes that are applicable to their export baskets (see, for example, UNCTAD 1993). Because of their more diversified export structure, the GSP benefited the more advanced DCs, mainly in South-east Asia, and will probably not by itself provide a basis for sustaining and diversifying LDC exports without complementary reforms.

The primary objective of reforming GSP schemes should be to grant LDC exports enhanced access to DMEC markets and to facilitate the administration of the scheme to enable LDCs to increase the utilization rate and reap greater benefits from various schemes. To this end, a variety of measures could be implemented, including the following.

First, product coverage of the schemes could be extended to a wider range of export items. Similarly, reducing preferential rates to zero for most or all products, and removing all ceilings and/or quantitative restrictions, would enhance product coverage.

Second, measures such as the application of full and global cumulation, simplification of the rules of origin, administrative procedures and documentation, and the introduction of derogation rules[22] would improve the harmonization of interscheme diversity, thus facilitating the utilization of the GSP. If all preference-giving countries include goods originating from other beneficiaries in the calculation of local content, this will expand trading opportunities as well as enhance regional and south–south trade.[23] The review of GSP schemes should seek to introduce these improvements which will go a long way to offset the negative impact of the erosion of preferences enjoyed under GSP stemming from market-access liberalization in the UR.

Financial and technical assistance
External assistance could be focused on short- and long-term issues. In the short term, net-food importing LDCs would require increased food aid and/or additional finance from donor countries and international financial institutions (IFIs) to cover anticipated increases in import bills.[24]

In general, assistance should be directed at the following areas: (i) removing obstacles (for example, legislative, institutional, or personnel) that could frustrate LDCs' compliance with the UR agreement and active participation in WTO activities; and (ii) identifying new trading opportunities based on existing export baskets of LDCs, for example, to increase the level of utilization of preferential regimes such as GSP.

Debt-relief measures to alleviate the debt overhang of LDCs, such as debt rescheduling, and in particular the auction of debts on secondary markets, could also release scarce resources for domestic use in the short to medium term.

In the long run, external assistance should concentrate on expanding domestic food production in food-deficit countries, and on promoting trade diversification in order to utilize new trading opportunities. Donor support would be necessary to enhance the competitiveness of LDC economies by facilitating access to new technology, enhancing technological capabilities, and providing training programmes to improve local skills to support domestic diversification efforts. Assisting DCs, in particular LDCs, to adjust successfully to a post-UR world should be of interest to DMECs as well. The increasing integration of DCs benefits both them and the DMECs. A growing proportion of industrial-country exports goes to DCs: it was about one-fifth in the late 1980s, is one-quarter at present, and it is projected to exceed one-third by the end of the next decade (World Bank 1995:1–2).

An adequate flow of external finance is particularly important because overcoming supply-side constraints in LDCs will require, in many cases, major investment programmes in physical infrastructure and social services. The private sector has a key role to play in LDC economies, but an expansion of public investment and social expenditure will be necessary to 'crowd in' private investment (Mosley et al. 1992, and White 1992, quoted in Kirkpatrick and Weiss, Chapter 2 in this book). Given the low levels of incomes and savings in most LDCs, the resources needed for these investments exceed those that could be mobilized from the domestic economy, hence the need for external supplementary financial assistance. Inevitably, this will necessitate a reversal of the decline in aid flows to LDCs: since 1992 there has been a 7.9 per cent decline in aid flows to LDCs (OECD 1994, quoted in Weston 1995:22).

In deciding the level and timeliness of, eligibility for, and/or access to, external financial assistance, some pertinent issues need to be considered, including the following. Are existing financing facilities adequate to contain the additional financial needs stemming from the UR?[25] What should be the nature of a new financing facility specifically designed to promote post-UR adjustment in LDCs? Should such a facility have conditionalities or specific criteria to be satisfied by needy countries? What should be the criteria for deciding the level of assistance for each country? Should all LDCs have unencumbered access to this new financing facility?

At the subregional or regional level, neighbouring countries can also help to improve market access for LDCs within a framework of intraregional trade.[26] Alternatively, joining a regional trading bloc, for example the EU, may help LDCs to counteract the potential dangers posed by regionalism, such as a deterioration in market access. In addition to this 'defensive reason', such an arrangement might entail some spin-offs for LDCs, including the 'import' of useful institutions, and enhancing the credibility of trade reforms (Collier and Gunning 1995:400).

4 CONCLUSIONS

Much of the prognosis about the effects of the UR is by no means certain, as the lack of clarity on some issues prevents unambiguous conclusions of specific effects from being made. More importantly, globalization and liberalization seem to have a momentum that defies easy prediction. This section briefly flags some issues that may yet influence the UR's effect on LDCs. These include the trend towards regionalism, the decreasing commodity intensity of final goods, organization and implementation of external assistance, and systemic effects of the UR.

One major concern for multilateralism is the drive towards regionalism. Between 1948 and 1994, 109 regional trading blocs were notified to GATT. Ironically, one-third of these were signed in the last half (1990–94) of the UR negotiating process[27] (*The Economist*, 16 September 1995, p. 27). If this proclivity for regionalism remains undiminished, the marginalization of LDCs could increase as most operate outside the major trading blocs or have asymmetrical and weak links with them.

The decreasing commodity intensity of final goods, an aspect of the technological revolution spurring globalization and liberalization, has far-reaching implications for LDCs. While natural-resource endowments have become less significant in production, LDCs' commodity dependence is yet to diminish.[28]

By incorporating in the Final Act measures for technical and financial assistance for LDCs, the UR acknowledges the need for external assistance to enable LDCs to restructure their economies, but the modalities for delivering these are as yet unclear. This creates the necessity for additional research to work out how external assistance should be organized and implemented. More research and rigorous cost–benefit assessment is also required at the global level to determine with more certainty the specific requirements or assistance needed by LDCs, as a group, from bilateral and multilateral sources.

If systemic costs and benefits are incorporated into this sort of analysis, it should assist LDCs to cope better with the UR in order to reap its long-term benefits. This is particularly important, first, because most estimates seem to have concentrated on LDCs' loss/gain of export earnings and market shares to the neglect of the UR's multiplier effects. The UR's systemic effects, for example on employment in the agricultural sector, have received little attention to date in UR impact analyses. While the contribution of agriculture to the GDP of LDCs is about 30 per cent in 1993, two-thirds of the labour force of LDCs was in the agricultural sector; on the other hand, only 5 per cent of the labour force in DMECs was engaged in agriculture in 1993 (see Table 11.4).

Second, the studies implicitly assume a counterfactual scenario of a continuation of the status quo *ex ante* if the UR had failed, which is unrealistic, as increased protectionism on the part of DMECs, a continuation of the unilateral liberalization by DCs, or some policy combination of these two were quite distinct possibilities. The counterfactual scenario, therefore, has to be explicitly and more realistically defined, taking into account not only the second-round effects of the UR, but also the possibility of governments failing in their obligations during its implementation. Assumptions underlying studies have to be standardized and/or made more transparent to allow for replicability and more definite results. At the specific country level, further research may be required to:[29]

1. estimate as accurately as possible the level of adjustment costs, for example, to quantify net benefits or losses by analysing transitional and long-term costs as well as benefits;[30]

Table 11.4   DMECs and DCs: share of agriculture in GDP and share of labour force in agriculture (percentages)

Region	Share of agriculture in GDP			Share of labour force in agriculture			
	1970	1980	1993	1970	1980	1993	1994
DMECs	4	4	2	13	8	5	4
Developing countries* *of which*	26	18	13	77	71	64	64
Africa	32	26	23	79	69	61	61
Asia	33	21	15	69	69	60	60
America	13	10	9	41	38	30	30
LDCs	41	42	31	81	76	69	69

Note: * Includes LDCs.

Source: Same as Tables 11.3a and b.

2. identify sector-specific obstacles to trade expansion and specify how these could be ameliorated;
3. explore ways of meeting the costs associated with the overall economic restructuring from domestic sources, and appraise the level and type of direct assistance required from bilateral and multilateral sources, for example, technical cooperation requirements for trade promotion and capacity building for trade-policy formulation and implementation; and
4. design a country-specific programme of action for economic restructuring considering 1 to 3 above.

The effects of the UR on LDCs must be monitored,[31] and measures must be put in place to deal rapidly with 'unanticipated' responses. There is the possibility of new barriers being erected that could limit LDC trade expansion: for example, escalation in the use of anti-dumping policies and countervailing duties, and abuse of the selective safeguard mechanism. Moreover, if the DMECs do not adhere to the special and differential treatment granted to LDCs in the Final Act (for example, inability to provide technical assistance for agricultural development), their economic adjustment during the transitional period could be jeopardized. The resolution of outstanding 'non-trade' issues, such as the relationship between the environment and labour standards on one hand, and trade on the other, could also have significant effects on the projected benefits of the UR for LDCs.

Multilateralism in the post-UR world has enormous potential benefits for international trade and development, but the UR is not a rose without thorns: the S and D treatment granted to LDCs is a tacit acknowledgement of the transitional costs LDCs would incur in conforming to the UR agreement. By creating an improved trading environment underscored by progressive liberalization in trade and capital markets, increasing competition and access to new technology, it threatens to push to the margin less-competitive countries, in particular LDCs.

Most studies assessing the impact of the UR are in agreement on its short-run costs, albeit marginal, for the LDCs. Net losses are expected to be greatest for the least industrialized, commodity-dependent and poorest countries in Africa, most of which are LDCs. In the long run, LDCs should be able to diversify their trade and enhance their net welfare from a more liberalized trading environment if bilateral and multilateral assistance materializes to enable them to restructure their economies to adjust to increased competition and utilize emerging market opportunities.

If, as predicted by some studies, preference erosion results in net loss of foreign-exchange earnings, it could deny LDCs the opportunity to utilize scarce domestic resources to finance the economic restructuring necessitated by the UR in the short run. Phasing out the MFA is likely to dampen incentives for LDCs to diversify vertically into higher value-added products in the short run, as they may be crowded out by the more-developed DCs already established in such markets.

However, LDCs are likely to derive major benefits as result of the impact of the UR in other areas of trade. First, reductions in tariff escalation in the major markets will enhance the production of manufactured exports in LDCs. Second, the dispute-settlement mechanism, substantially strengthened in favour of smaller countries under the UR, should be seen as of significant benefit to LDCs. Indeed, it should make it easier for them to assert their rights under GATT. Third, although the agreement on agriculture may entail short-run costs for net food-importing countries, with the reduction in agricultural export subsidies in OECD countries, LDCs as a group should be able to increase their exports of agricultural products to the developed countries in the long run if they can overcome critical supply-side constraints.

Generally, given most LDCs' structural weaknesses, which render their agricultural and industrial production inflexible and uncompetitive, this group of countries is unlikely to withstand unbridled competition in the post-UR era. In the short run, DMECs stand to increase their share of the world market for goods and services to a greater extent than the DCs, in particular the LDCs. In the long run, if LDCs make good progress in reducing supply-side constraints, the consequent trade expansion, particularly the enhanced production of non-traditional exports, should help them attain trade-diversification objectives: that is, diversify markets, and products and/or increase value-added content, and improve earnings stability.

Overall, the impact of the UR on LDCs depends on numerous intervening variables. Any a priori assessment is therefore, of necessity, rendered somewhat impressionistic. Nevertheless, to the extent that the UR promises an era of free trade in an increasingly globalized and liberalized environment, it does offer some opportunities, albeit limited, to LDCs, the exploitation of which depends on country-specific characteristics, as well as on the level of bilateral and multilateral assistance available to each country and to the LDCs as a group. Most importantly, the gains of LDCs depend on their own trade regimes and how Articles in the Final Act on the special and differential treatment of LDCs are interpreted and implemented.

NOTES

1. A version of this chapter was published in UNCTAD (1996).
2. Useful comments from Chandra Kant Patel and two anonymous referees are gratefully acknowledged. The usual disclaimer applies.
3. Technical assistance provided by UNCTAD and UNDP to developing-country teams was crucial in this respect.
4. The effects of the UR on DCs (and LDCs) have been the subject of numerous UNCTAD studies, for example, Trela 1995; UNCTAD 1990, 1991, 1994c and 1995a–d. See also UNCTAD 1995e, for a selected bibliography on this by UNCTAD and other international bodies.
5. A 'cause-and-effect' analysis is also problematic for some issues like erosion of preferences that may result from the UR, as it implicitly assumes a continuance of the *status quo ex ante*, which is doubtful in a post-UR world.
6. See, for example, GATT (1994b, 1995) and UNCTAD (1994a).
7. This excludes some major agricultural products or food of special interest to DCs, in particular, fish and fish products, forestry products, jute and hard fibres and their products and natural rubber, which together with minerals and metals are treated as belonging to the industrial sector (UNCTAD 1995e:9).
8. Much of this evidence is derived from analysis of old data on different products at the aggregate level using partial equilibrium models.
9. The estimates of costs and benefits for the various regions differ depending on the model used, the assumptions underlying it and the base and end years selected (see Weston 1995:6, for some specific estimates). There is, however, a consensus that losses may be greatest for the poorest countries, especially in the short run, and the largest gains may accrue to the DMECs followed by the middle-income countries and the NIEs. One model suggests that only 11 per cent of the global annual gains of about \$70 billion will accrue to developing countries (see Hamilton and Whalley 1995:34, and their end notes 5 and 6).
10. Some studies are, however, sceptical about the adverse impact of preference erosion (for some examples, see Weston 1995:7–9). For a detailed analysis on the market-access implications of the Final Act for LDCs, see UNCTAD (1992, Chapter V).
11. This excludes non-agricultural exports, for example minerals, which are practically duty free, even for those with MFN status. On the basis of this, some experts have argued that loss of preferences for such exports to the EU will make 'no real' difference for Africa as these make up more than half of its total exports (see Hamilton and Whalley 1995:41 and Weston 1995:8).
12. Generally, losses are estimated to be less than 5 per cent of total export earnings, and more than 10 to 20 per cent of export earnings in only a few cases (UNCTAD 1995a). Estimates of losses likely to result from loss of EU preferences in 1989 are as low as 0.5 per cent of total African exports and less than 0.3 per cent of Sub-Saharan Africa's exports in 1992 (for the loss of OECD preferences). It is also argued that the full impact of changes will be gradual as tariff cuts for other suppliers MFNs will be phased in over 6 years (Weston 1995:7).

13. Indeed, there is some scepticism about the adverse effects of the Final Act on agricultural policies on world prices and food-aid surpluses for two reasons. First, the agricultural policy changes agreed are not as wide ranging as was anticipated; and second, some of the observed changes in world prices will reflect ongoing agricultural liberalization policies in DMECs rather than the effects of the UR (Page and Davenport 1994:34).

14. Although some estimates suggest a net positive effect on SSA's agricultural trade balance as exports expand more than imports (DeRosa 1994:11, cited in Weston 1995:16), this is more likely to be so for middle-income rather than low-income countries (Weston 1995:16).

15. It should be noted in this connection that studies that have assessed the quantitative impact of the UR agreement on commodities since the conclusion of the Round have reported more modest results than earlier ones (see UNCTAD 1995e, for a survey of the studies; Part Two reviews the impact of the UR agreement on specific agricultural commodities covered by it).

16. The pessimism this entails for LDCs is tempered to some extent by the fact that NIEs face high costs of production (for example, labour costs) at home, and thus may continue to shift production facilities to LDCs; in particular, LDCs with technological, physical and social infrastructure stand to gain. Thus NIEs may lose some market share to some LDCs.

17. DCs in Latin America and Asia witnessed significant improvements over the last two decades in diversifying their export markets by reducing the value of commodity exports to DMECs from 80 and 60 per cent in 1970–72 to about 69 and 50 per cent, respectively, in 1990–92; but the value of commodity exports of African DCs (about two-thirds of which are LDCs) to the DMECs had remained constant at about 76 per cent over the same period, with the EU's share increasing by seven percentage points to 58 per cent (UNCTAD 1995e:Add.1, Table 2) probably because of the Lomé Convention.

18. Recent studies on African industrialization have, for example, exposed its weak technological capacity in terms of the ability to apply, adapt and modify new technology in the process of industrial production (see Lall 1993 and Park 1993, cited in Kirkpatrick and Weiss, Chapter 2 in this book).

19. The need to produce even primary exports more efficiently has become urgent given the declining shares of LDC exporters in world markets due, in part, to product innovation in DMECs and more efficient production and marketing of competing goods and services in more-developed developing economies.

20. It is estimated that this alone could potentially double developing countries' commercial service exports, currently estimated at about $180 billion (see World Bank 1995:3).

21. For example, one such study showed that the utilization rate of GSP schemes (that is, ratio of imports that actually received preferential treatment to covered imports) of OECD countries fell by 2.6 per cent in 1992 to 46.9 per cent in 1993. However, the value of total developing-country imports actually receiving preferences increased from $64.1 billion in 1991 to $79.0 billion in 1993. This could be explained by one characteristic of the schemes: quota restrictions are based on quantity (for example, weight, number of items) and not value based (that is, worth of products).

22. These rules provide that appeals for preferential treatment, on a product and country basis, should be addressed within a limited period, for example, three months, failing which the preference must be granted. Similar rules are already applied to African, Caribbean and Pacific (ACP) countries under the Lomé Convention.

23. Regional cumulation is granted by the EU to some regional groupings, for example, ASEAN, Andean Group and the Central American Common Market (CACM); Japan and the United States also operate similar but slightly different systems (Inama 1995:97–108).

24. This is also part of the recommendations of the Marrakesh Ministerial Decision.

25. It is doubtful if the existing facilities of the World Bank and the IMF would be adequate, in particular considering the conditionality attached to these facilities and some of the issues raised below.

26. This may not be entirely in consonance with a post-UR multilateral trade environment, but it could well be one way LDCs respond to the increasing trend towards regionalism. Moreover, two major problems that have increased the potential trade-diversion effects and limited

potential trade-creation effects of such a trade would have to be overcome first: high regional transportation costs and inefficient manufacturing activities (Kirkpatrick and Weiss, Chapter 2 in this book).

27. It is not clear how much of the interest in trading blocs was due, at the time, to the increased pessimism of the UR's successful conclusion. What is evident is that the drive towards regionalism is yet to diminish as more ambitious plans are on the horizon for extending old ones (for example, the North American Free Trade Agreement and others in the Latin American and Caribbean region into Free Trade Areas of the Americas), and creating new ones (for example, South Asian Preferential Trade Area to be set up by the seven-member ASEAN group by the year 2003).

28. The long-run decline in the prices of primary commodities, on the world market, relative to those of manufactures, since the 1970s, is unlikely to be reversed in the foreseeable future for several reasons, including: sluggish growth in the demand for primary commodities on world markets relative to the demand for other goods and services because of changing sectoral composition of world output in favour of services; increasing use of substitutes for, or greater economy in the use of, raw materials because of technological advances; and productivity increases ensuing from the application of new technology have expanded the supply of agricultural products, some of which are of particular interest to LDCs (Maizels 1987:543; Reinhart and Wickham 1994: 198–203).

29. Canada and Switzerland have already led the way by commissioning studies to determine the impact of the UR on selected aid recipients. But, as cautioned by Weston (1995:22), such studies need to be coordinated to avoid duplication.

30. This is particularly important as it has been argued that the tendency to put too much emphasis on analysing aggregate effects at the expense of individual-country analysis, product experience or possible future changes in production structures, underscores the estimated marginal losses attributable to preference erosion by many studies for developing countries, thereby weakening the case for compensation for their loss (Weston 1995:7).

31. The need for monitoring is recognized in the Final Act as stated in the Decisions on Measures in Favour of LDCs: expeditious implementation of all special and differential measures taken in favour of LDCs is to be ensured through, *inter alia*, regular reviews (para. 2 (i)).

REFERENCES

Awuku, E.O. (1994), 'How does the Uruguay Round affect the North–South trade?', *Journal of World Trade*, vol. 28, no. 2, pp. 75–93.

Collier, P. and J.W. Gunning (1995), 'Trade policy and regional integration: Implications for the relations between Europe and Africa', *The World Economy*, vol. 18, no. 3, May, pp. 387–410.

Davenport, M. (1994), 'Possible improvements to the generalized system of preferences', UNCTAD/ITD/8, Geneva.

The Economist, 16 September 1995.

FAO, *Production Yearbook* (various issues), Rome: FAO.

Ganesan, A.V. (1995), 'The implications of the Uruguay Round for the least developed countries', a report prepared for the UNCTAD Secretariat, March.

GATT (1993), 'An analysis of the proposed Uruguay Round Agreement, with particular emphasis on aspects of interest to developing countries', MTN.TNC/W/122-MTN.GNG/W/30, Geneva: GATT.

GATT (1994a), 'Increases in market access resulting from the Uruguay Round', *News of the Uruguay Round of Multilateral Trade Negotiations*, Geneva: GATT.

GATT (1994b), *News of the Uruguay Round of Multilateral Trade Negotiations: The Final Act of the Uruguay Round*, NUR 084, 5 April, Geneva: GATT.

GATT (1994c), 'Outcome of the Uruguay Round for developing countries', 3 October, Geneva: GATT.

GATT (1995), 'Provisions related to least developed countries in the Uruguay Round Agreements, legal instruments and ministerial decisions', P–Misc95. Prepared by the WTO Secretariat for UNCTAD Brainstorming Meeting, 18–19 May.

Hamilton, C. and J. Whalley (1995), 'Evaluating the impact of the Uruguay Round results on developing countries', *The World Economy*, vol. 18, no. 1, January, pp. 31–50.

Hoekman, B.M. (1989), 'Agriculture and the Uruguay Round', *Journal of World Trade*, vol. 23, no. 1, pp. 83–96.

Inama, S. (1995), 'A comparative analysis of the generalized system of preferences and non-preferential rules of origin in the light of the Uruguay Round Agreement', *Journal of World Trade*, vol. 29, no. 1, February, pp. 77–111.

Maizels, A. (1987), 'Commodities in crisis: An overview of the main issues', *World Development*, vol. 15, no. 5, pp. 537–49.

Page, S. and M. Davenport (1994): *World Trade Reform: Do Developing Countries Gain or Lose?*, London: Overseas Development Institute.

Raffer, K. (1995), 'The impact of the Uruguay Round on developing Countries', in Fritz Breuss (ed.), *The World Economy After the Uruguay Round*, Vienna: Schrifftenreihe Des Forschungsinstituts Fur Europafragen, pp. 169–92.

Reinhart, C.M. and P. Wickenham (1994), 'Commodity prices: Cyclical weakness or secular decline?', *IMF Staff Papers*, vol. 41, no. 2, pp. 175–213.

Trela, I. (1995), 'Phasing out the MFA in the Uruguay Round: Implications for developing countries', a report prepared for the UNCTAD project on 'The Impact of the Uruguay Round on Developing Countries'.

UNCTAD (1990), *Agricultural Trade Liberalization in the Uruguay Round: Implications for Developing Countries*, UNCTAD/ITP/48, a joint UNCTAD/UNDP/WIDER (UNU) study, New York: United Nations Publications.

UNCTAD (1991), *Trade and Development Report, 1991*, UNCTAD/TDR/11, United Nations publication, Sales No. E.91.II.D.15, New York: United Nations.

UNCTAD (1992), *The Least Developed Countries, 1992 Report*, TD/B/39(2)10, United Nations publication, Sales No. E.93.II.D.3, New York: United Nations.

UNCTAD (1993), 'The role of GSP in improving LDCs' access to markets: Some recent developments', TD/B/39(2)/CRP.7, Geneva.

UNCTAD (1994a), 'The outcome of the Uruguay Round: An initial assessment', Supporting papers to the *Trade and Development Report, 1994*, UNCTAD/TDR/14, Supplement, United Nations publication, Sales No. E.94.II.D.28, New York: United Nations.

UNCTAD (1994b), *Trade and Development Report, 1994*, UNCTAD/TDR/14, United Nations publication, Sales No. E.94.II.D.26, New York: United Nations.

UNCTAD (1994c), 'A preliminary analysis of the results of the Uruguay Round and their effects on the trading prospects of developing countries', TD/B/WG.4/13, Geneva, 10 June.

UNCTAD (1994d), *Handbook of International Trade and Development Statistics*, New York and Geneva: United Nations.

UNCTAD (1995a), 'Main conclusions of the brainstorming meeting on the Uruguay Round and LDCs and net food-importing developing countries', 18–19 May, Geneva.

UNCTAD (1995b), 'Preliminary analysis of opportunities and challenges resulting from the Uruguay Round Agreement on Textiles and Clothing', UNCTAD/ITD/17, a report by the UNCTAD Secretariat, 6 October.

UNCTAD (1995c), 'Report of the Expert Group Meeting on Trade Diversification in the Least Developed Countries', Geneva, 10–11 April.

UNCTAD (1995d), 'Translating Uruguay Round special provisions for least developed countries into concrete action: issues and policy requirements', TD/B/WG.8, Geneva, March.

UNCTAD (1995e), 'The Uruguay Round and international commodity trade and prices', TD/B/CN.1/30, Adds. 1 and 2, Geneva, 31 August.

UNCTAD (1995f), 'Report on evaluating the outcome of the Uruguay Round Agricultural Agreement using the Agricultural Trade Policy Simulation Model', mimeo, Report prepared by Professor Odd Gulbrandsen for the UNCTAD Secretariat, Geneva, 12 January.

UNCTAD (1996), *The Least Developed Countries 1996 Report*, TD/B/42(2)/11, United Nations publication, Sales No. E.96.II.D.3, New York: United Nations.

Weston, A. (1994), 'The Uruguay Round: Unveiling the implications for the least developed and low-income countries', a report prepared for the UNCTAD Secretariat, Geneva, September.

Weston, A. (1995), 'The Uruguay Round – Costs and Compensation for Developing Countries, Report to the Group of Twenty-four', UNCTAD/GID/MISC.31, Geneva.

World Bank (1995), *Global Economic Prospects and the Developing Countries*, Washington, DC: World Bank.

Index